I0187336

The Writings of

"FIONA MACLEOD"

UNIFORM EDITION

ARRANGED BY

MRS. WILLIAM SHARP

"Theseus . . . Wilt thou speak of the ancient trouble of thy race?"—Œdipus at Kolonos.

"For immaterial things, which are the highest and greatest, are shown only in thought and idea, and in no other way, and all that we are saying is said for the sake of them."—PLATO, *The Statesman.*

The Winged Destiny
Studies in the Spiritual History of the Gael

BY

"FIONA MACLEOD"
(WILLIAM SHARP)

NEW YORK

DUFFIELD & COMPANY

1910

Windham Press is committed to bringing the lost cultural heritage of ages past into the 21st century through high-quality reproductions of original, classic printed works at affordable prices.

This book has been carefully crafted to utilize the original images of antique books rather than error-prone OCR text. This also preserves the work of the original typesetters of these classics, unknown craftsmen who laid out the text, often by hand, of each and every page you will read. Their subtle art involving judgment and interaction with the text is in many ways superior and more human than the mechanical methods utilized today, and gave each book a unique, hand-crafted feel in its text that connected the reader organically to the art of bindery and book-making.

We think these benefits are worth the occasional imperfection resulting from the age of these books at the time of scanning, and their vintage feel provides a connection to the past that goes beyond the mere words of the text.

As bibliophiles, we are always seeking perfection in our work, and so please notify us of any errors in this book by emailing us at corrections@windhampress.com. Our team is motivated to correct errors quickly so future customers are better served. Our mission is to raise the bar of quality for reprinted works by a focus on detail and quality over mass production.

To peruse our catalog of carefully curated classic works, please visit our online store at www.windhampress.com.

WINDHAM PRESS
CLASSIC REPRINTS

CONTENTS

v

Contents

TO

J. A. G.

To you, dear friend, let me dedicate this bindweed of thoughts and dreams, which had their life by the grey shores you, also, love. Have you not wandered there often, seeking forgetfulness, and, wandering, found peace?

You are in your southern home, by calm waters where mine are foam-white, and under blue skies where mine are dark with cloud and wind: and yet, of all I know, few do so habitually dwell in that fragrant, forgetting and forgot, old world of ours, whose fading voice is more and more lost in the northern seas. The South is beautiful, but has not the secrets of the North. Do you, too, not hold Iona, motherland of all my dreams, as something rare and apart, one who has her own lovely solitude and her own solitary loveliness that is like no other loveliness? In your heart, as in mine, it lies an island of revelation and of peace. For you, too, is the enduring spell of those haunted lands where the last dreams of the Gael are gathered, dwelling in sunset beauty.

In this book I have dealt — as, I hope, in all I write — only with things among which my thought has moved, searching, remembering, examining, sometimes dreaming. Slightly to adapt a comment I read somewhere recently:—while it is true that certain ideas monopolise my imagination, I do not wilfully ignore the lesser nor even the ignoble things of life; above all, I do not dishonestly seek to seem unaware of or to hide them. It is only that I have no time to attend to them, being otherwise busy.

I think the fundamental idea of this book, as of all my thought in these things from which the book has risen like a phantom out of haunted woods, is utterable in the noble phrase of Renan: "J'avais le sentiment de l'infini et de l'éternel, et de là mes sourires pour les choses qui passent. Mais l'Esprit ne passe point." Nor am I so much concerned to set others right, for which I am not qualified, as to interpret, for which I may be: remembering as I do Goethe's words, "If you call a bad thing bad, you do little; if you call a good thing good, you do much." To each his interest. I shall rest content if I am of the horizon-makers, however humbly; if I may be among those who extend the horizons.

You who know the way of the wind in my mind know that I do not, as some say, " dwell only in the past," or that personal sorrow is the one magnet of my dreams. It is not the night-wind in sad hearts only that I hear, or the sighing of vain futilities; but, often, rather an emotion akin to that mysterious Sorrow of Eternity in love with tears, of which Blake speaks in *Vala*. It is, at times at least I feel it so, because Beauty is more beautiful there. It is the twilight hour in the heart, as Joy is the heart's morning. Perhaps I love best the music that leads one into the moonlit coverts of dreams, and old silence, and unawaking peace. But Music, like the rose of the Greeks, is " the thirty petalled one," and every leaf is the gate of an equal excellence. The fragrance of all is Joy, the beauty of all is Sorrow: but the Rose is one—*Rosa Sempiterna,* the Rose of Life. As to the past, it is because of what is there, that I look back: not because I do not see what is here to-day, or may be here to-morrow. It is because of what is to be gained that I look back; of what is supremely worth knowing there, of knowing intimately: of what is supremely worth remembering, of remembering constantly: not only as an exile dreaming of the land left behind, but as one travelling in narrow defiles who looks back for familiar fires on the hills, or upward to the familiar stars where is surety. In truth, is not all creative art remembrance: is not the very spirit of ideal art the recapture of what has gone away from the world, that by an imperious spiritual law is for ever withdrawing, to come again newly?

You wrote to me once, " Beware of the beauty that you seek." You would have me bow down only before the beauty that is beyond the last careful words of ivory and pale gold, beyond even the airs of the enchanted valleys where Music is.

And, to-day, with a wind of the south coming across glad water, and greenness uplifting itself from the grass to the foam of leaves on swaying elms, I realise in truth how small is the measure of beauty that any can give, saying " I have gathered this." Yonder yellow butterfly hovering over the grass-hid nest of the shrew-mouse . . . I think of it as a living flower of the sun, earth-wafted, wondering at the creature of the sod: but how poor that is compared with the excelling simplicity of the unknown peasant who, long ago, tenderly called the shrew-mouse *an dallag fheoir*, the little blind one of the grass, and the but-

To J. A. G.

terfly *dealan Dhé,* the little flame of God. The
one is the beauty of fantasy, the other is the
beauty of a child's mind matured in joy. And
so it is with Beauty. We dwell on this loveliness, or on that: and some white one, flame-
winged, passes us on the way, saying, " It is
Loveliness I seek, not lovely things."

In truth, Beauty is the light that we call
imagination — the radiance, the glow, the
bloom: we think of it as in those lines of
Prometheus Unbound:

> " Beloved and most beautiful, who wearest
> The shadow of that soul by which I live."

Beauty is less a quality of things than a
spiritual energy: it lies not in the things seen
but in harmonious perception. Yet, also, it
can dwell apart, in the sanctuary of this
flower or of that woman's face. But in itself
it is as impersonal as dew, as secret and divine and immortal—for, as you will remember,
Midir, the lord of sleep and youth and love,
the son of Angus, lord of death and the years
and the winged passions, was made of dew, of
the secret dews: Midir of the twilight, of the
secret and silent peoples, of the veiled im-
mortalities. It can exist for us in one face,
on one form, in one spirit, on the lifted waters,
on the hills of the west, in trampling marches

of sound, in delicate airs, but it is in all of these, and everywhere: wherever the imagination is become light, and that light is the light of flame. To each the star of his desire: but Beauty is beyond the mortal touch of number, as of change and time. Has any ever spoken more deeply of this than Plato, when in that vision of Perfect Beauty in the *Banquet* he writes: " It not like any face or hands or bodily thing; it is not word nor thought; it is not in something else, neither living thing, nor earth nor heaven; only by itself in its own way in one form it for ever Is."

Is it not he also, the wise and noble dreamer, who makes Socrates say in the *Phædrus*, " Beloved Pan, and all ye other gods . . . give me beauty in the inward soul."

The vision of the few. Yes. But a handful of pine-seed will cover mountains with the green majesty of forest. And so I too will set my face to the wind and throw my handful of seed on high:—

> Cuiridh mi m'aodann anns a' ghaoith
> 'Us tilgim baslach caoin an aird.

But you—you are of the little clan, for whom this book is: you who have gone upon dark ways, and have known the starless road, and perchance on that obscure way learned

To J. A. G.

what we have yet to learn.   For you, and such
as you, it is still a pleasure to gather bindweed of thoughts and dreams; still a pleasure
to set these dreams, these thoughts, to the
airs and pauses and harmonies of considered
speech.   So, by your acceptance of this book,
let me be not only of your fellowship but of
that little scattered clan to whom the wild bees
of the spirit come, as secret wings in the
dark, with the sound and breath of forgotten
things.

THE SUNSET OF OLD
TALES

'*Mieux que les scènes troublantes du jour, ces musiques et ces voix nocturnes me disaient l'espirit caché.*'
E. SCHURÉ, *Sanctuaires d' Orient.*

The Sunset of Old Tales

"And some were woven single, and some twofold,
and some threefold."

BLAKE: *Vala*, Night viii.

I do not know if in anything I have a
keener pleasure than in the hearing . . . by
the hearthside, or looking down into green
water, or on the upland road that strings glen
upon glen along its white swaying neck . . .
of the old tales and poems of beauty and
wonder, retold sometimes in an untarnished
excellence, sometimes crudely, sometimes so
disguised in the savour of the place and hour
that not then, and perhaps not for long, are
they recognised in accent or discerned in
feature. Perhaps this pleasure is the greater
because it is the pleasure of the tale-lover, for
the tale's sake, rather than of the tale-collec-
tor, for the quest's sake. I do not know how
many tales and fragments of tales and broken legends I have heard, now here, now there;

3

or what proportion of these was old, or what proportion of them was of the fantasy or dreaming mind of to-day, or how many retained the phrase and accent of the past in taking on the phrase of to-day and the accent of the narrator's mind. It is the light, the lift, the charm, the sigh, the cadence I want. I care less for the hill-tale in a book than told by the firelight, and a song is better in the wash of the running wave than in crowded rooms. Every sad tale and every beautiful tale should have a fit background for its setting; and I have perhaps grown so used to the shaken leaf, or the lifted water, or the peat-glow in small rooms filled with warm shadow and the suspense of dreams, as the background of *sgeul* and *rann* and *oran,* that I am become unwisely impatient of the common conditions. Yet even in these much lies with ourselves. I have a friend who says he can be happy with a gas-jet in a room in a street-house. He opens a window by the edge of an inch, if there is no wind crying in the chimney, so that a thin air may be heard rising and falling: and turns his back to the gas-jet: and keeps his eyes on the book before him. But are there many of his kind, who are unhappy, being kept in towns, and yet know how to become masters of illusion? I know a fam-

4

ily of distinction in one of our great cities who have never heard tale or song, legend or dream, or any breath of romance, except at entertainments in their own or another's house, or at a concert or at a theatre. I have heard them spoken of as rich people, as having more than they need or could ever use. They are poor people, I fear. In the pity I have for them I admit there is something, too, of dread. Could one fall into that estate? For they live what is called "life." But as they are never alone, and in a sense have always everywhere, a gas-jet, I cannot see that the existence they lead is life, that they *live*. If it were not for the imaginative solace of fires, those unconquerable allies of dreams and romance, I suppose the deep love for the things of which I speak would die away from the life of towns.

It would be a good thing to be a collector, and to know how to winnow the gathering, and where to range and where to place apart. We owe a debt, indeed, to the few who are truly fit for the task they have set themselves. But there are some minds which care very little to hear about things, when they can have the things themselves. It is not for the service of beauty, but only for the uses of formal knowledge, that one might desire a stuffed

5

cuckoo. But a cuckoo in a case—or a cuckoo in a cage, if one would live barred, which I cannot believe—is not a cuckoo. The bells in the grey cloud when, unseen, the cuckoo swims on the wind . . . that is the cuckoo.

I have good friends who have urged me to collect folklore. In a sense I have done so since I was a child. But I do not care to go pencilling through the Highlands or from isle to isle. The tale or song thus sought loses its charm for me. I like to be taken by surprise when, beyond the hawthorn in bloom, a swallow swoops, and I know that spring is come; or when, in the beech-thicket, the mavis suddenly calls the five long calls of joy, and the thrill of June is felt; or when, above the fern, in a windless moonlit silence, the night-jar throbs the passion of midsummer.

And, too, I should be uneasy if I had to do more than listen. For I remember a friend's telling how a " folklorist " rejoiced a year or two ago over strange tales gathered out of the wilds of Inverness, and builded on them a theory, and gave much delighted perplexity to himself and others, till another specialist broke the enchantment by pointing out that the so-called oriental survivals were no more than a year old, being, in fact, nothing else than Gaelic renderings of parts of *The Ara-*

bian Nights, translated by an enthusiast, who wished to bring to the Gael something of accepted worth.

I have sometimes given of this sea-drift and wind-drift which has remained with me, as I chanced to remember, or as the theme invited. And I have written, too, of the charm of these old-world legends and romances in their modern survivals or often bewildering changes.

But if ever I yielded to this quest as a possessing eagerness it would be to catch the last reflections of the sunset of old tales. And not the least curious would be those which have lapsed into all but forgetfulness. I take, almost haphazard, six of these, much as I find them in my notes, or as accident has awakened in my memory; and a seventh, " The Wayfarer," I have added partly because it also has, in these old Gaelic lands, the sunset hue of an immortal tale told in supreme beauty so many years ago; and partly because I have not yet had opportunity to include it fittingly since its original appearance some years back in *Cosmopolis.* These tales, or their like, that in some form have travelled across so many lands and seas, have lived on so many tongues and seen time rise and fall like the punctual tides, and are now fading

7

into forgetfulness with the passing of the last western tongue as ancient as they, are very slight. But they have this to their gain, that they are on the rainbow-side of the sunset, and that few tales of the kind will now be told by the crofter or hill-shepherd or islesman, or by old or young at the *ceilidh*, or by those who stand back more and more from the ways and the cross-ways.

THE TREUD NAN RÒN

"What have I heard but the murmur of sand:
What have I seen but foam . . ."
(Refrain of a Gaelic Song.)

Last August, sailing one day on the Lynn
of Morven in a black-green calm, though from
Cruachan to Nevis a storm darkened the Appin hills with cloud and wind, I heard from a
man of Lorne a seal-story that was not so
much a tale as a fragment of old legend.
There is a low sandy isle among the isles of
Lorne, lying in Morven waters between the
Corrie of the Stags and the island of Lismore.
It is called, I think, Faileag-mhara, which is
to say, little lawn or meadow of the sea: a
good name, for its pretty beaches and bent-
held sands enclose grassy spaces, where the
tern descends to her rude nest and the scart
and guillemot sometimes breed. My Lorne
friend spoke of it as the isle of the piocach,
because that fish, the saithe, is often to be
caught in plenty, in quiet twilights, off its
north shore. It might be called, also, the isle

9

of shells, for many beautiful shells lie in its
little bays and pools. And a poet might call it
the isle of voices, for it is always either in
some low tranced song, or shaken with a wild
music; and, besides, it is like a listening ear
of the sea, held to a mysterious sighing from
the dark mountains of Morven, or from the
continual whispering of the tides of Appin
running by the head of Lismore. In storm it
is like a harp hung among the branches of
tormented trees: men have heard terrifying
cries and an intolerable wailing when passing
it in the mist and the blindness of tempest.

On the still noon of which I write I had
seen a dark head rise from the purple-sha-
dowed blueness of the sea about fifty fathoms
away, and had remarked to my companion
that the seal yonder was " an old man," as the
saying is, and of great size.

" Ay, he is well known here. It's the big-
gest bull I've seen this side the west o' Jura.
They say he's fèy. Howsoever, he'll bide no
seal near him—neither man-seal nor woman-
seal. He had a mate once. She swam too
near a *geòla,* a yawl as we might be saying in
the English, where a woman leaned in the
moonshine an' played a foreign thing like
what we call the cruit-spannteach. A man
took a gun an' put a ball into her side. She

came up three times, crying like a child or
bleating like a lamb-lost ewe maybe: it was
between the one and the other, and ill to
hearken. The bull yonder dashed at the stern
o' the yawl an' broke the steering-gear. The
failm was torn away, ay an' I tell you the
crann sgòidc swung this way an' that—the
boom swung this way an' that, for all the
calmness of the calm. The man with a gun
tried to shoot the man-seal, but couldn't. The
singing woman with the foreign music went
below crying: and I am not wondering at that
if she had seen the eyes of the woman-seal.
I've seen the pain in them, I have. I've seen
tears in their eyes. I saw one once away out
by Heiskir, that was made mateless and childless one red sunset, an' leaned on a rock staring motionless acrost the black an' white o'
the tost sea. She did not move when a ball
struck the rock, an' sent splinters flyin'. She
did not turn her head, no not by this or that.
She stared out acrost the black an' white. It
wasn't where the bull died, or where her
young sank. It was out acrost the black an'
white o' the tost sea. The red of the set was
in her eyes. They were redder: ay, I saw
that. The black was green about the rock,
an' the splash had the whiteness of snow, an'
the mussels and dog-whelks on the rock glis-

11

tered in the shine. A scart flew by her scream-
in', an' the terns wailed. She just stared.
Her head was up, an' she stared an' stared an'
stared an' stared. The shooters left her alone.
It was dark when I sailed east o' that."

"How long has that old man been here?"
I asked.

"I am not knowing that. No one knows
that. There's a man over yonder, John Stuart
up Ballachulish way, who told me it was nine
hundred years old. Is that foam? Maybe,
maybe. Did ye ever hear tell of the story of
the Seal of the Shiant Isles? No? It was like
this: though for sure, it's no story, but only
a saying.

"He was an old bull-seal, an' there's no
man knows or ever knew the years he had.
He was grey with the sea and time. Padruig
Dhomnullach, the Heiskir bard, made a song
on him. He said he had the years back to
the days when Oisin was beautiful as the
west wind on the yellow banks o' May. Ay,
that he swam the Moyle, when the swans o'
Lir were on it, with their singing beyond all
singing for sweetness and pain. An' that he
was older than them: older than the *sgeul* or
the *shennachie*, than the tale or the teller. His
name was Ròn, an' he was the first o' the
clan. He was the son of the King of Ireland,

and a brother of a son of that King. His mother was a beautiful woman of the sea in the north isles. She was called Sea-Sand. Perhaps it was because her hair was yellow as the sands of the sea. Perhaps it was because she was like the sand that is now here an' now there, and is sometimes so light that a mew's foot does not stir it and sometimes so smilin' and treacherous that a man sinks in it to his death. An' one day his brother came over to him with a message. They played a game on the shore. It was with great curved shells, an' they were thrown against the wind they were, an' a skilful and crafty throwing is needed for that, they with the holes in them an' the shape like partans of the sea. But that day the wind caught one of the shells in the midway of the hurl, an' it swung sideway an' struck Ròn on the whiteness of the brow. He cried a cry, an' was down. And when the King's son saw that, he had fear. Men would say he had put death on his brother. So he ran from that place. He looked back, an' he saw sand blowing upon the body, an' falling upon it, and heard a moaning an' a crying. Then he knew it was Sea-Sand keening the son of her love. And he saw the wave running up the shore, an' she meeting it. And then she lifted Ròn an'

threw him in the wave, an' he rose like a
man an' fell down like a seal, for tall he was,
an' handsome he was, but he had no arms now
an' no legs, but only a slimness and long body.
'The sea for your home,' she cried, an' that
crying was on the wind. And that's how
Ròn took to the sea, but remembers the shore
for ever an' ever. He an' his. Ay, *air chuan,
air mhuir, air chorsa,* in the deep ocean, in
the narrow sea, by the shores."

And after that he told me how Ròn took a
woman of the land and kept her in a pool of
the rocks. And the young they had were as
good in the sea as on the land: and they had
brown eyes that the salt did not sting, and
long brown hair like seaweed, and their songs
were wild.

And thinking of this that I was told on the
Lynn of Morven, my mind was often troubled with some other confused memory.
What had I known of this before: when had
I heard the like, and if so, where? It was
only to-day, at the flying of a bird and the
falling of its shadow across a flapping sail,
that, in a moment, I know not how, I found
myself thinking of an old Greek tale of how a
prince of Salamis, Telamon, slew his brother
at quoit-throwing on the shore, and he too, a
king's son, son of Aeacus, of Aegina: and

how that brother's name was Phocus, which is
to say a seal: and how the name of Aeacus'
sea-love, and the mother of Phocus, was
Psammatheia, which is Sea-Sand, sand of the
sea.

THE MAN ON THE MOOR

"Woe for the doom of a dark soul. . . ."
SOPHOCLES.

"The desert groweth. Woe unto him who con-
taineth deserts."
NIETZSCHE.

On the mainland of Ardnamurchan there is
a house by the shore, built of grey stones,
against which the yellow flags and gallingale
run up like surf, and behind which a long
slope of bracken looks like the green sea beyond rocks when the wind is heavy on it,
though with no more to see than a myriad
wrinkling. There is no other house near, nor
boat on the shore: and I saw or heard never
a sheep, but the few thin beasts of Anndra
MacCaskill browsing the salt grass by the
long, broken, wandering dune where the rocks
lie in a heavy jumble. It is a desolate place.
I saw no birds in all the bramble, never a
finch in the undershaws, nor shilfa in the
tansy-wastes. Even on the shore the white
wings of the gulls and terns were not catch-

ing the light: I saw nothing but three birds,
a dotterel flying and wailing, a scart black-
green on a weedy rock, and a grey skua hawking the sighing suck of the ebb. The light
was that of storm, though the twilight was already gathering in every corrie and hollow:
and in October the day falls soon. The sea
south was a dark, tossing waste, with long,
irregular dykes of foam that ran and merged
when you looked at them, but were like broken walls on fields of black rye when you saw
them only through the side of the eyes.
South-west and west long splashes of red
flame ruddied the wild sea and brought the
black to blue. It was not this year, nor last,
nor the year before, that I heard that of which
I now write: but I remember it all as though
it were of yesterday. A bit of loneroid, gale
or bog-myrtle as it is called in the south, wet,
with the light green and the dark green on
the same stem, will often, in a moment, bring
Tighnaclachan before me, so that I see just
that desolate shore and no other shore, and
hear the scattered lamenting of the few sheep
yonder, and see that scart on the weedy rock
plucking at its black-green feathers, or that
grey skua with its melancholy cry hawking the
sighing shallows of the ebb beyond the ledges,
to this side of the house itself, half windowless

17

yet it may be, and with the byre-doors open and falling back and rotting.

It was a matter of no moment that took me there: partly to meet one coming another way, partly to see Dionaid Maclure, a frail old woman who kept the place for Neil Mc-Neil, her brother. I had walked some three miles, and was tired; not with the distance, but with a something in the wind, and perhaps from the singular gloom of the place at that hour in that grey loneliness, caught between deserted lands and a sea never quiet, an angry troubled waste, perpetually lamenting, continually shaken with fierce wraths.

As I came close to Tighnaclachan, I saw no smoke above the boulder-held thatch. The ragged pony I had seen there before was not in the airidh beyond. It was with relief I heard the clucking of a hen somewhere. The only other living thing I saw was a magpie by a pool of rain-water, stalking with sharp cries of anger its own restless image.

Yet it was here that, before I heard the tale Neil McNeil told me, I heard words from old Janet which put a beauty into that lonely un-homely place for me, then and for always. I forget what led to the beauty in the old heart, and stirred it: but I remember the shape it took on the old lips. She had given me tea,

an we had sat awhile in the brown dusk by
the comforting red glow of the peats, and then
I told her something, I forget what—perhaps
of some one we knew, perhaps a bit of a tale,
or a song maybe, likely the sigh of a ballad or
song—when she leaned to me, and said, " It's
a blessing they are, a healing and a blessing:
ay, so they are, the moonlight an' the dew.
When we're young, summer's sweet wi' them:
when we're old, they're in the heart still. It's
the song left, the memory o' the song, a sweet
air, when the bird's flown for aye. Ay, my
dear, an' there's more than that to be said.
God made the sun an' the day: the Holy
Spirit, the night an' the stars; but Christ
made the moonlight an' the dew."

She was tender and sweet, old Dionaid:
fair in life and fair in death. Strange that
the beauty of a single thought can thence-
forth clothe the desolation in loveliness, and
change the grey air and the grey sea and the
grey face of a seared land into a sanctuary of
peace, as though unknown birds builded there,
doves of the spirit. I remember, once, on the
waste of Subasio behind Assisi, that some
one near me said the barrenness was terrible,
more lifeless and sad than any other solitude.
To me, at that moment, as it happened, this
was not so: the hill glowed with the divine

19

light, that came, not from the east welling it
or the west gathering it, but from the immortal life of the heart of St. Francis—and a
storm of white doves rose with flashing wings,
so that I was dazzled: and only when I saw
that they were not there did I know I had seen
the prayers and joy of a multitude of hearts,
children of him to whom the wind was
" brother " and the grass " sister."

But now I must go back to that of which
I meant to write. I have given the lonely
setting of the place where, when we came in
at dayfall for the porridge, Neil McNeil—a
tired man, tall, gaunt, grey-black, with cold
blue eyes like the solander's—told me of the
man MacRoban, or MacRobany.

There is no need to tell of what kept me
there till long after dark was come, with the
flowing tide making so heavy a noise among
the loose rock that at times our words sounded
hollow and far away: nor of all that we
three, waiting there, talked: nor what dreams
and thoughts came into that flame-lit dark
room in the desolate house by the sea. When
Neil spoke once, unquestioned, it was after
a long silence, when we were unconsciously
listening to the loud *tick-tack, tick-tack* of
the great wall-clock as though we were eager
almost to a strained anxiety to hear urgent

tidings, some news expected or feared, or half-guessed, coming mysteriously, on quivering lips: with a foreign sound, broken, meshed in obscurity—hearing at the same time the gathering clamour in the sea's voice, the hoarse *scroach-an-scroach* of the flung surge on the dragged reluctant beach, and the loud-demanding cry of the wind behind the confused and trampling noise of the tide, that by the sound was in the house itself and away inland.

"I can't tell you much about what you asked," he began slowly. "There isn't much to tell. You've been in or near that place away in the Italian country, and may know more than I know. It was this way, then, since I must tell you the little I know. You thought, that day we talked about it, the name was MacCroban. But I'm not knowing if there's any such name: any way it is not the man's name, the man I'm thinking of, the man I have in my mind. His name was Mac-Róban, or MacRóbany."

"Was?"

"Ay."

Tick-tack . . . tick-tack . . . and the loud anger of the sea at the door. I was glad when Neil went on.

"He had no home. I met him a long way

inland—on the Moss of Achnacree, beyond
Morven, across the Sound of Lorne. It was
at the edge o' dark, and he was lying with his
head on a stone. I stooped and spoke to him.

" ' Poor man, have you the heavy sickness
on you?' I asked, and again in the English,
when he did not answer.

" ' It is dying you are,' I said. ' I fear,
poor man, it is near death you will be if you
lie there.'

" ' I will give you all things,' he said in a
thin voice, weary as a three-day wind in the
east: 'Ay, I will give you secrets and all
things, if you will give me death.'

" ' And for why that?' I asked.

" ' I die like this every night,' he said, ' and
there are three of us. I am not knowing
where my two brothers will be, in what land,
west or east: my brother John, and my
brother Raphael. But they, too, are like this,
like what I am, like what you see me here.
They have their heads on stones, in a waste
place. They call upon death. If any man
stoops as you do, over John, my brother, he
will say what I say—" I will give you all, I
will give you all secrets, I will give you
knowledge and power, if you will give me one
thing, if you will give me death." And if any
man stoops over Raphael, my brother, he will

say that also—that John our brother would say, and that I say.'

"At that I thought the poor man had the black trouble.

"'No,' he said, as though he knew my thought. 'It is not madness I have, but old, old weariness.'

"'And what will your name be?' I asked.

"'Here I have been, in this country, for seven years, wandering. And here my name, by some chance of change, is MacRoban, or MacRobany. And that is no ill change, for it means son of Roban or Robany, and that is what I am. But no,' he added, 'it is not the name you have now in your mind. It is an older name than that. It is a name that has the sand of the desert on its feet. It is a name written on the weeping wall in the Holy City of Zion.'

"I looked at the man, though the darkness was fast falling through the greyness. I remember a crying of many curlews in that waste place, and the suddenness of snipe drumming in a wet hollow a stone's-throw beyond where two lapwings never stopped wheeling and wailing.

"'And who will you be?' I said. My voice was hard, for the cold of a fear was in my bones.

23

"'My name is Robani,' he said, 'Daniel Robani. I am Daniel Robani, and my brother John is Johannes Robani, and my brother Raphael is Raphael Robani. And there's no weariness like our weariness. And every night we lie down to die, but we never die.'

"Then I knew the poor man was mad, and seeing I could not lift him, I gave him my cloak and hurried on to the clachan of Ledaig beyond the Moss to get help. I saw the minister, a stranger come for a month, but a good man and kind. He came with me. We saw no man. We found my cloak, but no man.

"Next day the minister had me into his room. 'Tell me again what words he spoke,' he said to me. I told him. Then he leaned from his chair, and said to me: 'Neil McNeil, you have dreamed a dream or seen a mystery. Best go to your home now, and in silence: ay, go away without word of this. For I do not know what is dream and what is vision, and what is truth and what madness. But hear this: In the tenth year of this century we live in, a great vase or jar of marble was found in the excavated ruin of an ancient city in the southlands of Italy, called Aquila—which is to say, Iolair, Eagle

24

—and in that jar was a copper plate. On the one side was engraved in the Hebrew, " A plate like this has gone unto every tribe." On the other side, and also in the Hebrew, was engraved the Death Warrant of Jesus of Nazareth, called Jesus the Christ. And of the four witnesses who signed the condemnation of the Christ the names of three were the names of three brothers, Daniel Robani, and Johannes Robani, and Raphael Robani.' "

Neil ceased abruptly. The noise of the waves was as a multitude of hands batting the walls of the house: the wail and cry of the wind was like a dreadful Spirit. Before the red glow of the peat-fire we sat silent. *Tick-tack, tick-tack:* and the calling of the sea, the calling of the sea.

THE WOMAN AT THE CROSS-WAYS

" . . . fiercest is the madness that springeth from inappeasable desires."—PINDAR, Nem. xi.

I do not know in how many old literatures that tradition survives of a being of the veiled world who can at will pass from diminutive shape to a sombre and terrifying aspect. It may not be at will, always, for those shadowy beings who are seen only by loosened passions may be creatures that feed upon these passions, as creatures of the wilds upon sudden pastures. And as they are fed, these shy divinities change: that which was small is become great: that which was human is now inhuman: the stream flowing past in the darkness is become Terror whispering, the wind among the shaken grasses on the moor is Fear, clothing herself in shadows.

A friend and kinsman, who at one time had an other-world sight beyond that of any I have known, told me lately that the reason why he had put a chain upon that hound of supernatural vision and kept it in a secret

26

place in his mind and never willingly let it loose upon the dreams and thoughts and deed-shapes of men and women, was because of this, that often he had seen the disembodied passions and desires. Sometimes, he said, they were like swallows flying about the eaves of a house, sometimes like crested demons standing with a spear upon the dark brows of advancing tempest, sometimes like trees waving many arms and with starlike eyes in their dim cavernous depths. And often, he told me, these changed, as the embodied passions and desires cried out to them with longing and proud laughters, or waited like children in a wood, or bade them slake their thirst at other wells, or commanded them return whence they came, or, in a shaken dread, were still, or, with scornful eyes, silent. And as they were fed, so did these disembodied passions and desires grow; or as they were denied, so did they dwindle; but most were ravenous with hunger, and were glutted with sweet prey.

"And when the world that we call the other world is become as open to the eyes as this world-in-the-veils that we call our own," he said, "one must either see too much, or be content to shroud his eyes and see only as others see: and that way I have chosen."

So, I think often, may it be with those
beings of the wastes. Some there may be
that do not change—creatures of the woods;
the *Ceasg*, lovely and harmless, in the flowing brown depths of the hill-stream; the
Grianuisg, that herds flocks of white doves;
the green *Glastig*, that milks the wild deer;
the *Mòrglas*, sitting silent on a high boulder
in unpeopled glens at twilight. But these
have their life apart from us. They are the
offspring of another father, as the slim wom-
en of the trees and the waves, as the blind
grey-girl of the cliffs whom the hawks and
wild falcons feed and guard. Many fear her,
and have heard her crying in rain, or when
the broken winds wail among crags and
ledges.

But of the others, many change; some at
will, to appal or to deceive or to evade; some
because they are as shadows that shrink to
daisies or increase to vast and menacing
shapes just as the mind that perceives them
mirrors them.

Of these, I think, is the woman of tears,
the *Beantuiream*, the weeping woman, the
woman of mourning, she who keens the sorrow of death in lonely places. How many
have heard that lament, by running water in
the dusk, by pools where the grey owl hawks

the grey moth, on moors when the lapwings sleep and even the curlews are not crying under the moist down-dropping stars.

Sometimes she is seen as the Washer of the Ford, a tall, gaunt woman, chanting the *Seis-Bhais*, the Death-Dirge, as she washes the shroud of him who sees her; and sometimes she may suddenly grow great and terrible, and inhabit darkness, and the end is come. Sometimes she is seen as the *Nigheag Cheag a Chroin*, the little washer of sorrow, perhaps singing low while she steps the stones of a ford, or moves along the dim banks where the dew is white on sorrel and meadowsweet, *a leineag cheag bhais na lamh* . . . her little shroud of death in her hand . . . *a caoineadh chroin na ceul*, the keen of sorrow in her mouth for him or her whose death is near.

I heard once of a meeting with the Woman of Tears told by one whose brother was he who had seen and heard: but of these neither died at that time. It is not of that I am thinking, however, but of something in the brother's tale as he told it, and as it was told to me.

"It was this way," said he who told me: " . . . when Micheil went home that night, he went by the old packhorse road on the high moor, for the rains had made a bog of the highway for more than a mile near Alltdhu, that was our house, a big stone house with the three byres to it. He was cold and hungry, for he had not touched sup or bite since noon of the day; and if he was sad it was not for any who called our hearts their home, but because of his tiredness, it may be, or the darkness and the wet, or mayhap for a song's lament that was on his lips or in his mind, for he was aye fond of sweet sorrowful lilts.

"But when he was come to within the nearness of a mile, the rain was up, and the half-moon shone. It was so still he could hear the snipe drumming in the bog below Creag-dhu. There wasn't a sound else, no, not a sound, but only the stillness of stillness. 'Tis a place, yon, for the cryin' o' peewits an' the whaup's lamentings: but on this night one might have heard the grey moth dancing above the eyes o' the heather.

"Micheil hated the deepness of that silence, and it was worse when the snipe were still again. He whistled, but the sound went so far out upon the moor, and was so unlike the thing he had made, that he was troubled. He went on slowly with the heavy dislike on him

for the noise of his feet.   Sorrows were in his
mind by now, and the lamenting of the heart
that is never at peace because the things that
cannot be are so great and desirable and the
things that are look so broken and poor and
desolate.

"When nigh upon Donnusk Water he
stopped: to see the stones of the ford, he
said: though he knew the stones, and that
the water was shallow, and was aflow below
them at that.

"He thought it was myself at first.

"'Is it you, John?'" . . . he said in the
whisper that he thought would be the loud
voice.

"He saw then it wasn't me; no, nor any
man: but a woman, or a girl, stooping over
the water.

"Perhaps he thought it was Elsie the cow-
woman, or our niece Kirsteen: he did not
think so, but to hide the whisper in his
mind he lifted that thought on to the banks
above it.

"'*Galasaidh*' . . . he called, his voice falling like a splashing stone.

"'*Will that be you, Cairstine?*' he called
again, but lower, and he looked behind him
when he had spoken.

"Then he saw the woman or the girl look

31

round. He had not heard her singing before, but he heard it now. By that sorrowful lamentation, low and sweet forbye, and by the tears that glistered white on the grey face, he knew it was the *Nigheag Cheag a Chroin.*

"Micheil was a man who would not let fear eat his heart. He gave a low sob, and waited till the sickness of the cold sweat was gone: then he licked the dryness of his lips.

"'Peace to you, good woman,' he said.

"'And so you know me, *mo cuat,*' she answered to him, putting down on the grass the whiteness of the *leinag cheag bhais*, the little white shroud of death.

"'I know you, Woman of Tears,' he said, 'though why is it calling me *mo cuat* you are, for I am no lover of yours? And that whiteness there on the grass, sure it is for a child or a maid, that?'

"'Let me look at you,' she said.

"He saw her tall now, and dark: bigger than the great alder on the bank not far from her.

"'Do you remember?' she said.

"Micheil was still at that. 'No,' he whispered, when the high reed near him was no more shaken with the breath of his pulse.

" 'You will never be forgetting me, Micheil Macnamara. As for that whiteness there, it is the cloth of blindness.'

" '*Mo Bròn*,' Micheil moaned; 'sorrow upon me!'

" 'Look at me,' he said.

" Micheil put his gaze at her. It was no woman now he saw, not even a *bandia*, but a power or dominion, he thought. She had her feet far down among roots of trees, and stars thickening in her hair as they gather in the vastness and blackness of the sky on a night of frost.

" 'Are you Death?' Micheil sobbed, his knees shaking with the awe that was on him.

" 'I am older than Death,' she said. Her voice was beyond and above and behind and below; but it was no more than the lowness of a low wind in the dusk.

" Then he heard a chanting, as of trees in a wind, and of waves rising and falling in caverns by the sea: but he did not know, and never knew, if it was in the tongue of the Gael he heard, or in what tongue. But it would be the Gaelic, for sure: for Micheil had little English, then or after. And the words that he heard were somewhat as are these words, but remembered dimly they are, as in a dream:—

33

"'I am she who loveth Loneliness,
And Solitude is my breath.
I have my feet on graves,
And the resurrection of the dead is my food,
For the dead rise as a vapour
And I breathe it as mist,
As mist that is lickt up of the wind.
I am she who stands at the pools:
I stand at the meeting of roads,
The little roads of the world
And the dark roads of life and death,
And the roads of all the worlds of the Universe.
I am Anama-Bhroin, the Soul of Sorrow:
I am she who loveth Loneliness,
And I have the Keys of Melancholy and of Joy.
My lover is Immortality,
For I am a Queen,
Queen of all things on earth and in the sea,
And in the white palaces of the stars
Built on the dark walls of Time
Above the Abyss.'

" But this that was Solitude clothing herself in voice was remembered by Micheil, as I say, only as words in a dream. These may not be the words, but only the dimness of the colour of the words. He heard no more, and saw no more. And when I found him in the morning he was stiff in cold sleep. It was a day and a night and another day before he spoke, and told me what I have told. He wrote it too, later, on a paper: and so neither forgot."

But why, this evening, have I copied all
this from notes taken some five or more
years ago? It is not because both John and
Micheil Macnamara are dead.

It is because, to-day, lying in a solitary
place, with the crying of curlews on the
west wind, I was reading a book that I
had last read in the alien tongue of a great
French poet, on a day when another wind of
the west stole up across the purple blueness
of the Gulf of Corinth, and passed away in
the radiance beyond the Steeps of Delphi.
And, as I read the ancient Hymn in the
as fine English of another translator, I
found myself remembering . . . something
. . . I knew not what: and then I remembered.

For a time I wondered if the Greek mystic
and poet had, in his own hour and day, seen
a like vision and uttered it in beauty, such as
the islander Micheil had confusedly seen and
confusedly given again in broken words and
crude music. Then I took up the volume,
and read again (while a whisper was in the
coarse grass and tangled bracken, and far
away over the heather the curlews wailed
above the long low flowing tide of the west
wind) :—

"I am Hecatê of the Ways, of the Cross-

35

The Woman at the Cross-Ways

*Ways, of the Darkness, of the Heaven and
the Earth and the Sea; saffron-clad Goddess
of the Grave, exulting among the spirits of
the dead; Perseia, lover of loneliness; Queen
who holdest the Keys of the world . . ."*

THE LORDS OF WISDOM

"Knowing that knowable spirit, let not death
disturb you."—*The Prashna Upanishad.*

A friend writes to me asking what is "the
wisdom of the wild bees"? He read the
phrase, he says, in something I wrote once,
and also in an Oban paper last year, quoted
there as a Hebridean saying. I am not sure
if I have heard it in English. But in Gaelic,
either as "the old wisdom of the bees," or
"the secret knowledge of the bees," the
phrase occurs in tales of the islanders of
Tiree, Coll, Iona, Colonsay, and Islay as
naturally as phrases such as *cho marbh ri
sgadan,* "as dead as a herring," or *cho luath
ris na luinn,* "as swift as the wave-tops"; or
as, in tales of second-sight, *mar thubradh
anns an dailgionn,* "as was spoken in the
prophecy"; or as, in tales of love, *a ghraidhean mo chridhe,* "thou dear one of my
heart"; or as, in the telling of the "*Tri
Broin nan Sgeulachd*" ("The Three Sorrows
of Story-Telling"), or other old tales, men-

37

tion of the *slacan druidheachd*, the magic wand, or being *fo gheasaibh*, under enchantment.

In Iona, some years ago, I heard an old woman speak of the robin-redbreast as " St. Columba's Companion," and of the wild bees as his children: " They have Colum's wisdom," she said. But I imagine that, in most instances, the phrase is used without much thought of the lost or time-worn meaning, as are used the other phrases I have given. " Ask the wild bee for what the Druids knew," and " ask the children of the heather where Fionn sleeps," and the like, point to an old association of the wild bee and ancient wisdom. And, doubtless, the story-teller of to-day might naturally use figuratively or directly allude to a creature so familiar to him; as, last year, in one of the isles, a shepherd speaking to me ended his narrative with " and I would go to that country, and look till I found, if I had the three wisdoms of the bee, that can find its way in the grass, and over the widest water, and across the height of hills." Here, of course, is meant the natural knowledge of the bee, not the wisdom of druid, or of Colum Cille, or of the masters of illusion, or of the *cumhachdan siorruidh shuas*, the everlasting powers above. I re-

member a line too, as part of an invocation
or oath, though I cannot recall the latter
exactly. The line was fifth or sixth, and
ran, " by the wisdom of the air-travellers," or
words to that effect (possibly birds in their
migration, and not bees, were meant). The
invocation, if such it were, began:—

> " 'Air a ghrian anns an iarm,
> Air an adhar os do chionn,
> Air an talamh os do bhonn,
> Air an dreighinn naoimh,'

and invoked also other things of earth and
elemental things. And not long ago I heard
a phrase used by a Gaelic preacher so nearly
in the words of a great writer that I thought
it was a quotation from some poem or legendary tale familiar to me, and it was not for
some time, in " Who was it put wisdom on
the bee, teaching her the direction of the
fields of the air, and the homeway to the hive
on hillside or in glen; or who showed the salmon to leave the depths of the sea, and come
up narrow streams; or who gave the raven
the old wisdom of the hills? " . . . that I
recognised an unconscious iterance of Bacon's
noble measure:—" Who taught the raven in
a drowth to throw pebbles into an hollow
tree where she spied water, that the water

might rise so as she might come to it? Who taught the bee to sail through such a vast sea of air, and to find the way from a field in flower a great way off to her hive? Who taught the ant to bite every grain of corn that she burieth in her hill, lest it should take root and grow?"

In Ross, I was told by a man of the Gairloch, they speak . . . in a folk-tale, I think he said, but possibly colloquially . . . of the bees as "lords of wisdom" or "the little kings of wisdom." It is a fine phrase, that . . . the lords of wisdom: and not one to forget.

Oftenest, however, the allusions to the bee are, doubtless, to its "knowingness" rather than to its "wisdom"; its skill in tracking the pathless ways, its intuition of the hour and season, of the way of the wind, of the coming of rain, of gathering thunder.

But I recall from childhood a memory of another kind: though I cannot say, now, how much is old thought drowned in dreams, or how much is due to the ceaseless teller of tales who croons behind the heart and whispers the old enchantment in the twilights of the mind.

One day when the young Christ was nine years old he saw Mary walking by a thicket.

He ran and hid in the thicket, and sent three wishes of love to her, and gave to each the beat of two wings and the pulse of song. The first rose on wings of blue and sank into the sky, carrying a prayer of Mary. The second rose on white wings and fled seawards by the hills of the west, carrying a hope of Mary. The third rose on wings of green, and sank to the grasses, carrying a dream of Mary.

Then a voice came from the thicket: a voice so sweet as to send the birds to the branches . . . *chuireadh e na h'eoin 'an crannaibh:*—

"The Yellow Star, O Mary, to the bird of the blue
    wing! . . .
The rainbow, O Mary, to the white bird! . . .
The wild bee, O Mary, to the green bird! . . ."

At that, Mary worshipped. "O God in the thicket," she said, "sweet the songs and great the beauty. But lo! the birds are gone." Then Christ came out of the thicket, and took her hand. "Mother," said the child, "no trouble to your heart, dear, because of the Yellow Star. Your prayer was that my Father would not forget His secret promise. The sun is steadfast, and so I say that the Yellow Star is set upon your prayer. And

41

no trouble to your heart, Mother, because of the Rainbow to the white bird: for your hope was for the gates of the west and the hidden gardens of Peace: and even now the gates are open, and spices and balms are on the green wave that flows the long way east of the sun and west of the moon. But as to the wild bee, Mother, of that I cannot speak."

At that, Mary was sad, for she knew that when a Druid of the east had told her to give her son the friendship of the wind, of the blown dust, of the grass, of the leaf, and of the wild bee, she had done all those things but the last. So she stood and wept.

Then the young Christ, her son, called to a bee that was among the foam-white pastures.

"What was your dream, Mother?" he said.

"My dream," said Mary, "was that I should know death at the last, for in the flesh I am a woman, and that of me that is mortal desireth death."

So Christ asked the wild bee. But the bee said, "Can you see the nine hundred and ninety-nine secret roads of the air?"

"No," said the child.

"It is on one of these roads," said the wild bee, "that Mary's dream went."

So when Mary, sad at heart, but in this thing only, went back to the house where she dwelt and made ready the supper for that day's end, Christ gave friendship to the wild bee, and became a bee, and floated above the pastures. And when he came home at twilight he knew all the secrets of the little people of the air.

That night, after the meal was done, he stood looking at Mary and Joseph.

" I have known many wisdoms," he said, " but no wisdom like the wisdom of the wild bee. But I have whispered to them a secret thing, and through the years and the ages they will not forget. And some of the children of men shall hear the wild bees, and many shall call upon them; and to that little clan of the unwise and foolish, as they shall ever be accounted, I will send the wild bees of wisdom and of truth."

And Joseph said, " Are the bees then so wise? "

But Mary whispered: " I do not think it is of the wild bees of the pastures that the Christ my son speaks, but of the wild bees of the Spirit."

Christ slept, and put his hand in **Mary's,** and she had no fear: and that of her which was of heaven deepened in joy, and that of

43

her which was mortal had peace. But Joseph lay awake, and wondered why to a little clan of those held foolish and unwise should come, as secret wings in the dark, the sound and breath of an ancient wisdom.

THE WAYFARER

"This bright one who is Joy . . ."—*The Katha Upanishad.*

". . . then Salome asked of Him, 'How then may the woman dwell with the man?' And Jesus answered her: 'Eat all fruit save that which is bitter.'"
—*Clement of Alexandria.*

I

Among those in the home-straths of Argyll who are now grey, and in the quiet places of whose hearts old memories live green and sweet, there must be some who recall that day when a stranger came into Strath Nair, and spoke of the life eternal.

This man, who was a minister of God, was called James Campbell. He was what is called a good man, by those who measure the soul by inches and extol its vision by the tests of the purblind. He had rectitude of a kind, the cold and bitter thing that is not the sunlit integrity of the spirit. And he had the sternness that is the winter of a frozen life. In his heart, God was made in the image of John Calvin.

With this man the love of love was not
even a dream. A poor strong man he was,
this granite-clasped soul; and the sunlight
faded out of many hearts, and hopes fell away
to dust before the blight of the east wind of
his spirit.

On the day after his coming to Strath Nair,
the new minister went from cottage to cottage. He went to all, even to the hill-bothy
of Peter Macnamara the shepherd; to all save
one. He did not go to the cottage of Mary
Gilchrist, for the woman lived there alone,
with the child that had been born to her. In
the eyes of James Campbell she was evil.
His ears heard, but not his heart, that no
man or woman spoke harshly of her, for she
had been betrayed.

On the morning of the Bell, as some of
the old folk still call the morrow of the Sabbath, the glory of sunlight came down the
Strath. For many days rains had fallen,
hours upon hours at a time; or heavy, drop-
ping masses of vapour had hung low upon
the mountains, making the peaty uplands
sodden, and turning the grey rocks into a
wet blackness. By day and by night the
wind had moaned among the corries along
the high moors. There was one sound more
lamentable still: the incessant *méhing* of the

desolate, soaked sheep. The wind in the corries, on the moors, among the pines and larches; the plaintive cruel sorrow of the wandering ewes; never was any other sound to be heard, save the distant wailing of curlews. Only, below all, as inland near the coast one hears continuously the murmur of the sea, so by night and day the Gorromalt Water made throughout the whole reach of Strath Nair an undertone as of a weary sighing.

But before nightfall on Saturday the rain ceased, and the wet wind of the south suddenly revolved upon itself beyond the spurs of Ben Maiseach. Long before the gloaming had oozed an earth-darkness to meet the falling dark, the mists had lifted. One by one, moist stars revealed hollows of violet, which, when the moon yellowed the fir-tops, disclosed a vast untravelled waste of blue, wherein slow silent waves of darkness continuously lapsed. The air grew full of loosened fragrances; most poignantly, of the bog-myrtle, the bracken, and the resinous sprays of pine and larch.

Where the road turns at the Linn o' Gorromalt there is an ancient disarray of granite boulders above the brown rushing water. Masses of wild rose grow in that place. On

this June gloaming the multitudinous blooms
were like pale wings, as though the fabled
birds that live in rainbows, or the frail creatures of the falling dew, had alit there, tremulous, uncertain.

There that evening, the woman, Mary
Gilchrist, sat, happy in the silences of the
dusk. While she inhaled the fragrance of
the wild roses, as it floated 'above the
persistent green odour of the bent and
the wet fern, and listened to the noise of
Gorromalt Water foaming and surging out
of the linn, she heard steps close by her.
Glancing sidelong, she saw " the new minister," a tall, gaunt man, with lank, iron-
grey hair above his white, stern, angular
face.

He looked at her, not knowing who she
was.

Mary Gilchrist did not speak. Her face,
comely before, had become beautiful of late.
" It's the sorrow," said the Strath folk simply,
believing what they said.

Perhaps the dark eyes under the shadowy
hair deepened. The minister, of course,
could not see this, could not have noted so
small a thing.

"God be with you," he said at last in
Gaelic, and speaking slow and searchingly;

"God be with you. This is a fine evening, at last."

"God be with you, too, Mr. Campbell."

"So; you know who I am?"

"For sure, sir, one cannot live alone here among the hills and not know who comes and who goes. What word is there, sir, of the old minister? Is he better?"

"No. He will never be better. He is old."

When he spoke these words, James Campbell uttered them as one drover answers another when asked about a steer or a horse. Mary Gilchrist noticed this, and with a barely audible sigh shrank a little among the granite boulders and wild roses.

The minister hesitated; then spoke again.

"You will be at the hill-preaching to-morrow? If fine, the Word will be preached on the slope of Monanair. You will be there?"

"Perhaps."

He looked at her, leaning forward a little. Her answer perturbed him. The Rev. James Campbell thought no one should hesitate before the free offering of the bitter tribulation of his religion. Possibly she was one of that outcast race who held by Popish abominations. He frowned darkly.

"Are you of the true faith?"

"God alone knows that."

"Why do you answer me like that, woman? There is but one true faith."

"Mr. Campbell, will you be for telling me this? Do you preach the love of God?"

"I preach the love and hate of God, woman! His great love to the elect, his burning wrath against the children of Belial."

For a minute or more there was silence between them. The noise of the torrent filled the night. Beyond, all was stillness. The stars, innumerous now, flickered in pale uncertain fires.

At last Mary Gilchrist spoke, whispered rather:

"Mr. Campbell, I am only a poor woman. It is not for me to be telling you this or that. But for myself, I know, ay, for sure, I know well, that everything God has to say to man is to be said in three words—and these were said long, long ago, an' before ever the Word came to this land at all. An' these three words are, ' God is love.' "

The speech angered the minister. It was for him to say what was and what was not God's message to man, for him to say what was or was not the true faith. He frowned blackly awhile. Then, muttering that he would talk publicly of this on the morrow,

was about to pass on his way. Suddenly he
turned.

" What will your name be? If you will tell
me your name and where you live, my good
woman, I will come to you and show you
what fearful sinfulness you invite by speaking of God's providence as you do."

" I am Mary Gilchrist. I live up at the
small croft called Annet-bhan."

Without a word, Mr. Campbell turned on
his heel, and moved whitheraway he was
bound. He was glad when he was round the
bend of the road, and going up the glen.
God's curse was heavy on those who had
made iniquity their portion. So this was the
woman Gilchrist, whom already that day he
had publicly avoided. A snare of the Evil
One, for sure, that wayside meeting had been.

It had angered the new minister to find
that neither man nor woman in Strath Nair
looked upon Mary Gilchrist as accursed. A
few blamed; all were sorrowful; none held
her an outcast. To one woman, who replied
that Mary was the sinned against, not the
sinner, that black misfortune had been hers,
Mr. Campbell answered harshly that the All-
wise God took no store by misfortune—that
at the last day no shivering human soul could
trust to *that* plea. Even when John Mac-

allum, the hill-grieve, urged that, whether
Mr. Campbell were right or wrong, it was
clear nothing could be done, and would it not
be wisest for one and all to let bygones be
bygones, each man and woman remembering
that in his or her heart evil dwelled somewhere—even then the minister was wrought
to resentment, and declared that the woman,
because of her sin, ought to be driven out of
the Strath.

In the less than two days he had been in
Strath Nair this man had brought upon that
remote place a gloom worse than any that
came out of the dark congregation of the
clouds. In many a little croft the bright
leaping flame of the pine-log or the comfortable glow of the peats had become lurid.
For the eye sees what the heart fears.

Thus it was that when the Sabbath came
in a glory of light, and the Strath, and the
shadowy mountains, and the vast sun-swept
gulfs of blue overhead took on a loveliness
as though on that very morrow God had re-
created the earth and the universe itself, thus
it was the people of the Strath were down-
cast. Poor folk, poor folk, that suffer so because of the blind shepherds.

But before that glory of a new day was
come, and while he was still striding with

bitter thoughts from the place where he had left the woman Gilchrist, Mr. Campbell had again cause for thought, for perplexed anger.

As he walked, he brooded sullenly. That this woman, this lost one, had ventured to bandy words with him! What was she, a fallen woman, she with an unhallowed child up there at her croft of Annet-bhan, that she should speak to him, James Campbell, of what God's message was!

It was then that he descried a man sitting on a fallen tree by the side of the burn which runs out of the Glen of the Willows. He could not discern him clearly, but saw that he was not one of the Strath-folk with whom he had talked as yet. The man seemed young, but weary; yes, for sure, weary, and poor too. When he rose to his feet in courteous greeting, Mr. Campbell could see that he was tall. His long fair hair, and a mien and dress foreign to the straths, made him appear in the minister's eyes as a wayfarer from the Lowlands.

"God be with you. Good evening," Mr. Campbell exclaimed abruptly, in the English tongue.

The man answered gravely, and in a low, sweet voice, "God be with you."

"Will you be for going my way?" the minister asked again, but now in the Gaelic, for he knew this would be a test as to whether the man was or was not of the Strath.

" No. I do not go your way. Peradventure you will yet come my way, James Campbell."

With a start of anger the minister took a step closer. What could the man mean, he wondered. Still, the words were so gently said that hardly could he put offense into them.

" I do not understand you, my good man," he answered after a little; " but I see you know who I am. Will you be at the preaching of the Word at Monanair to-morrow; or, if wet, at the house of God close by the Mill o' Gorromalt ? "

" What Word will you preach, James Campbell ? "

" Look you, my man, you are no kinsman of mine to be naming me in that way. I am Mr. Campbell, the minister from Strathdree."

" What word will you preach, then, Mr. Campbell? "

" What word? There is but one Word. I will say unto you, as unto all men who hearken unto me on the morrow, that the Lord God is a terrible God against all who trangress His holy law, and that the day of repentance is wellnigh gone. Even now it may be too late. Our God is a jealous God, who doth not brook delay. Woe unto those who in their hearts cry out, 'To-morrow! To-morrow!'"

For a brief while the man by the wayside was still. When he spoke, his voice was gentle and low.

" Rather do I believe the Word to be that which the woman Mary Gilchrist said to you yonder by the linn: that God is love."

And having said this, he moved quietly into the dusk of the gloaming, and was lost to sight.

James Campbell walked slowly on his way, pondering perplexedly. Twice that evening he had been told what the whole message of God was—an evil, blasphemous, fair-seeming doctrine, he muttered, more fit for the accursed courts of her who sitteth upon seven hills than for those who are within the sound of the Truth. And how had the false wisdom come? He smiled grimly at the thought of the wanton and the vagrant.

Before he slept that night he looked out upon the vast and solemn congregation of the stars. Star beyond star, planet beyond planet, strange worlds all, immutably controlled, unrelinquished day or night, age or æon, shepherded among the infinite deeps, moving or-

derly from a dawn a million years far off to
a quiet fold a million years away, sheep shepherded beyond all change or chance, or no
more than the dust of a great wind blowing
behind the travelling feet of Eternity—what
did it all mean? Shepherded starry worlds,
or but the dust of Time? A Shepherd, or
Silence? But he who had the wisdom of God,
and was bearer of His message, turned to his
bed and slept, muttering only that man in his
wretchedness and sin was unworthy of those
lamps suspended there to fill his darkness for
sure, for God is merciful, but also to strike
terror and awe and deep despair into the
hearts of that innumerable multitude who go
down daily into a starless night.

And when he had thought thus, he slept:
till the fading bitterness of his thought was
lost too in the noise of Gorromalt Water.

II

A great stillness of blue prevailed on the
morrow. When sunrise poured over the shoulder of Ben Maiseach, and swept in golden
foam among the pines of Strath Nair, it was
as though a sweet, unknown, yet anciently
familiar pastoral voice was uplifted—a voice

full of solemn music, austerely glad, rejoicing
with the deep rejoicing of peace.

The Strath was as one of the valleys of
Eden. The rain-washed oaks and birches wore
again their virginal green; the mountain-ash
had her June apparel; the larches were like
the delicate green showers that fall out of the
rainbow upon opal-hued clouds at sunsetting;
even the dusky umbrage of the pines filled
slowly with light, as tidal sands at the flow.

The Gorromalt Water swept a blue arm
round the western bend of the Strath; brown,
foam-flecked, it emerged from the linn, tu-
multuous, whirling this way and that, leaping,
surging.

In the wet loneroid, in the bracken, in the
thyme-set grass, the yellow-hammers and
stonechats remembered, perhaps for the last
time in this summer-end, their nesting songs,
their nestling notes.

From every green patch upon the hills the
loud, confused, incessant bleating of the ewes
and four-month lambs made a myriad single
crying—a hill-music sweet to hear.

From the Mill o' Gorromalt, too, where little Sine Macrae danced in the sunlight, to
the turfed cottage of Mary Gilchrist high on
the furthest spur of Maiseach, where her
child stretched out his hands to catch the sun-

57

rays, resounded the laughter of children. The blue smoke from the crofts rose like the breath of stones.

A spirit of joy moved down the Strath. Even thus of old, men knew the wayfaring Breath of God.

It was then the new minister, the Interpreter, brought to the remembrance of every man and woman in the Strath that the Lord God moveth in shadow, and is a jealous God.

The water-bell of the Mill, that did duty on the preaching Sabbaths, began its monotonous call. Of yore, most who heard it had gone gladly to its summons. When John Campbell had preached the Word, all who heard him returned with something of peace, with something of hope. But now none went save unwillingly; some even with new suspicions the one against the other, some with bitter searchings, some with latent dark vanities that could not bloom in the light.

And so the man delivered the Gospel. He "preached the Word," there, on the glowing hillside, where the sun shone with imperious beauty. Was it that while he preached, the sky darkened, that the hillside darkened, the sunglow darkened, the sun itself darkened? That the heart of each man and woman darkened, that the mind of each darkened, that

58

every soul there darkened, yea, that even the white innocence of the little children grew dusked with shadow? And yet the sun shone as it had shone before the tolling of the bell. No cloud was in the sky. Beauty lay upon the hillside; the Gorromalt Water leaped and danced in the sunlight. Nothing darkened from without. The darkening was from within.

The Rev. James Campbell spoke for an hour with sombre eloquence. Out of the deep darkness of his heart he spoke. In that hour he slew many hopes, chilled many aspirations, dulled many lives. The old, hearing him, grew weary of the burden of years, and yet feared release as a more dreadful evil still. The young lost heart, relinquished hope.

There was one interruption. An old man, Macnamara by name, a shepherd, rose and walked slowly away from where the congregation sat in groups on the hillside. He was followed by his two collie dogs, who had sat patiently on their haunches while the minister preached his word of doom.

"Where will you be going, Peter Macnamara?" called Mr. Campbell, his voice dark with the same shadow that was in the affront on his face.

"I am going up into the hills," the old man

answered quietly, " for I am too old to lose sight of God." Then, amid the breathless pause around him, he added: "And here, James Campbell, I have heard no word of Him."

"Go," thundered the minister, with outstretched arm and pointed finger. "Go, and when thine hour cometh thou shalt lament in vain that thou didst affront the most High God!"

The people sat awed. A spell was upon them. None moved. The eyes of all were upon the minister.

And he, now, knew his power, and that he had triumphed. He spoke to or of now one, now another poor sinner, whose evildoing was but a weakness, a waywardness to guide, not a cancer inassuageable. Suddenly he remembered the woman, Mary Gilchrist.

Of her he spoke, till all there shuddered at her sin, and shuddered more at the chastisement of that sin. She was impure; she dwelt in the iniquity of that sin; she sought neither to repent nor to hide her shame. In that great flame of hell, which she would surely know, years hence—a hundred years hence—a thousand, ten thousand, immeasurably remote in eternity—she would know then, when

too late, that God was, indeed, a jealous God
—in unending torture, in ceaseless——

But at that moment a low *hush* grew into a
rising crest of warning. The wave of sound
spilled at the minister's feet. He stared,
frowning.

"What is it?" he asked.

"Hush!" some one answered. "There's
the poor woman herself coming this way."

And so it was. Over the slope beyond
Monanair Mary Gilchrist appeared. She was
walking slowly, and as though intent upon the
words of her companion, who was the wayfarer with whom Mr. Campbell had spoken
at the Glen of the Willows.

"Let her come," said the minister sullenly.
Then, suddenly, being strangely uplifted by
the cold night-wind in his heart, he resumed
his bitter sayings, and spoke of the woman
and her sin, and of all akin to her, from Mary
Magdalene down to this Mary Gilchrist.

"Ay!" he cried, as the newcomers approached to within a few yards of where he
stood, "and it was only by the exceeding overwhelming grace of God that the woman, Mary
Magdalene, was saved at all. And often, ay,
again and again, has the thought come to me
that the mercy was hers only in this life."

A shudder went through the Strath-folk,

but none stirred. A sudden weariness had come upon the minister, who had, indeed, spoken for a long hour and more. With a hurried blessing that sounded like a knell, for the last words were, " Beware the wrath of God," Mr. Campbell sat back in the chair which had been carried there for him.

Then, before any moved away, the stranger who was with Mary Gilchrist arose. None knew him. His worn face, with its large sorrowful eyes, his long, fair hair, his white hands, were all unlike those of a man of the hills; but when he spoke it was in the sweet homely Gaelic that only those spoke who had it from the mother's lips.

" Will you listen to me, men and women of Strath Nair?" he asked. He was obviously a poor man, and a wanderer; yet none there who did not realise he was one to whom all would eagerly listen. And so the man preached the Word. He, too, spoke of God and man, of the two worlds, of life and death, of time and eternity. As he spoke, it was as though he used, not the symbols of august and immortal things, but, in a still whiteness of simplicity, revealed these eternal truths themselves.

Was it that as he preached, the sky, the hillside, the sunglow, the sun itself lightened;

that the heart of each man and woman lightened, that the mind of each lightened, that even the white innocence of the little children grew more fair to see?

The stranger, with the eyes of deep love and tenderness—so deep and tender that tears were in women's eyes, and the hearts of men were strained—spoke for long. Simple words he spoke, but none had ever been so moved. Out of the white beauty of his soul he spoke. In that hour he brought near to them many fair immortal things, clothed in mortal beauty; stilled shaken hearts; uplifted hopes grown dim or listless. The old, hearing him, smiled to think that age was but the lamp-lit haven, reached at last, with, beyond the dim strait, the shining windows of home. The young grew brave and strong; in the obscure trouble of each heart, new stars had arisen.

There was but one interruption. When the wayfarer said that they who could not read need not feel outcast from the Word of God, for all the Scriptures could be interpreted in one phrase—simply, " God is love "—the minister, James Campbell, rose and passed slowly through the groups upon the hillside.

" Listen," said the wayfarer, " while I tell you the story of Mary Magdalene."

Then he told the story again as any may

read it in the Book, but with so loving words, and with so deep a knowledge of the pitifulness of life, that it was a revelation to all there. Tears were in the heart as well as in the eyes of each man and woman.

Then slowly he made out of the beauty of all their listening souls a wonderful thing.

Mary Gilchrist had kneeled by his side, and held his left hand in hers, weeping gently the while. A light was about her as of one glorified. It was, mayhap, the light from Him whose living words wrought a miracle there that day.

For as he spoke, all there came to know and to understand and to love. Each other they understood and loved, with a new love, a new understanding. And not one there but felt how sacred and beautiful in their eyes was the redemption of the woman Mary Gilchrist, who was now to them as Mary Magdalene herself.

The wayfarer spoke to one and all by name, or so to each it seemed; and to each he spoke of the sobbing woman by his side, and of the greatness and beauty of love, and of the pitifulness of the sorrow of love, and of the two flames in the shame of love, the white flame and the red. The little green world, he said,

this little whirling star, is held to all the stars
that be, and these are held to every universe,
and all universes surmised and yet undreamed
of are held to God Himself, simply by a little
beam of light—a little beam of Love. It is
Love that is the following Thought of God.
And it is love that is of sole worth in human
life. This he said again and again, in familiar words become new and wonderful. Thus
it was that out of the pain and sorrow, out of
the passion and grief and despair of the heart
of the woman Mary, and out of the heart of
every man, woman, and child in that place, he
wrought a vision of the Woman Mary, of
Mary the Mother, of Mary whose name is
Love, whose soul is Love, whose Breath is
Love, who is wherever Love is, sees all and
knows all and understands all; who has no
weariness, and who solves all impurities and
evils, and turns them into pure gold of love;
who is the Pulse of Life, the Breath of Eternity, the Soul of God.

And when he had ceased speaking there was
not one there—no, not one—who could see
the glory of the beauty of his face because of
the mist of tears that were in all eyes.

None saw him go. Quietly he moved down
the path leading to the green birches at
the hither end of the Glen of the Willows.

There he turned, and for a brief while gazed silent, with longing blue eyes full of dream, and pale face stilled by the ecstasy of prayer.

All stood beholding him. Slowly he raised his arms. Doves of peace flew out of his heart. In every heart there a white dove of peace nested. Mayhap he who stood under the green birches heard what none whom he had left on the hill-slope could hear—the whispering, the welling, the uplifted voice of spirits redeemed from their mortal to their immortal part.

For suddenly he smiled. Then he bowed his head, and was lost in the green gloom, and was seen no more.

But in the gloaming, in the dewy gloaming of that day, Mary Gilchrist walked alone, with her child in her arms, in the Glen of the Willows. And once she heard a step behind her, and a hand touched her shoulder.

"Mary!" said the low, sweet voice she knew so well, "Mary! Mary!"

Whereupon she sank upon her knees.

"Jesus of Nazareth, Son of God!" broke from her lips in faint, stammering speech.

For long she kneeled trembling. When she rose, none was there. White stars hung among the branches of the dusky green pyramids of the Glen of the Willows. On the hillside beyond, where her home was, the moonlight lay, quiet waters of peace. She bowed her head, and moved out of the shadow into the light.

QUEENS OF BEAUTY

" Empires become drifted sand, and the queens of
great loveliness are dust. They shall not come
again, towered cities of the sands, palaces built upon
the sea, roses of beauty that blossomed for an hour
on the wind that is for ever silently and swiftly
moving out of darkness and turning a sunlit wing
and then silently moving into darkness again. But
the wind is changeless in that divine continual advent, and the sunlit wing is that immortal we call
Beauty, the mirage hung upon the brows of life."—
The Ancient Beauty.

There is a Gaelic saying—both in legendary lore and folk-song—of the beauty of the
" Woman of Greece," of " the Greek woman,"
na mna Greuig.

It is, of course, Helen of Troy who is
meant. I do not know if that story of love
and death and beauty has survived in some
measure intact—that is, perfect in episode if
fragmentary in sequence—or if it exist only
in a few luminous words, or merely in allusion. Something of the old romance of Hellas, something of the complex Roman mythus,

have come down on the Gaelic tide, little altered, or altered only in the loss of the temporal and accidental. But they are sometimes hard to trace, and often are as lost in the old Gaelic legendary lore as the fragrance of moor-rose or orchis in the savour of wild-honey.

"Who were the three most beautiful women of old?" I asked a man, a native of the Gairloch of Ross, one day last summer. We were old friends, for we had often been out on the sea together in rough weather and calm, and I had ever found him somewhat like the sea in this, that he could be silent all day and yet never be other than companionable, and had mysterious depths, and sudden revelations. So I was always glad to sail with him when the chance came.

On this day—it was between Gometra and Ulva, where the fierce tides of the Atlantic sometimes cast up cones from the pine-woods of Maine, or driftwood of old wreckage from the Labrador headlands—we were in a *bàta-da-chroinn*, or wherry, and spun before the wind as though swept along by the resistless hand of Manan himself. The sea was a jubilation of blue and white, with green in the shaken tents of the loud-murmuring nomad host of billows. The sky was cloudless in

the zenith, and a deep blue; of a pale blue in
the north and east; but in the south a moun-
tainous range of saffron and salmon-pink
cloud rose solidly above the horizon-cutting
isles. A swirl of long-winged terns hung
above a shoal of mackerel fry, screaming as
they splashed continually into the moving
dazzle. Far in the blue depths overhead I
saw two gannets, like flecks of foam that the
wind had lifted. And that was all: not another bird, not a boat, no trailed smoke down
by Iona or over by Tiree, not a single sail,
suspended on the horizon like the wing of
the fabled condor that moves but does not
stir.

"Who were the three most beautiful wom-
en of old?"

He took a time to answer. He stared
down into the green water slipping past, as
though seeking there some floating image
of a dim, beautiful face, as though listening
for some sigh, some cadence, from the old
lost world, from Tir-fo-Tuinne, the Land-un-
der-wave, the drowned sleeping world with
the moving walls of green and the moving
roof of blue.

"I do not know," he said at last. "I do
not remember. There are many songs, many
tales. But I've heard this: that there will

be seven lovelinesses of beauty in a woman's beauty . . . the beauty of Malveen, the daughter of Oisin; the beauty of Deirathray, the love of Finn; the beauty of Yssul of the North; the beauty of Emer, the wife of Cuchulain; the beauty of Gwannolê, the Queen of the Saxons; the beauty of the Greek woman, for whom all men strove and died; the beauty of the woman who came out of the south." And after he had spoken I thought that in the first of these is the beauty of sorrowful things; and in the second, the beauty of great love; and in the third, the beauty of wildness; and in the fourth, the beauty of faith; and in the fifth, the beauty lit at the torches of death; and in the sixth, the beauty that fires men to take up spears and die for a name; and in the seventh, the beauty of the poets that take up harp and sorrow and the wandering road.

Once before, elsewhere, I had asked this question, and had a different answer, though it held three names of those names now said. "Well, now," said my informant, an old woman of Arisaig, "and who, they, but the Sweet Love of the Sons of Usneach (Usna), and the wife of the Hero of Madness, and the fair Woman of Greece." She knew all about Deirdre, or Dearshul or Darshool, the be-

71

loved of Finn, and the bride of the eldest of the Sons of Usna; and all about Emer, the wife of Cuchulain, the hero of the Gael; and of how the white beauty and great love of these women live for ever in song and story, and in the passion of women's hearts and in the shaken minds of men. But she knew nothing of "the fair woman of Greece," nor of that land itself, thinking indeed it was " a great and glorious town, a shining and prosperous and kingly town, in the southlands of Ispân (Spain)."

Of some of those of whom my boatman spoke, he knew little. Of Malveen (Malmhin) he knew only that her name sang like a shell in the cadence of an old *iorram*, or boatsong, of the Middle Isles: and he had heard the story of Oisin and Malvina in Dr. Clerk's Gaelic variant of *Ossian*, told often at this or that ceilidh by the winter-fire. Darshul, or Deirdre, he called Darathray; the only occasion on which I have heard the name of that fair torch of beauty so given. Her story he knew well. "The best of all the tales that are told," he said. Of Yssul he knew nothing, but that she was the love of a king's son, and that she and Drostan lie below the foam of a wild sea. Gwannolê, the queen of the Saxons, he knew to be Arthur's queen, and

72

he had heard of Mordred, king of the Picts,
though not of Lancelot. He knew Helen's
name, and had a confused memory of the
names of those who loved and died for her,
and of the fate of Troy: all got from his
mother, who was the daughter of a minister
of Inverness. He knew nothing of " the
woman who came out of the south." When
pressed, he said with a smile, " Her name
will be Ashlyenn " (*Aisling*, a Dream), " I'm
thinking." But later he spoke suddenly. It
was when my thoughts had wandered elsewhere, and when I was watching the cloud-
spray circling over the Treshnish Isles, with
two winds meeting: and for a moment I could
not recover the clue to what lay in his words.

" Perhaps the woman out of the south
would be the woman of the woods, that Mer-
lyn loved, and who put him under spells of
silence and sleep. She had the wild beauty,
they say. She was not a woman of a man
and a woman, but the deathless one of the
nameless folk and a woodwoman. She is in
songs and tales. It may be that woman that
had the loveliness, for no man will ever have
seen her but will always sing of her."

I think, however, that this last legendary
beauty is older, and more native to the western Gael. I think, though it is only a sur-

73

mise, that if not Niamh, Oisin's beautiful love of the other world, it must be of one to whose surpassing beauty there is allusion in the most ancient Gaelic chronicles, and of whom, doubtless, the wandering bards of Eire and Alba long sang as of the Rose of Beauty. " But the fairest of the women who came into Erin with the sons of Milidh was Feale, the wife of Luaidh, son of that Ith who had been slain by the Tuath de Danann, and who had lived alone in the western regions of Espân, in an inland valley, until she was wooed by Luaidh, the son of Ith, surnamed Laidceann, for his love of poetry: and men said concerning Feale that she was too beautiful to live."

In a verse rescued from oblivion by Alasdair Carmichael of Uist, these and other names of beauty, pagan and mythological and Christian, are strangely blended.

Is tu gleus na Mnatha Sithe,
Is tu beus na Bride bithe,
Is tu creud na Moire mine,
Is tu gniomh na mnatha Greuig,
Is tu sgeimh na h'Eimir aluinn,
Is tu mein na Dearshul agha,
Is tu meann na Meabha laidir,
    Is tu taladh Binne-bheul.

[*Thine is the skill of the Fairy Woman, and the virtue of St. Briget, and the faith of Mary the Mild, and*

74

*the gracious way of the Greek woman, and the beauty
of lovely Emer, and the tenderness of heartsweet Deirdre, and the courage of Maev the Great Queen (lit., the
strong), and the charm of Mouth o' Music.*]

The names stir. What a great thing in
beauty is this, that after kingdoms are fallen
and nations are drifted away like scattered
leaves, and even heroic names are gone upon
the wind, a memory of loveliness endures, as
a light that time cannot touch, as a fragrance
that death cannot reach. This is the immortality of the poet's dream. It is a great destiny
to raise thrones and win dominions and build
kingly cities. But cities can be ground into
dust, and dominions can be as palaces built
upon the sea, and the highest throne can
become as the last yellow leaf shaken in the
winds of autumn. But great beauty . . .
that is a memory for ever. When one of
the queens of a troubling loveliness dies, it
is only as it were a mortal hour of beauty
that is gathered back into the night: all of
what is immortal passes into the dreams of
men, is the beauty beyond beauty in the
perfect song, the ineffable suspense in music.
It endures, that immortal memory, that immortal dream. It is whispered and told and
communicated in every Spring. It is on
every wind of the west.

75

ORPHEUS AND OISIN

"They asked me if I had seen a white fawn in my dreams, and whether the trees of the secret valley had advised me to love."—CHATEAUBRIAND, *Atala*.

A friend wrote to me some time ago to say that he had seen a quaint tale in old Scots called "Orpheo and Heurodys." I imagine this to be the reprint in Laing's *Remains of Ancient Scottish Poetry*. But, also, he asked if I had come upon any Gaelic variant of the tale of Orpheus and Eurydice. I had not, nor have I. True, I have heard that a tale of one Heurodys has been told, now here, now there. But I have not met any who has heard it told. That a variant of the story of Orpheus and Eurydice survives, however, seems fairly certain. But one would suspect a modern derivation, if it were too pat and retained too strong a savour of the original. There can be an erring on the other side also, however. The late ferrymaster at Iona once told an English lady who was seeking for folklore (and made a book of her strange

gleanings, for she had a singular method of
gathering, in that she would tell a tale and
then ask if the listener had ever heard of its
like) that he had a tale that would interest
her; for, he said, though it was not of a king's
son in the ancient days who went to hell to
seek his love, his story was of one Christina
Ross, who believed she was loved by the
prince of darkness, and one day, sure enough,
she was seen no more. At that, her lover,
Rory M'Killop, the piper from Mull, disap-
peared too. But months on months later he
came again, and said he had been in Gehenna:
and that he saw Christina and told her to follow his piping and all would be well, but if
she stopped to take sup or bite, or called to
him that he should once look back, it would
be o'er the hills an' far away he would be, and
she forlorn for evermore. And the M'Killop
had played well, as he himself averred; none
ever better. But Kirsty Ross had stopped
to pull a fine red apple from a branch, and,
forgetting, had called to him, so that he had
looked back—and the next moment there
was a great gulf between them, he on the
edge of the world again, and she there for
ever, with a heap o' dust in her hand.

And when I asked him afterwards why he
had told such a farrago of nonsense, for I

77

knew he had but given tongue to the moment's whim, he said, " What harm in that now? . . . for sure the lady had her story as she wanted, and as for the truth, well, didn't Rory M'Killop of Heiskir go off with Kirsty Ross, and come back a year later, saying he had been in the Americas, and his wife dead now, God rest her."

But I have wondered often if the ancient Gaelic tale of Oisin and Niamh—the later-life tale of the Son of Fionn and his otherworld love, in the days of his broken years and gathered sorrows—has not in it the heart of the old Greek story. Rather, it may have in it, not an echo, but a like strain of the primitive mythopœic imagination: as the featherwrack on the rocky shores of Ithaka and that gathered on Ultima Thule are one and the same.

For Oisin, too, went to the otherworld to gather love, and to bring back his youth; but even as Orpheus had to relinquish Eurydice and youth and love, because he looked to take away with him what Aidôneus had already gathered to be his own, so Oisin, the Orpheus of the Gael, had to come away from the place of defeated dreams, and see again the hardness and bitterness of the hitherworld, with age and death as the grey fruit

on the tree of life. And if the end of the one
is hidden—for some say he was slain by the
jealous gods, who love not that any soul
should whisper the secret of their mysteries,
and some that he was destroyed by the in-
furiated bacchanals, and some that he wandered lonely till his sorrow came over him
like snow, so that he lay down beneath it and
slept and was no more seen of men—so too
is hidden the end of the other. For Oisin
did not dwell evermore in the pleasant land
whither his youth had gone and he to seek
it, but came back to find the world grown
old, and all he had loved below the turf, and
the taunts of the monks of Patrick in his ears,
and the bell of Christ ringing in the glens and
upon the leas. Nor does any know of his
death, though the Gaels of the North believe
that he looked his last across the grey seas
from Drumadoon in Arran, where that Avalon of the Gael lies between the waters of
Argyll and the green Atlantic wave.

It may well be that the old Greek tale of
Orpheus seeking Eurydice in the kingdom
of things ended and gathered, and the old
Gaelic tale of Oisin and Niamh, and the
mediæval tale of Ponce da Leon, and the
folk-tale (told me again, for in one form or
another I have heard it often, a year-back on

green Lismore) of the shepherd of the isles
who loved a soulless, smiling woman of the
otherworld and followed his fay into the darkness of the earth below a leafless thorn, and
was lost to the world for months, till he was
seen one May-day walking among the yellow
broom crowned with hawthorn and with a
rowan branch in his hand, smiling and dumb,
and with eyes cold as cold blue water—it may
well be that these legendary tales are but the
ever-changing mortal utterance of what is
unchanging, the varying accent of the un-
varying desire of the soul, to recapture that
which has gone away upon the wind, or to
take from the brows of the wind of what is to
come the secret coronals of strange blossom
wet still with immortal dews. It may well
be that each is but an expression of the need
for youth, which is the passion of life, and
the instinct of the imagination to breathe itself into a passionate moment of emotion, and
the impulse of all the emotions and all the
passions.

Orpheus loved, and Eurydice was gathered
untimely as a flower in its beauty; but are we
not all lovers as Orpheus' was, loving what is
gone from us for ever, and seeking it vainly
in the solitudes and wilderness of the mind,
and crying to Eurydice to come again? And

are we not all foolish as Orpheus was, hoping by the agony of love and the ecstasy of will to win back Eurydice; and do we not all fail, as Orpheus failed, because we forsake the way of the otherworld for the way of this world?

Many of us, do we not love Niamh, and come again from enchantment, and find all things grown old, the apples of Avalon become sere without and full of dust within? Many of us, do we not follow a fay who has stolen our joy, to go crowned a brief while with illusions, or to hold in nerveless hands the disenchanted wand of the imagination? Many of us, are we not continually adventuring upon a quest as futile as that of Ponce da Leon, who, for the sake of a dream, was blind to the other founts of youth that were within his reach, and so forsook all that he might cross the world to find what was in his own mind?

Whether the story of Oisin, the Gaelic Orpheus, be a wanderer from archaic mythology, or arose clanless among the Gaelic hills—from moonseed, as is said of the tufted canna that floats its fairy snow-beards on the moorland air—matters little. The tale, at least, has a beauty that is certainly its own. Oisin, also, was the son of one who loved a woman of the deathless folk; for as the Thracian king Œagrus loved Calliope, of the divine race, so Fionn, the Agamemnon of the Gael, loved one of the Hidden People —a daughter of the people of the mounds, as we would say, of the Sidhe. Each became the arch-poet of his race: both were taught and inspired by divine genius, the Thracian by Apollo, the Gael by Angus of the Sun-locks—Angus Og, the Balder of the west.

The dwellers in the underworld and all the great kings and lords in Hades knew the enchantment of the lute of Orpheus; and when Oisin went to the otherworld with Niamh, the sleeping kings and the spellbound heroes and all the secret clans of Midir were thrilled with wonder, and rejoiced with proud laughter. The one went out with the Argonauts, and crossed the foam of the Symplegades, and beheld war as a pageant: the other went with the clans of the Fianna, and crossed the wild waters of the Moyle, and at Moytura saw great tides of spears and swords flashing upon a sea of red, and beheld nations meet and dwindle and perish, so that when the sun set it was as though it dragged away the land in great cloths of crimson, dripping like a veil over the untraversed sea and all the battle-worn shores of the west.

Orpheus and Oisin

Both loved with great, unforgetting love,
and in the end knew weariness and death:
and the one, it is said, died in a Thracian
valley, calling upon his lost love in the underworld; and the other, it is said, died by
Drumadoon in the isle of Arran of Argyll,
old and blind, with his hand in the hand of
Malveen, but on his lips this sigh to his long
lost, forbidden love . . . *O Niamh, thy kisses
were sweet as the blue joyous wine of the wave
to the Sea-wind.*

Some of the oral legends have it that the
mother of Oisin was a mortal, bewitched by a
woman of the Sidhe: others, that she was
herself Fionn's *leannan-shee*, or fairy-love
. . . and I have heard her called Niamh,
Moän, Liban, and other sweet perilous names.

But the common legend[1] is that Fionn
wearied of his white love, and wedded a
daughter of a great lord of the Ultonians.
Then "the other" put the spell of the *Fath-
fith* on her, so that she was changed to a
hind of the hill.

[1] So well summarized, in particular, by Mr. Alasdair Carmichael—and an idea of how difficult a
summary sometimes is may be gained from the fact
that the late Mr. Campbell of Tiree had gathered
and sent to Mr. Carmichael no fewer than fourteen
variants of the First Song of Oisin, the Song to his
Hind-Mother

83

When her hour was come, she swam the deep water of Loch-nan-'ceall that is near Arisaig in West Argyll, to the little isle in it that is called Sanndraigh.

And there her child and Fionn's child was born. When the swoon of the birthing was past, she forgot, and that of her which was a hind licked the brow of her young. Then she remembered, and licked no more; but, looking, saw that though the enchantment lay upon her still, the spell was broken for her little son. But hair like a fawn's hair grew upon the brow she had licked: and that is why the youngest and fairest of Fionn's sons was given the name of Oisin, the Fawn.

The child was taken to his father's Dûn, and the hind leapt away through the bracken, and swam the loch, and took to the hills—for the fear of Bran and Luath and Breacleit, Fionn's great hounds, was upon her.

Oisin and his mother did not meet again for years upon years. One day, when passing from boyhood to youth, he went with the hunters to the hill of the mountain-deer, but because of a mist he strayed and found himself at last alone and in a solitary place, a green glen set among leaning blue hills, with water running from a place of high piled rocks. He saw a hind pasturing there, more

graceful and beautiful than any deer he had
ever seen: so great was its beauty that he
looked at it as a girl who had never seen an
image in water might look at her mirrored
face in a pool. Then the spirit of the huntsman stirred within him, and he lifted his
spear. The hind looked at him, with sad
wistful eyes, brown as hill-water, and slowly
he lowered the spear.

"Thrust me not with thy spear, Oisin,"
said the hind, "for I am thy mother that bore
thee on the isle Sanndraigh in Loch-nan-
'ceall. Alone I see thee, and hungry and
weary. Come back with me now to my
home, fawn of my heart."

They went slowly, side by side, across the
green grass to a great rock that in slope was
the height of nine men, and was smooth as
the blade of a sword. The wife of Fionn
breathed upon it, and a hollow was come, and
when they had gone in there was no hollow
but only a great rock with a slope that was
in size the height of nine men and was as
smooth as the blade of a sword.

Then, to his exceeding joy, Oisin saw that
his mother was spellbound no more, but was
a woman, and lovely and young. When they
had kissed long with great love, she gave him
food to eat and sweet heather-ale to drink,

85

and then sang songs of a music sweeter than any he had ever heard.

For three days it was thus with them, with the sleep of peace at night, where was no night, and the waking of joy at morn, where was no morn, but where Time lay asleep, as the murmur of the unresting sea in the curved hollows of a shell.

Then Oisin remembered Fionn and the hunters, and said he would go out to see them, and set their sorrow at rest. But before he went out of that spellbound place he made a song for his mother, the first of the songs of Oisin, that would be a *sian* to guard her from the hounds and spears of Fionn and his hunters. Then once more the hollow opened in the smooth cliff of the great rock, and he was in the glen again among the blue hills, and saw a kestrel flying at a great height as though scorning the spread greenness of the land and the spread greyness of the wrinkled sea. And when Oisin was come again to the Dùn of Fionn, there was great wonder as well as great joy, for it was not three hours as it seemed, nor yet three days, as he thought, but three years, that he had been in the secret place of the rocks, and known the food and drink and music of enchantment.

Orpheus and Oisin

In truth, this tale, as the tale of the other
Orpheus, is but an ancient and familiar strain
which is the burthen or refrain of unnumbered songs of the spirit, in every race, in
every age: as in every literature, in every
age, one may hear the same sigh as in the old
Scots song:

> "For I'm wearied wi' hunting,
> An' fain would lie doon."

These old myth-covering tales—whether we
call them Greek or Aryan or what else—are
as the grass that will grow in any land: and
the grass of the Vale of Tempe or on the
slope of Helicon does not differ from the
grass in green Aghadoe or that on the scarps
of Hecla by the Hebrid seas. It was but
the other day I told an eager listener a tale
of one Faruane (*Fear-uaine*, a " green man ")
who lived " in the old ancient days " in a
great oak, and had so lived for generations—
for a honeycomb of ages, as the phrase runs
—and did nothing but watch the clouds sail
above the branches and the shadows glide
between the tree-boles, and live on sunlight and dew. Then one day, as he was
walking lightly on the moss, he saw another
world come into the old untroubled wood,

and that "world" was a woman. She was young as Niamh the undying, and beautiful as Emer the fair, and bewitching as Liban of the spells; and Faruane grew weary of his calm immortal dream, and longed unwittingly for sorrow and death, for he did not know these companions of the soul, nor even that he longed, nor could he know that a soul was other than a perishable thing of the earth as he himself was. So he moved softly in the sun-warmed dusk of the branches, and came upon the girl (whose name was Moän) among the fern where she stood like a fawn with wide eyes. He was too beautiful for her to fear, and too beautiful for her not to love, and though Moän knew that to give herself in love to a wood-spirit was to live three years in a dream and then die in body and to go away in soul, she put from her all desire of the things she knew and let Faruane kiss her on the lips and take her hand and lead her into the green glades, to be forgotten, beyond the murmuring forest, save in a song that lived like a breath of remembered passion in the gloamings of a thousand years.

But for three years Faruane and Moän knew the Spring rapture and the Summer joy and the Autumn peace and the Winter sleep of the children of earth. She remembered nothing, for her soul was filled with beauty; and she desired nothing, for her mind was hushed with dreams and honied with content.

But when she died, which was as a child falling asleep in a shadowy place of moss and rustling leaves, Faruane faded from the light, and his death was as a sunbeam passing from a green branch; for he had seen her soul stoop and kiss him and go away to its own place, where he could not follow. But they had daughters, and these lived to the fulness of the green hour, which is calm and unaging through many generations of our fevered mortal day. They in turn bore children to other sons of the greenness, the semblance of Moän but in all else of the seed of Faruane; so that they are like the offspring of the clan of men, but fear them and love them not, and may not dwell with them nor near them, nor wed with them. But they love the shadows of leaves, and the sun ripens them as fruit, and they are forgotten, and have no dreams but the dream that is their life.

And what, then, is this fantasy of a dreaming mind in the west but kin to the sweet fantasy of a dreaming mind in Hellas of old —though the island poet, or singer of Arcady with a silver flute, making beauty in the hot noon by a plane-shadowed fount, as a child makes a coronal of daisies and wild thyme, called Moän Mêropê, and sung of her wood-lover as Dryas? For both knew of the shy green god of the oak, and had seen the off-spring of him and the mortal woman of his love, the fawn-eyed, withdrawing Dryads of the haunted trees.

It is in this sense that the things of the imagination do not die, but change with the changing hours—as the wild parsley and the hyacinth come into the woods at the first flute-notes of April, and were as young last year, or will be under the yet unfallen dews, as they were a thousand years ago, in Arcadian valleys or in the glens of the Gael.

THE AWAKENING OF ANGUS ÒG

One noon, among the hills, Angus Òg lay
in sleep. It was a fair place where he lay,
with the heather about him and the bracken
with its September gold in it. On the
mountain-slope there was not a juniper tall
enough, not a rock big enough, to give poise
to a raven: all of gold bracken and purple
heather it was, with swards of the paler ling.
The one outstanding object was a mountain
ash. Midway it grew, and leaned so that
when the sun was in the east above Ben
Monach, the light streamed through the
feather-foliage upon the tarn just beneath:
so leaned, that when the sun was on the sea-
verge of Ben Mheadhonach in the west, the
glow, lifting upward over leagues of yellow
bracken, turned the rowan-feathers to the
colour of brass, and the rowan-berries into
bronze.

The tarn was no more than a boulder-set
hollow. It was fed by a spring that had
slipped through the closing granite in a dim
far-off age, and had never ceased to put its

cool lips round the little rocky basin of that
heather-pool. At the south end the ling fell
over its marge in a curling wave: under the
mountain-ash there was a drift of moss and
fragrant loneroid, as the Gaels call the bog-
myrtle.

Here it was, through the tides of noon,
that Angus Òg slept. The god was a flower
there in the sunflood. His hair lay upon the
green loneroid, yellow as fallen daffodils in
the grass. Above him was the unfathomable
sea of blue. Not a cloudlet drifted there,
nor the wandering shadow of an eagle soaring from a mountain-eyrie or ascending in
wide gyres of flight from invisible lowlands.

Around him there was the same deep
peace. Not a breath stirred the rowan-
leaves, or the feathery shadows these cast
upon his white limbs: not a breath frayed
the spires of the heather on the ridges
of Ben Monach: not a breath slid along the
aërial pathways to where, on Ben Mheadhonach, the sea-wind had fallen in a garth of
tansies and moon-daisies, and swooned there
is the sun-haze, moveless as a lapsed wave.

Yet there were eyes to see, for Orchil
lifted her gaze from where she dreamed her
triune dream beneath the heather. The goddess ceased from her weaving at the looms

of life and death, and looked broodingly at
Angus Og—Angus, the fair god, the ever-
young, the lord of love, of music, of song.

"Is it time that he slept indeed?" she
murmured, after a long while, wherein she
felt the sudden blood redden her lips and the
pulse in her quiet veins leap like a caged
bird.

But while she still pondered this thing,
three old Druids came over the shoulder of
the hill, and advanced slowly to where the
Yellow-haired One lay adream. These, however, she knew to be no mortals, but three
of the ancient gods.

When they came upon Angus Òg they
sought to wake him, but Orchil had breathed
a breath across a granite rock and blown the
deep immemorial age of it upon him, so that
even the speech of the elder gods was no
more in his ears than a gnat's idle rumour.

"Awake," said Keithoir, and his voice was
as the sigh of pine-forests when the winds
surge from the pole.

"Awake," said Manannan, and his voice
was as the hollow booming of the sea.

"Awake," said Hesus, and his voice was
as the rush of the green world through space,
or as the leaping of the sun.

But Angus Òg stirred not, and dreamed

93

only that a mighty eagle soared out of the
infinite, and scattered planets and stars as
the dust of its pinions: and that as these
planets fell they expanded into vast oceans
whereon a myriad million waves leaped and
danced in the sunlight, singing a laughing
song: and that as the stars descended in a
silver rain they spread into innumerable for-
ests, wherein went harping the four winds of
the world, and amidst which the white doves
that were his kisses flitted through the gold
and shadow.

"He will awake no more," murmured
Keithoir, and the god of the green world
moved sorrowfully apart, and played upon a
reed the passing sweet song that is to this
day in the breath of the wind in the grass, or
its rustle in the leaves, or its sigh in the lap-
ping of reedy waters.

"He will awake no more," murmured Manannan, and the god of the dividing seas
moved sorrowfully upon his way; and on the
hill-side there was a floating echo as of the
ocean-music in a shell, mournful with ancient mournfulness and the sorrow-song of
age upon age. The sound of it is in the ears
of the dead, where they move through the
glooms of silence: and it haunts the timeworn
shores of the dying world.

94

The Awakening of Angus Òg

"He will awake no more," murmured
Hesus; and the unseen god, whose pulse is
beneath the deepest sea and whose breath is
the frosty light of the stars, moved out of the
shadow into the light, and was at one with it,
so that no eyes beheld the radiance which
flowered icily in the firmament and was a
flame betwixt the earth and the sun, which
was a glory amid the cloudy veils about the
west and a gleam where quiet dews sustained
the green spires of the grass. And as the
light lifted and moved, like a vast tide, there
was a rumour as of a starry procession
sweeping through space to the clashing cym-
bals of dead moons, to the trumpetings of
volcanic worlds, and to the clarions of a thousand suns. But Angus Òg had the deep immemorial age of the granite upon him, and
he slept as the dead sleep.

Orchil smiled. "They are old, old, the
ancient gods," she whispered: "they are so
old, they cannot see eternity at rest. For
Angus Òg is the god of Youth, and he only
is eternal and unchanging."

Then, before she turned once more to her
looms of life and death, she lifted her eyes
till her gaze pierced the brown earth and rose
above the green world and was a trouble
amid the quietudes of the sky. Thereat the

95

icy stars gave forth snow, and Angus Òg
was wrapped in a white shroud that was not
as that which melts in the flame of noon.
Moreover, Orchil took one of the shadows of
oblivion from her mystic loom, and put it as
a band around Ben Monach where Angus
Òg lay under the mountain-ash by the tarn.

.   .   .   .   .

A thousand years passed, and when for the
thousandth time the wet green smell of the
larches drifted out of Winter into Spring,
Orchil lifted her eyes from where she spun
at her looms of life and death.   For, over the
shoulder of the hill, came three old Druids,
advancing slowly to where the Yellow-haired
One lay adream beneath the snow.

"Awake, Angus," cried Keithoir.

"Awake, Angus," cried Manannan.

"Awake, Angus," cried Hesus.

"Awake, awake," they cried, "for the
world has suddenly grown chill and old."

They had the grey grief upon them, when
they stood there, face to face with Silence.

Then Orchil put down the shuttle of mystery wherewith she wove the threads of her
looms, and spoke.

"O ye ancient gods, answer me this.
Keithoir, if death were to come to thee, what
would happen?"

" The green world would wither as a dry leaf, and as a dead leaf be blown idly before the wind that knows not whither it bloweth."

" Manannan, if death were to come to thee, what would happen? "

" The deep seas would run dry, O Orchil: there would be sand falling in the place of the dews, and at last the world would reel and fall into the abyss."

" Hesus, if death were to come to thee, what would happen? "

" There would be no pulse at the heart of earth, O Orchil, no lift of any star against any sun. There would be a darkness and a silence."

Then Orchil laughed.

" And yet," she said, " when Angus Òg had the snow-sleep of a thousand years, none knew it! For a thousand years the pulse of his heart of love has been the rhythmic beat of the world. For a thousand years the breath of his nostrils has been as the coming of Spring in the human heart. For a thousand years the breath of his life has been warm against the lips of lovers. For a thousand years the memory of these has been sweet against oblivion. Nay, not one hath dreamed of the deep sleep of Angus Ŏg."

97

"Who is he?" cried Keithoir. "Is he older than I, who saw the green earth born?"

"Who is he?" cried Manannan. "Is he older than I, who saw the first waters come forth out of the void?"

"Who is he?" cried Hesus. "Is he older than I, who saw the first comet wander from the starry fold; who saw the moon when it was a flaming sun, and the sun when it was a sevenfold intolerable flame?"

"He is older!" said Orchil. "He is the soul of the gods."

And with that she blew a frith across the palm of her hand, and took away the deep immemorial age of the granite that was upon the Fair God.

"Awake, eternal Spring!" she cried. And Angus awoke, and laughed with joy; and at his laughing the whole green earth was veiled in a snow of blossom.

"Arise, eternal Youth!" she cried. And Angus arose and smiled; and at his smiling the old brown world was clad in dewy green, and everywhere the beauty of the world was sweet against the eyes of young and old, and everywhere the pulse of love leaped in beating hearts.

"Go forth, eternal Hope!" she cried. And Angus Òg passed away on the sunflood, weaving rainbows as he went, that were fair upon the hills of age and light within the valleys of sorrow, and were everywhere a wild, glad joy.

.   .   .   .   .

And that is why, when Orchil weaves dumbly in the dark: and Keithoir is blind, and dreams among remote hills and by unfrequented shores: and Manannan lies heavy with deep sleep, with the oceans of the world like moving shadows above him: and Hesus is grown white and hoar with the frost of waning stars and weary with the burden of new worlds: that is why Angus Ōg, the youthful god, is more ancient than they, and is for ever young. Their period is set. Oblivion is upon the march against their immemorial time. But in the heart of Angus Ōg blooms the Rose of Youth, whose beauty is everlasting. Yea, Time is the name of that rose, and Eternity the beauty and fragrance thereof.

CHILDREN OF WATER

"O, hide the bitter gifts of our lord Poseidon."—
ARCHILOCHUS OF PAROS.

Children of Water

"Ri traghad
's ri lionadh . . .
Mar a bha
Mar a tha
Mar a bhitheas
Gu brath
Ri tragadh
'S ri lionadh."

(Ebbing and flowing . . . as it was, as it is, as it
shall be evermore—the ebb and the flow.)

Students of Gaelic mythology will remember that Tuan—who, under the grey cloud
and by the whispering rushes of the west,
gave out the same ancient wisdom as Pythagoras gave by Ionian Krôton, or as Emped-
ocles gave by Sicilian Acragas—remembered
his many transformations. He had been, he
said, an eagle and a stag and a salmon in
deep waters, and had known other changes.
In like manner the Sicilian sophist remembered that he had been " a youth and a
maiden and a bush and a bird and a gleaming fish in the sea "; and the greatest of
Greek mages declared that again and again

he had lived in a changed body, as old raiment discarded or new raiment donned.

But I am not now concerned with this
problem, that, like a wind at twilight, has
troubled with furtive shadows the waters of
many minds. As with a greater problem, it
may be folly to believe it, but a worse folly
to hold it incredible. And, too, in the end,
when we are tired of the tide-play of the
mind and sink into the depths and silences and
think from there, what are the thousand
words that say no against the one word that
says yes? I recall from childhood a story of
a man who, for the gain of a great wisdom,
sold to the Prince of Pride the whole substance and reach of his mortal period, retain-
ing only a single minute out of all this incalculable treasure. He lived to the stipulated
hour, and at the end of his hundredth year
knew all that the wisdom of man has gathered out of the silence in which he moves,
shadow of an eddy of wind between the two
vast Alps of Time and Death. And on the
shore of the last minute of the last hour of
the hundredth year—when he had sighed, and
said there was no more to know, and that
the last dream had been dreamed—he remembered his one minute he had kept unbartered.
So he took it, and held it before his eyes, as

we hold a crystal lens: and in that minute he saw backwards a thousand years, and beheld the long trail of his wandering lives; and saw forward, and beheld the ways and the cross-ways, the pillar of dust and the leaning banner of mist; and saw downward, and beheld many empires in the caverns of old seas, and below these, outworn ages, and below these, space and stars; and saw upward, and beheld human wisdom like dew, a thin vapour, vanishing, and then a congregation of mighty spirits and dominions, princes of the elements, overlords of destiny, throneless and throned gods, and then a majesty of light, and then seven heavens like seven stairs, and then a myriad blaze of world-apart wings and an illimitable swinging of uncountable suns, and knew, then, that his wisdom had but crossed the first marches of infinitude, had but reached the leaning horizon of eternity. In the hundred years he had learned all that the pride of the mind could teach, and it was as nothing: in the one minute of his soul he had seen behind and beyond, beneath and above, and in knowing the nothingness of knowledge had entered the inheritance of wisdom.

I think, rather, of another interpretation of the old wisdom of these dreamers of time and change. Are they not prophets of that restless spirit which is the heritage of many troubled souls, that instinct for spiritual wandering, that deep hunger for experience, even if it be bitter, the longing for things known to be unattainable, the remembrance which strives for re-birth, the insatiable thirst for the beauty of mirage, the brooding discontent with or fiery rebellion against the tyranny of accident and circumstance? To these, it is not enough that one life be the guerdon of birth: not even that many lives slip from level to level: not even that the accident of sex be as varied as the accident of race or the accident of conditions. They would know flight, as the seamew or the osprey: they would know the waterways, as the creatures of the wave: they would know the wind, as the leaf on the bough knows it, as the grass knows it, as the grey thistle in a stony place: they would know, even, the rapture of the upbuilded bow along the bastions of storm, or where the arch leans in moist rose and green and purple over still streams and inland valleys—would know, even, the elemental passions of wind and rain and of the unloosened fires. There is no limit to this troubled desire. It is the madness, perhaps, of many minds dwelling habitually, and from generation to generation, among things hard to endure, in the grey countries of rain and wind: it is the madness, also, of some in whose hearts is not and never can be any peace, the sons and daughters of longing, the children of thirst.

For in truth there is a restlessness unlike any other restlessness in the vagrant spirit of man: a disquietude that is of the soul as well as of the body, the tossed spray of forgotten and primitive memories. And yet, perhaps, all this obscure tumult in the dark is only the dream of those unquiet minds who are the children of water.

Long ago, when Manannan, the god of wind and sea, offspring of Lîr, the Oceanus of the Gael, lay once by weedy shores, he heard a man and a woman talking. The woman was a woman of the sea, and some say that she was a seal: but that is no matter, for it was in the time when the divine race and the human race and the soulless race and the dumb races that are near to man were all one race. And Manannan heard the man say: "I will give you love and home and peace." The sea-woman listened to that, and said: "And I will bring you the homelessness of the sea, and the peace of the restless wave, and love like the wandering wind." At that the man chided her, and said she could be no

woman, though she had his love. She laughed,
and slid into green water. Then Manannan
took the shape of a youth, and appeared to
the man. "You are a strange love for a sea-
woman," he said: "and why do you go putting your earth-heart to her sea-heart?" The
man said he did not know, but that he had no
pleasure in looking at women who were all
the same. At that Manannan laughed a low
laugh. "Go back," he said, "and take one
you'll meet singing on the heather. She's
white and fair. But because of your lost love
in the water, I'll give you a gift." And with
that Manannan took a wave of the sea and
threw it into the man's heart. He went back,
and wedded, and, when his hour came, he
died. But he, and the children he had, and
all the unnumbered clan that came of them,
knew by day and by night a love that was
tameless and changeable as the wandering
wind, and a longing that was unquiet as the
restless wave, and the homelessness of the
sea. And that is why they are called the
Sliochd-na-mara, the clan of the waters, or
the Treud-na-thonn, the tribe of the sea-
wave.

And of that clan are some who have turned
their longing after the wind and wave of the
mind — the wind that would overtake the

waves of thought and dream, and gather them and lift them into clouds of beauty drifting in the blue glens of the sky.

How are these ever to be satisfied, children of water?

CUILIDH MHOIRE

Εὔιππον, εὔπολον, εὐθάλασσον.
—SOPHOCLES.

Within a hundred years ago many of the
islefolk, and not only in the more remote
places, openly or furtively practised what are
called pagan rites. Many of these dwelt with
water, more particularly with the water of the
sea: for to the people in the west the sea is
an ever present power to be feared, to be pro-
pitiated, to be beguiled if possible, to be re-
garded as a hard foster-mother, perhaps:
hardly to be loved. I have never heard any
definition of the sea more impressive than that
of a fisherman of the isle of Ulva, whom I
knew. " She is like a woman of the old tales
whose beauty is dreadful," he said, " and who
breaks your heart at last whether she smiles
or frowns. But she doesn't care about that,
or whether you are hurt or not. It's because
she has no heart, being all a wild water."

I have read often of the great love of the

islesmen for the sea. They love it in a sense
of course, as the people of the land love uplands and wild moors, and the movements of
clouds over stony braes or above long pastures
by low shores and estuaries. Nor are they
happy away from it. How could they be,
since the wave is in their hearts. Men and
women who are born to the noise of the sea,
whose cradles have rocked to the surge or
croon of the tides, who have looked on the
deep every day in every season of every year,
could not but feel towards it as a shepherd
feels towards the barest hills, as a forester
feels for the most sombre woods, as the seed-
sower and the harrower feel for monotonous
brown lands which swell upward till they bear
the rounded white clouds like vast phantom
flowers. In this sense they love it, and truly.
Some love it for itself, and its beauty. A few
love it with passion, feel its spell irresistible,
magical. " A wild mare, a mocking beautiful
woman, and the blue sea in foam, for the joy
of these I would give the world and time,"
says a Gaelic poet. But it is not of the ex-
ceptions I speak: it is of the many. These do
not love what they have so much cause to
dread; what holds so many little fortunes in
so great and loose a clasp; what shuts off
from so many desires; what has so common

a voice of melancholy; what makes an obvious destiny take the measure of fatality, an implacable doom. For them, when the sea is not a highway, it is a place of food, the Cuilidh Mhoire or Treasury of Mary, as the Catholic islesmen of the Southern Hebrides call the sustenance-giving waters. When neither, it is most likely to be a grave, the cold drifting hearths of the dead.

As to those I speak of, the people in many parts were good Christians for most days, and then one day other selves hidden under taught faiths and later symbols would stand disclosed. Above all, when certain days of traditional sanctity recurred, it was customary to perform rites of a druidic or pagan remembrance, in the face even of priests of a Faith that has ever turned stern eyes on all rites of the eager spirit of man save its own. And what the people were then, in the many, they still are in the few; though now for the most part only where the Great Disenchantment has not yet wholly usurped the fading dominion of the Great Enchantment.

It was the custom, then, and still is in some isles, for mothers to wet brow or finger of their new-born in the flow of the tide at the end of the third week of the child's life. The twenty-first day, if a Sunday, was held to be

the most fortunate, and a Thursday next to
it: but a Friday was always to be avoided,
and a Saturday was held in some fear, unless
the child was dark in hair and eyes and colour.
It was above all needful to see that this wave-
baptism happened when the tide was at the
flow. If it were done at the ebb, woe to that
child and that mother: soon or late the "bap-
tized" would be called, to sink in deep gulfs
and be homeless and no more seen—and, in
the west, for the dead to have no green grave
for sleep-covering is a nakedness of sorrow
ill to endure for those left to mourn.

I remember, when I was a child, being taken
to have tea in the cottage of one Giorsal Macleod, in Armadale of Sleat, who had lost both
husband and son through this sea-hallowing
rite having been done at the ebb. Her husband was a young man, and had never spoken
to her of the fear of his mother, who through
a misjudgment in a time of weakness and
fever had "waved" him after the turn of
the ebb. But one day when Annra Macleod
came in to find Giorsal crying because unwittingly she had done a like thing, he laughed
at her folly, and said that for himself he cared
no whit one way or the other whether the
child were dipped in this hour or in that.
But before the month was out, and on a calm

113

night and just as the herring had risen, Annra's feet tangled in the nets, which fell back with him, and he sank into the strong ebb, and was sucked away like a fading shadow. And seven years from that day little Seoras, the boy, when fishing for *piocach* in the haven, stumbled from the coble's heavy bow and into the swift-slipping greenness. He was good at the swimming, and could easily have saved himself on so calm a day and with the coble not a fathom-reach off : but he was an ebb-child, and his fate was on him, and he was called out to deep water and death. His mother saw this. And when she spoke of her sorrow she used invariably the words, " *A Dhia* (O God), 'twas a long-laid death for my cold darling : 'twas I that did it with that dip in the ebb, I not knowing the harm and the spell, *A cuislin mo ghraidh, A m'ul-aidh 's m'agh!* (O pulse-let of my love, O my treasure and joy !) "

In those days I speak of, the people used to have many sea-rites, and, almost in all the isles, on *La' Chaluim-Chille* (St. Columba's Day) in particular. Offerings of honey-ale or mead, fluid porridge, kale-soup, precious bread even, were given to the god of the sea. As the darkness of Wednesday night gave way to dawn on Maundy Thursday, as Mr.

Carmichael relates in his beautiful *Carmina Gadelica*, the man deputed by the islefolk would walk into the sea up to his waist, and then, while he poured out the offering, would chant

> A Dhe na mara
> Cuir todhar 's an tarruinn
> Chon tachair an talaimh
> Chon bailcidh dhuinn biaidh.

> "O god of the sea,
> Put weed in the drawing wave
> To enrich the isle-soil,
> To shower on us food."

" Then those behind the offerer took up the chant and wafted it along the seashore on the midnight air, the darkness and the rolling of the waves making the scene weird and impressive."

That I have not seen; and now I fear the god of the sea has few worshippers, and knows no scattered communes of bowed chanters at midnight.

But this, though also I have not seen, I know of at first hand. A man and his three sons, on an island which I will speak of only as south and east of the Minch, went secretly on the eve of St. Columba's Day a year ago, and took a pail of milk from the byres, and a jug of running water of a well-spring, and a small loaf of bread from the oven, and a red faggot from the fire held in a cleft stick. The youngest son threw the fire into the sea, crying, " Here's fire for you!" And the other sons poured on the black flood the surf-white milk and the rain-grey water, crying, " Here's clean water for you!" and " Here's the kindly milk for you!" And the father threw the loaf of bread on the wave, and cried " Peace to your hunger!"

That was all, and they did it secretly, and the sons (it is said) half to please their father. Only one or two neighbours knew of it, and they silent before the minister; but somehow it came to the man's ears, and like most of his kind he was angry at a thing beyond him and his understanding, and spoke in contempt to one wiser than himself (I do not doubt), and threatened him with a public exhorting from the pulpit, so that Mr. M—— sullenly promised no more to do the thing his forebears had done for generation upon generation.

" After all, the minister was right," said some one to me, who had heard the tale: " for Mr. M—— was only holding by a superstition."

I did not make the obvious retort, but said

simply that it was better to hold by old things of beauty and reverence than to put a blight on them.

I do not say the minister was wholly wrong. He spoke according to his lights. Doubtless he had in remembrance some such passage as that in Deuteronomy where the ban is put upon any one who will suffer his son or his daughter to go through fire, or upon any that draw omen from the cry of fowls, or upon the interpreter of signs. And compelled by that stubborn thraldom to the explicit word which has been at once the stern strength and the spiritual failure of all the Calvinistic denominations (in our religion-harried Scotland at least), he spoke in numbed sympathy and twilight knowledge.

Since, I have tried to learn if Mr. M—— had knowledge of the ancient meanings of that sea-rite, and if other words, or chant, or *urnuigh-mhara* or sea-prayer, had been used by his elders. But, as yet, I have not learned. I have wondered often if this broken and all but silent rite were a survival of a custom before ever St. Colum was heard of. The bread offering and that of the milk are easy of understanding. But why should one give fresh water from an earth-spring to that salt, unstable wilderness; why offer to it a flame of fire, to it whose pale crescents of light or moving green lawns beneath swaying cataracts are but the glittering robe over a cold heart, than which no other is so still everlastingly in an ancient and changeless cold?

SEA-MAGIC

"Manan mil air sloigh . . ."

In one of the remotest islands of the Hebrides I landed on a late afternoon in October a year ago. There was no one on the island except an old man, who was shepherd for the fourscore sheep which ate the sweet sea-grass from Beltane till Samhain:[1] one sheep for each year of his life, he told me, " forby one, and that will be right between them an' me come Candlemas next." He gave me water and oatcake, and offered to make me tea, which I would not have. I gave him the messages I had brought from the distant mainland of the Lews, and other things; and some small gifts of my own to supplement the few needs and fewer luxuries of the old islander. Murdo MacIan was grateful, with the brief and simple gladness of a child. By mistake a little mouth-organ, one of those small untuneful instruments which children delight in and can

[1] "Beltane till Samhain": 1st May till Summerend (31st October).

buy for a few pence, was in my package,
along with a " poke " of carvies, those little
white sweets for buttered bread dear to both
young and old—though even they, like all
genuine products of the west, great and small,
are falling away in disuse! The two had been
intended by me for a small lass, the grand-
child of a crofter of Loch Roag in the wester-
side of the Lews; but when the yacht put in
at the weedy haven, where scart and gillie-
breed and tern screamed at the break of silence, I heard that little Morag had " taken
a longing to be gone," and after a brief ailing
had in truth returned whence she had come.

And for the moment neither snuff nor to-
bacco, neither woollen comforter nor knitted
hose, could hold Murdo as did that packet of
carvies (for the paper had loosened, and the
sugary contents had swarmed like white ants)
and still more that sixpenny mouth-organ. I
saw what the old man eagerly desired, but was
too courteous and well-bred even to hint: and
when I gave him the two things of his longing
my pleasure was not less than his. I asked
him why he wanted the *cruit-bheul*, which
was the nearest I could put the Gaelic for the
foreign toy, and he said simply that it was because he was so much alone, and often at
nights heard a music he would rather not be

hearing. "What would that be?" I asked.
After some hesitation he answered that a
woman often came out of the sea and said
strange foreign words at the back of his door,
and these, he added, in a whinnying voice like
that of a foal; came, white as foam; and went
away grey as rain. And then, he added, "she
would go to that stroked rock yonder, and put
songs against me, till my heart shook like a
tallow-flaucht in the wind."

Was there any other music? I asked. Yes,
he said. When the wind was in the west, and
rose quickly, coming across the sea, he had
heard a hundred feet running through the wet
grass and making the clover breathe a breath.
"When it's a long way off I hear the snatch
of an air, that I think I know and yet can
never put name to. Then it's near, an there's
names called on the wind, an' whishts an' all.
Then they sing an' laugh. I've seen the sheep
standing—their forelegs on the slit rocks that
crop up here like stony weeds—staring, and
listening. Then after a bit they'd go on at the
grass again. But Luath, my dog, he'd sit close
to me, with his eyes big, an' growling low.
Then I wouldn't be hearing anything: no more
at all. But, whiles, somebody would follow
me home, piping, and till the very door, and
then go off laughing. Once, a three-week

back or so, I came home in a thin noiseless rain, and heard a woman-voice singing by the fire-flaucht, and stole up soft to the house-side; but she heard the beat of my pulse and went out at the door, not looking once behind her. She was tall and white, with red hair, and though I didn't see her face I know it was like a rock in rain, with tears streaming on it. She was a woman till she was at the shore there, then she threw her arms into the wind an' was a gull, an' flew away in the lowness of a cloud.

While I was on the island the wind had veered with that suddenness known to all who sail these seas. A wet eddy swirled up from the south-east, and the west greyed, and rain fell. In a few minutes clouds shaped themselves out of mists I had not seen and out of travelling vapours and the salt rising breaths of the sea. A long wind moved from east to west, high, but with its sough falling to me like a wood-echo where I was. Then a cloudy rain let loose a chill air, and sighed with a moan in it: in a moment or two after, great sluices were opened, and the water came down with a noise like the tide coursing the lynns of narrow sea-lochs.

To go back in that falling flood would be to be half-drowned, and was needless too: so

I was the more glad, with the howling wind and sudden gloom of darkness and thick rain, to go in to Murdo's cabin, for it was no more than that, and sit by the comfortable glow of the peats, while the old man, happy in that doing, made tea for me.

He was smiling and busy, when I saw his face cloud.

" Will you be hearing that? " he said looking round.

" What was it? " I answered, for I thought I had heard the long scream of the gannet against the waves of the wind high above us.

Having no answer, I asked Murdo if it was the bird he meant. " Ay, it might be a bird. Sometimes it's a bird, sometimes it's a seal, sometimes it's a creature of the sea pulling itself up the shore an' makin' a hoarse raughlin like a boat being dragged over pebbles. But when it comes in at the door there it is always the same, a tall man, with the great beauty on him, his hands hidden in the white cloak he wears, a bright, cold, curling flame under the soles of his feet, and a crest like a bird's on his head."

I looked instinctively at the door, but no one stood there.

" Was the crest of feathers, Murdo? " I asked, remembering an old tale of a mes-

senger of the Hidden People who is known
by the crest of cuckoo-feathers that he
wears.

" No," he said, " it wasn't. It was more
like white canna blowing in the wind, but with
a blueness in it."

" And what does he say to you? "

" His say is the say of good Gaelic, but with
old words in it that I have forgotten. The
mother of my mother had great wisdom, and
I've heard her using the same when she was
out speaking in the moonlight to them that
were talking to her."

" What does he tell you, Murdo? "

" Sure, seldom he has anything to say. He
just looks in the fire a long time, an' then goes
away smiling."

" And who did you think it was? "

" Well, I thought it might be Mr. Macalister, him as was drowned on St. Bride's
day, the minister over at Uiseader of Harris;
I've heard he was a tall, fine man, an' a
scholar, an' of great goodness an' fineness.
And so I asked him, the second time he came,
if may be he would be Mr. Macalister. He
said no, an' laughed the bit of a laugh, and
then said that good man's bones were now
lying in a great pool with three arches to it,
deep in the sea about seven swims of a seal

124

from Eilean Mhealastaidh, the island that lies under the shadow of Griomaval on the main-land of the Lews.[1]

"An' at that," added Murdo, "I asked him how he would be knowing that."

"'How do you know you are a man, and that the name on you is the name you have?' he said. An' at that I laughed, and said it was more than *he* could say, for he did not seem to have the way of a man an' he kept his name in his pocket."

"With that he touched me an' I fell into an *aisling*.[2] And though I saw the red peats before me, I knew I was out on the sea, and was a wave herded by the wind an' lifted an' shaken by the tide—an' a great skua flyin' over saw my name floating like a dead fish an' sank to it an' swallowed it an' flew away. An' when I sat up, I was here on this stool before the peats, an' no one beside me. But the door was open, an' though there was no rain the flagstone was wet, an' there was a heavy wet-ness in the room, an' it was salt. It was like a spilt wave, it was."

"[1] Seven swims of a seal." A seal is supposed to swim a mile on one side without effort, without twist; and then to change to the other side and swim in the same way the next mile; and so on.

[2] An *aisling: i.e.* a swoon with remembrance.

I was silent for a time, listening to the howling of the wind and the stumbling rush of the rain. Then I spoke.

" But tell me, Murdo, how you know this was not all a dream?"

" Because of what I saw when he touched me."

" And what was that?"

" I have the fear of it still," he said simply. " His arms were like water, and I saw the sea-weed floating among the bones in his hand. And so I knew him to be a *morar-mhara*,[1] a lord of the sea."

" And did you see him after that?"

" Yes."

" And did he say anything to you then?"

" Yes. He said to me after he had sat a long time staring in the fire: ' Murdo, what age have you?' An' I told him. I said I would have eighty years come Candlemas. He said, ' You've got a clean heart: an' you'll have three times eighty years of youth an' joy before you have your long sleep. An' that is a true word. It will be when the wild geese fly north again.' An' then he rose and went away. There was a mist on the sea, an' creepin' up the rocks. I watched him go into it, an'

---

[1] "Morar" (or Morair), a lord, as Morair Gilleas-buig Mhic 'Illeathain" (Lord Archibald Maclean).

I heard him hurling great stones an' dash-
ing them. *'These are the kingdoms of the
world,'* I heard him crying in the mist. No,
I have not been seeing him any more at all:
not once since that day. An' that's all, *Bàn-
Morar.''*

That was many months ago. There is no
one on the island now: no sheep even, for
the pastures are changed. When the wild
geese flew north this year, the soul of
Murdo MacIan went with them. Or if he
did not go with them, he went where Manan promised him he should go. For who
can doubt that it was Manan, in the body
or vision, he the living prince of the waters,
the son of the most ancient god, who,
crested as with snow-white canna with a
blueness in it, and foot-circt with cold curling flame—the uplifted wave and the wandering sea-fire—appeared to the old islander?
And if it were he, be sure the promise
is now joy and peace to him to whom it
was made.

Murdo must have soothed his last hours
of weakness with the *cruit-bheul,* the little
mouth-organ, for it was by the side of his
pillow. In these childish things have we our
delight, even those few of us who, simple of
heart and poor in all things save faith and

wonder, can, like Murdo MacIan, make a brief happiness out of a little formless music with our passing breath, and contentedly put it away at last for the deep music of immortal things.

FARA-GHAOL

"The sea's never so full that it can't drown
sorrow."

Gaelic saying.

" 'Heart of rock!' cried the sea to the land:
'Fara-ghaol (false love)!' cried the land to
the sea."

Fragment of a Gaelic "iorram."

"Gur truagh nach mi 's mo leanu a bha
A muigh fo sgath nan geug O!"
"Would that I and my baby were
Under the shade of the tree, O!"

A Uist lullaby.

At a running water, that comes out at a
place called Stràth-na-mara, near the sea-gates
of Loch Suibhne, there is a pool called the
Pool of the Changeling. None ever goes that
way from choice, for it is not only the crying
of the curlèw that is heard there, or the
querulous wailing lapwing.

It was here that one night, in a September
of many storms, a woman stood staring at
sea. The screaming seamews wheeled and
sank and circled overhead, and the solanders

129

rose with heavy wing and hoarse cries, and the black scarts screeched to the startled guillemots or to the foam-white terns blown before the wind like froth. The woman looked neither at the seafowl nor at the burning glens of scarlet flame which stretched dishevelled among the ruined lands of the sunset.

Between the black flurries of the wind, striking the sea like flails, came momentary pauses or long silences. In one of these the woman raised her arms, she the while unheeding the cold tide-wash about her feet, where she stood insecurely on the wet slippery tangle.

Seven years ago this woman had taken the one child she had, that she did not believe to be her own but a changeling, and had put it on the shore at the extreme edge of the tide-reach, and there had left it for the space of an hour. When she came back, the child she had left with a numbness on its face and with the curse of dumbness, was laughing wild, and when she came near, it put out its arms and gave the cry of the young of birds. She lifted the *leanav* in her arms and stared into its eyes, but there was no longer the weary blankness, and the little one yearned with the petulant laughing and idle whimpering of the

130

children of other mothers. And that mother
there gave a cry of joy, and with a singing
heart went home.

It was the seventh year after that finding
by the sea, that one day, when a cold wind
was blowing from the west, the child Morag
came in by the peat-fire, where her mother
was boiling the porridge, and looked at her
without speaking. The mother turned at that,
and looked at Morag. Her heart sank like a
pool-lily at shadow, when she saw that Morag
had woven a wreath of brown tangled sea-
weed into her hair. But that was nothing
to the bite in her breast when the girl began singing a song that had not a word in
it she had ever heard on her own or other
lips, but was wild as the sound of the tide
calling in dark nights of cloud and wind, or
as the sudden coming of waves over a quiet
sea in the silence of the black hours of
sleep.

" What is it, Morag-mo-rùn? " she asked,
her voice like a reed in the wind.

" It's time," says Morag, with a change in
her eyes, and her face shining with a gleam
on it.

" Time for what, Morag? "

" For me to be going back to the place I
came from."

" And where will that be? "

" Where would it be but to the place you took me out of, and called across? "

The mother gave a cry and a sob. " Sure, now, Morag-a-ghràidh, you will be my own lass and no other? "

" Whist, woman," answered the girl; " don't you hear the laughing in the burn, and the hoarse voice out in the sea? "

" That I do not, O Morag-mo-chree, and sure it's black sorrow to you and to me to be hearing that hoarse voice and that thin laughing."

" Well, sorrow or no sorrow, I'm off now, poor woman. And it's good-bye and a good-bye to you I'll be saying to you, poor woman. Sure it's a sorrow to me to leave you in grief, but if you'll go down to the edge of the water, at the place you took me from, where the runnin' water falls into the sea-pool, you'll be having there against your breast in no time the child of your own that I never was and never could be."

" And why that, and why that, O Morag, lennavan-mo? "

" Peace on your sorrow, woman, and good-bye to you now "; and with that the sea-changeling went laughing out at the door, singing a wave-song so wild and strange the mother's woe was turned to a fear that rose like chill water in her heart.

When she dared follow—and why she did not go at once she did not know—she saw at first no sight of Morag or any other on the lonely shore. In vain she called, with a great sorrowing cry. But as, later, she stood with her feet in the sea, she was silent of a sudden, and was still as a rock, with her ragged dress about her like draggled seaweed. She had heard a thin crying. It was the voice of a breast-child, and not of a grown lass like Morag.

When a grey heron toiled sullenly from a hollow among the rocks she went to the place. She was still now, with a frozen sorrow. She knew what she was going to find. But she did not guess till she lifted the little frail child she had left upon the shore seven years back, that the secret people of the sea or those who call across running water could have the hardness and coldness to give her again the unsmiling dumb thing she had mothered with so much bitterness of heart.

Morag she never saw again, nor did any other see her, except Padruig Macrae, the innocent, who on a New Year's eve, that was a Friday, said that as he was whistling to a seal down by the Pool at Stràth-na-mara he heard

some one laughing at him; and when he looked
to see who it was he saw it was no other than
Morag—and he had called to her, he said, and
she called back to him, " Come away, Padruig dear," and then had swum off like a seal,
crying the heavy tears of sorrow.

And as for the child she had found again
on the place she had left her own silent breast-
babe seven years back, it never gave a cry or
made any sound whatever, but stared with
round, strange eyes only, and withered away
in three days, and was hidden by her in a
sand-hole at the root of a stunted thorn that
grew there.

At every going down of the sun thereafter,
the mother of the changeling went to the
edge of the sea, and stood among the wet tangle of the wrack, and put out her supplicat-
ing hands, and never spoke word nor uttered
cry.

But on this night of September, while the
gleaming seafowl were flying through the
burning glens of scarlet flame in the wide purple wildness of the sky, with the wind falling and wailing and wailing and falling, the
woman went over to the running water beyond
the sea-pool, and put her skirt over her head
and stepped into the pool, and, hooded thus
and thus patient, waited till the tide came in.

SORROW ON THE WIND

"The parable of Pythagoras is dark, but true;
Cor ne edito . . . Eat not thy heart."—BACON,
Essay, xxvii.

"There's sorrow on the wind, my grief, there's
sorrow on the wind!"—*Song*.

I give here, in narrative form, a story of
two, one of whom I knew; and some will
know "Father Angus," from whom also I
heard it. Rury Macarthur died over a year
ago, but not in his own place. He had gone
away after Maev left, and settled behind the
mainland coast, on an inland-lying farm where
the cry of the seamew never came and where
even from the last ridges of the upland the
grey line of the sea never wavered on the
horizon. "It was the wet poor land and the
loneliness out yonder that brought him here,"
the neighbours said. But I, who knew him,
think that there was in his mind another reason also. It is for that I credit the singular
story of a herd-lad, who said his master could
never abide the crying o' peewits, and that he

had time upon time seen him lift an arm and
shake it at the score or more wheeling lapwings, saying at them swift, hoarse words in
Gaelic; but that once, when a single peewit
kept drifting and wailing above him as he
walked up Netherton Brae, the tears were
coming out of his eyes and down his face, like
an old woman crying silently in the gloaming.

" Why will you not give up the girl, Rury? "
asked Father Angus M'Ian, as he and Rury
Macarthur walked along the grey machar, in
the fading hours of a chill July day which had
been all noise of wind and thin crying lash of
rain and the endless wailing of mew and tern,
with the desolate and lonely *sruch* of the tide-
lifted or tide-left wrack and the dull wave
beating.

" Why will you not give up the girl? She
has no heart, they say: and it would only be
sorrow you'd be having, if you took her to
your hearthside."

Rury Macarthur made no answer, but
walked on, his grey eyes staring out across the
long thistled greyness of the sandy machar,
and upon the dull grey and wan green of the
tumbling sea, that sometimes seemed like a
flood coming swift across a narrow down-
borne ridge, and sometimes was like an idle

and formless mist being furtively rolled back
and mysteriously gathered by obscure withdrawing hands.

"I'm not denying she has the fine looks,
Rury: indeed an' it's true that she has the
song and music of beauty. There is no other
girl in Barra like Maev, just as I don't know
one there or in any of the home-isles that has
the old name either. But she doesn't want
marriage, you say: nor to leave her grandmother, who is old and blind: and for this
and for that, an' I know not what all."

"She doesn't wish the thought of going
away from the sea," said Rury dully. "It
isn't the grandmother, no nor yet marriage. I
would have old Janet with no thought but
gladness: and Maev, if she hasn't the hawk's-
hunger for me, hasn't her thought on any
other. It's not that, Father Angus. It's the
sea-water. It's because I have my croft away
up yonder in the hollow of the great strath.
There's nought but leaning heads of hills,
north, south, east, and west: an' moorland an'
bog sloping up against them. You will not
have sight of the sea from any place on Tynavhona; no, not if you go up above the summer shielings, but at one place only, and that
will be at the Cave of the Wailing Woman on
the south-east shoulder of Sliav-Gorm. And

Maev will not come to that loneliness of Tynavhona : no, that she will not."

"Loneliness? Why the girl lives at the
very heart of it . . . not a croft near, in the
wildness of this machar of the west! Loneliness at Tynavhona! Why there are five or
seven crofts within sight of you, and Donald
Maclellan's big farm, and not a mile from
your door is the clachan of the Kern, it that
would be calling itself a *bailê* but for the fear
the crows would fly with the big news to the
Morair's factor!"

"Well and that may be, an' is so, Father
Angus. But it's loneliness for Maev. She
has the wave of the sea in her heart. Ay,
that's it. She has a wave in her heart. She
hears the tides as you hear the church-bell of
Our Lady of the Sea. You wouldn't be
without the good sound of the bells, Father
Angus: and if you were in a place where
there would not be the holy bells, no, not
once, you would be listening to them in your
sleep, and at this hour and at that, you never
knowing when or how, but something in you
suddenly saying *Whisht*. An' if any day you
heard them in the glen, or on the moor, or on
the slope of the hill, or by the byres maybe, ay,
or in your room with book and oil-lamp beside
you, would you not start an' be on your feet

with the beating heart in you, and your eyes
like a stoat's in the dark, smelling the wind?
Ay, you would have the restlessness, you
would, and the fever: and then, or if not then,
soon, ay, soon or late, you would rise and go
away. You would follow the call of the bell.
Ay, Father Angus, an' that is a true word.
And what that call of the bell would be
to you, the sound of the water an' the whis-
perin' of the waste and all that's in the sea
for good and evil (*peace to it, the good sea;
I'd say no evil of it, or of any whose place
it is*)—ay, all that and more, is the sea-call
to Maev."

" It's all a dream, Rury. The girl's a bit
fey with youth an' loneliness."

" Dream or no dream, Father Angus, it's a
daylong sorrow for me. I asked her to come
up to Tynavhona an' I would give her all I
could an' be asking no more than she cared to
give. There's no need for her to work at
what she has not the liking for. There's Morag an' Sine an' Mary to do all that's needed.
' You've a peewit's heart,' I said to her, ' and
I don't want to be lyin' beside you at night,
listening to the wind and fearing that if I
sleep you'll be up and away on wild wings.'
She laughed at that. ' It's not a peewit's heart
I have,' she said, ' but the heart of a tern.

139

You might blow a breath and I'd drift to your
feet like flyin' bog-cotton, with a sigh an' a
cry: an' if it's another wind or breath that
blows, then I drift away like bog-cotton too,
an' with a sigh an' a cry, an' it's to the shore
I go, to the shore in the dark, where there's
nothing but blackness and noise of water an'
whiteness of foam. An' there you cannot
come, Rury, no, not for all your lovingness.
No, no, the peewit to the moor, and the tern
to the saltness and wildness of the water.
Give me a peewit's heart, an' I'll come to
Sliav-Gorn, I'll come to your hidden moors!'
An' I pleaded an' argued, Father Angus, but
no word more than that could I get. . . .
'Give me a peewit's heart, an' then I'll come
to your hidden moors.' "

"Well, and have you not asked again? The
girl's thought may have changed. You know
the way the herring have: for a score years,
it may be, they will come from the wildness of
the sea round one headland, and in the same
week of the same month: and then all of a
sudden, when the boats are dappling the
haven, they sink fathoms deep, and take a
veer like a scythe going through green grass,
and are gone like a shadow, and will not be
seen again for weeks maybe, for months perhaps, perhaps not for years on years. It's

their way. And there's women as incalculable
as that."

"Yes, Father Angus, an' for sure I have,
an' again an' again too. And it was only three
days ago that I went to her, for the last time.
I said it was for the last time, and she said
that was well, for she could never have any
word more to put upon that thing between us.
Old Janet is passing swift, she said, and when
that is come which cannot be long coming,
then she will go away. She has the thought
of the lonely islet in her mind, I know: the
little bit of rock and grass out yonder that's
called Eilean Caorach. She said once she
would be glad to be there alone for a time.
And then, when she goes away to the great
towns, the mainland towns or the English
towns or in the Americas—for go she will,
and be lost and broken like a wounded seamew, and sink and be sucked down like that
seamew, oh yes, I know that well, as a man
hears death whispering a long time before the
cry and the silence — when Maev will go
away to these towns, and with the man she
loves then, or dreams she loves, or with one
who will master her and have her secret anger, then all that's in and around
Eilean Caorach, and all about Ardnatoon
where she now is, will be in her heart, like

moonlight in a pool of water. For her heart's of water."

"What were her words, Rury?" asked Father Angus quietly.

"They would be like this," Rury answered, after a pause. "They would be like this: 'Put your trouble away, *Ruaridh a gradach*. Give it to the peewits up at Tynavhona, but don't be hearing them calling my name for ever and ever. I loved you, I thought, but I have not that thought on me, now. But it would not matter—no, it would not matter. You told me I had a wave of the sea in my heart. I'm not knowing that, nor why, nor the meaning to it. But it may be. I can't love you, for you have a heart like a mountain. It would always be there: I could never get out of sight of it. There would be no going this way and that way. It is a good mountain—but, oh yes, I have the wave in my heart. I cannot be staying ever in one place, Rury. No, that I cannot. I could not be living month-in month-out at Tynavhona. Where would I be for the sea? There is no water up there. But you would have gladness to be living, here, anywhere—yes, yes, I know that, *caraid dileas*, but there's no change in *you*. There's no wave of the sea in *your* heart. You have not the understanding of all this,

Rury? No, nor is it with me any better. But I cannot be living here any more. In the time of the sorrow that's coming it's to Port-na-long I'll go, to sail away, and I shall not be back again: no, never here. It is no sorrow I am wishing you: peace be with you. Forget.' And that was all."

"Well, Rury, I have the true sorrow for you. It's a hard thing to be in the fowler's snare, as the saying is. What old tale is there that is not full of the sighing an' sorrow of vain love and wild beauty that's like a flame leaping in the wind an' falling away to ashes and black grief?"

"Ay, it is a hard thing, Father Angus."

The two walked on awhile, in silence. The grey hour grew dusky with thick shadow, though there was no night there in Barra, at that season: only, in times of gloom and storm, a coming of dull shadow into the half-night and half-day.

A guillemot flew with rapid whirling scream overhead. The harsh cries of scarts came from the weed-covered rocks at the sea's edge. Terns drifted past like flying foam, with a wail that fluttered behind their flight as a blown feather idly whirled in the wake of the wind. From the peat bog beyond the machar, they could hear cries and sounds that might

143

be the drumming of snipe or the harsh screech of the solander or the melancholy flute of the binne-bheul, but were not quite as these are, coming as they did out of a gloom full of menace and the obscure furtive ways of untrodden morass.

Father Angus sighed as he thought of the smallness of the little island-world that was all in all to him and his. How vast and grey and illimitable seemed the long machar, how vaster and sadder and more illimitable the sea beyond, how vast and shadowy the inland hills. The lifting of a Hand, nay but the least breath of the Unknowable, and these hills would be as blown dust, and the machar as a handfull of ground sand, and the great sea no more than a cup of water spilt and thrown upon the wind. How futile all human longing, all passion of the heart, all travail of the spirit, beside this terrible reality of wind and vastness, of wind baying like a hound in a wilderness—a wilderness where the hound's voice would fall away at last, and the hound's shadow fade, and infinitude and eternity be beyond and above and behind and beneath.

But in Rury's heart there was only a dumb revolt against the blind forces. He did not know them, nor what they did, and even in his secret mind he did not put his hatred upon

them. That would be to bring swift evil upon
him. They hear, the everlasting ones. They
hear a whisper in the dark: the wise will
keep even thought of them screened from the
proud, unrelenting eyes. But in his heart he
hated them. It was they who put a wave of
the sea between him and all his hopes. If
Maev were a woman as other women—perhaps, even, he thought, if he could love as
other men— But no, it was their will that
some should be children of water, and no love
and no hope and no supplications would avail,
no, not till the whole world was drowned in
the sea, or till the sea was gathered to the
leaning lips of the sky, as the sun sucks the
midsummer dew.

The night-wind rose out of the west. In
the vastness of shadowy gloom over sea and
land it moved like a lamenting voice, a creature blind and without form, homeless, seeking what is not to be found; crying sometimes,
as a lance slanting on the wind, an ancient
sorrow; deepening sometimes in an immense,
gathering, multitudinous sound, as though the
tides of night broke against the shores of the
stars.

THE LYNN OF DREAMS

"Men shall die who have an ear for harmonies. . . ."—*Boinn of the Sidhe* (in *The Black Linn
of Fraech*).

"Ah, son of water, daughter of fire, how can ye
twain be one?"—*The Little Book of the Great Enchantment.* '

"And lest that evil Destiny which puts dust upon
dreams, and silence upon sweet airs, and still songs,
and makes the hand idle, and the mind an ebbing
leaf, and the spirit as foam upon the sea, should
take from this dreamer what he had won, the god
of enchantment and illusion gave the man a broken
heart, and a mind filled with the sighing of weariness."—*The Ancient Beauty.*

There was a man—let us call him John o'
Dreams—who loved words as the many love
the common things of desire, and as the few
love the beautiful things of the arts. He was
known in that world, at once so narrow and
so wide, where the love of perfected utterance
in prose or verse is become an ideal. What
he wrote was read with eagerness: for those
who turned to his books knew they would find

there not only his own thought, which was deep, and his own imagination, which had a far-wandering wing, but a verbal music that was his own; a subtle use of the underplay of world-life, the colour, meaning, romance, association, suggestiveness, shadowy hints of words; the incommunicable charm.

He loved his art, and he had much to say, and above all longed to capture into rhythm and cadence the floating music that haunted him, and the wonder of life that was his continual dream. But he had a fatal curiosity. Year by year this had grown upon him. He desired to know the well-springs: he desired the well-spring of all literature. At first he sought closely into the art of the rarest masters, now in verse, now in prose: the masters of the dim past, working in the pale gold of antique Greek or the ivory of Catullus, or playing on silver flutes like the obscure singers of the Anthology; or the masters of a later time moulding molten brass like Dante and Milton, or achieving a supreme alchemy like Shakespeare, or shaping agate and porphyry like Leopardi, or white cornelian like Landor, or chrysoprase and green jade like Leconte de Lisle and Walter Pater. But nowhere in these did he find the final secret he sought. No, nor

147

in any other; nor in any language inhabited
by beauty—neither in the limpid excellence
of French, since Villon quickened it with a
mocking sweetness till Verlaine thrilled it with
a sound like a lost air in still woods, so subtle,
so evanishing, so little of the world about us,
so much of the other world on whose leaning
brows are mystery and shadow: nor in the
sweet and stately passage of the tongue of
Florentine and Roman: nor in the deep, troubled tongues of the North, from Weimar to
Christiania: nor in the speech, accompanied
by clarions and chants, of the spellbound
lands of Spain: nor in the great language,
like "a mighty army marching with banners," of the English nations.

Then he turned to his own shaped and coloured utterance, and looked into that; and
into his own mind so far as he could see on
this side its pinnacles and sudden gulfs; and
into his own soul so far as he could sink into
these depths. But neither in those still depths,
nor in that wide cold region of shade and
shine, nor even in that shaped thought and
coloured utterance out of which came the
beautiful phantoms of his imagination, could
he find the silver cord, the thin invisible line
that only the soul knows, when it leaves its
mortality, as fragrance leaves a rose at dusk.

Then a great sadness fell on him, and he wrote no more.

For long he had been in touch with that otherworld of which he had so often written; and now he dwelled more and more in that company of the imagination and of remembrance.

Dark, pathless glens await the troubled thought of those who cross the dim borderlands. To dwell overlong, there; to listen overlong, there; overlong to speak with those, or to see those whose bright, cold laughter is to us so sad (we know not why), and whose tranquil songs are to us so passing forlorn and wild; overlong to commune with them by the open gate, at the wild wood or near the green mound or by the grey wave; is to sow the moonseed of a fatal melancholy, wherein when it is grown and its poppy-heads stir in a drowsy wind, the mind that wanders there calls upon oblivion as a lost child calling upon God.

But, in that intercourse, that happens sometimes which cannot otherwise happen.

And so it was that one day while he of whom I write lay dreaming by a pool, set by a river that ran through a wood of wind and shadow, a stranger appeared by his side. He knew from whom this woodfarer came, for his eyes were cold and glad and no shadow fell on the bracken. Perhaps he knew—it may well be, he knew—more than this: for the cry of the plover was overheard, and the deceitful drumming of snipe was near, and these are two witnesses of him, Dalua, the Master of Illusions, the Fool of Faery—the dark brother of Angus Òg and of Airill Ail na'n Òg, beautiful lords of life and youth.

So when the stranger spoke, and said he would lead to the Lynn of Dreams, and reveal to him there the souls of words in their immortal shape and colour, and how the flow of a secret tide continually moves them into fugitive semblances of mortal colour and mortal shape, the man dreaming by the waterside gladly rose, and the two went together, under the shadow of old trees, to the Lynn of Dream.

When come to that place, where timeless rocks shelved to a deep water, green as a leaf, the mortal and the immortal stooped.

And there the dreamer of whom I write saw his heart's desire bending like a hind of the hill and quenching her thirst. For there he saw the images of beautiful words, as he knew them in their mortal shape and colour, clothe themselves in drifting thought, and often become the thought whose raiment they seemed—or stand, like reeds in shadow, and let the drifting thought take them and wear them as crowns, or diadems, or crested plumes.

And looking deeper he saw the souls of words, in their immortal shape and colour. These would not come from the violet hollows where they moved in their undying dance of joy, nor could the supplication of yearning thoughts reach them.

He saw, too, the flow of the secret tide that continually moved these children of joy into semblance of mortal beauty, images known in happy hours or seen in dreams, but often such as he had never known either in waking dream or in sleeping trance. These he saw ceaselessly woven and unwoven and rewoven. The clusters of many Pleiades made a maze in that living darkness. His soul cried aloud for joy.

When, startled by the wail of a plover at his ear, he looked round, he saw that he was by the riverside again. The stranger stood beside him.

" What have I seen ? " he stammered.

" I gave you a cup to drink, and you drank. It is the Cup of which Tristran drank when he loved Yseult beyond the ache of mortal love : the Cup of Wisdom, that gives madness and death before it gives knowledge and life."

The man was alone then, for the Master of Illusions had gone: Herdsman of thoughts and dreams that wander upon the Hills of Time.

But on the morrow, that led many unchanging morrows, the dreamer of whom I have spoken knew that the learning of the secret he had won was in truth the knowledge that is immortal knowledge, and therefore cannot be uttered by mortal tongue or shaped by mortal thought or coloured by mortal art.

He paid the eric for that wisdon. It is the law.

When again he strove to put beauty into the shimmering, elusive veil of words, he knew with bitter pain that he had lost even the artistry that had once been his. After too deep wisdom he stumbled in the shallows of his own poor troubled knowledge.

For a time he struggled, as a swimmer borne from the shore.

It was all gone: the master-touch, the secret art, the craft. He became an obscure stammerer. At the last he was dumb. And then his heart broke, and he died.

But had not the Master of Illusions shown him his heart's desire, and made it his?

MÄYA

"Those whispers just as you have fallen asleep—
what are they and whence?"—COLERIDGE, *Anima
Poetæ*.

Less has been written of the psychology of
waking dreams than of the psychology of the
dreams of sleep. Surely they are more wonderful, and less lawless, if that can be without
law which is invariable in disorder. I do not
mean the dreams which one controls, as the
wind herds the clouds which rise from the sea-
horizons: but the dreams which come un-
awares, as, when one is lying on the grass and
idly thinking, there may appear in the passing
of a moment the shadow of a hawk hovering
unseen. They are not less irresponsible and
unaccountable: they come, reinless and wild,
across unknown plains, and one hardly hears
the trampling of their feet or sees the flashing of tameless eyes before the imagination is
carried away by them. In a twinkling, the
world that was is no more, and the world that
now is has neither frontiers nor height nor

153

depth, and the dancing stars may be under-
foot, and from the zenith to the horizons may
lean the greenness of the domed sea, and
clouds be steadfast as the ancient hills, and
dreams and passion and emotions be the
winged creatures who move through gulfs of
light and shadow.

Sometimes it happens that, in sleep, dreams
have a rhythmical order, a beauty as of sculpture. It is rare: for when the phantoms of
the silent house are not wild or fantastic or
futile, they move commonly as to a music
unheard of us, and are radiant or sombre as
though an unseen painter touched them with
miraculous dyes. But, once perhaps, the
dreamer may rejoice in a subtle and beautiful
spiritual architecture: and look upon some
completed vision of whose advent he has had
no premonition, of whose mysterious processes
he has no gleam, and whose going will be as
lordly as its coming, without touch of ruin or
of faded beauty.

Who builds these perfected dreams? What
wings, in the impenetrable shadow wherein
one has sunk, have lifted them to the verge
where the unsleeping soul can perceive, and,
perceiving, perhaps understand?

These are not the distempered images of
broken remembrance: they are not the foam

idly fretting the profound suspense of the deep. Nor is the mind consciously at work, building, or shaping, or controlling. As the shadow comes, they come: but as the shadow of some shape of beauty thrown in moonlight in some enchanted garden, a garden wherein one has never been, a shape upon which none has ever looked, a thing of life, complete and wonderful. Strange imaginations arise, as birds winged with flame and with heads like flowers: the unknown is become familiar. When not an image is made by that subtle artificer within; when not a thought steals out to whisper or to shape; when the mind is as a hushed child in the cradle, hearing a new and deep music and unknowing the sea, listening to a lullaby beyond the mother-song and unknowing the wind . . . who, then, fashions those palaces upon the sea, those walls of green ice among the rose-garths of June, those phantoms of bright flame sleeping in peace among dry grass or moving under ancient trees of the unfalling branch and the unfading leaf?

Surely in these is a mystery beyond that of the unquiet brain in a body ill at ease, or beyond that of the mind when like a sleuth-hound it slips out on the trail of old dreams and fleeing imaginations?

When first I began to notice these lamps

of beauty hung in unexpected paths, whether in the twilights of bodily sleep or when the mind was in that trance of the spirit akin to the slumber of the body, I strove to understand, to trace, to go up to the hidden altars and look on the forbidden ecstasy. But, soon, an inward wisdom withheld me. And so for years I have known what has been my whim to call by a name: *The Secret Garden, the White Company, and Music.*

Of what I have seen there, and what music heard, and by whom I have been met and with whom gone, it is not my purpose to speak. Dreamland is the last fantasy of the unloosened imagination, or its valley of Avalon, or the *via sacra* for the spirit, accordingly as one finds it, or with what dower one goes to it. The ways are hidden to all save to those who themselves find. *"Thou canst not travel on the Path till thou hast become the Path itself."*

If these unaccountable waking and unsought dreams bore any immediate or later relation to the things held by the mind, or recently held, or foreseen, one would the more readily believe that the inner mind was working slowly and in its own way at what the outer intelligence had not reached or had ignored. But sometimes they have no recognisable bearing. Sometimes, indeed, they are as fragmentary as the phantasmagoria of sleep. A friend told me this:—" Speaking to a friend on ordinary matters, suddenly I saw him quite clearly walking swiftly along a shore-road unknown to me, a road northern in feature and yet in detail as unfamiliar to me as though set in an unvisited land. He was wild and unkempt, but walked with uplifted head and swiftly. His head and right shoulder were meshed in a net, which trailed behind him. His left arm gleamed as though it were of silver, or mailed like a salmon. His left hand was a flame of fire that was as though entranced, for it neither hurt the unconscious walker nor burned anything with which it came in contact. The vision came and went more swiftly than I have taken time to tell of it, and had no bearing, so far as I know, then or later, on anything concerning either him or myself. A few days later, certainly, he told me that he had been thinking some time before of the symbolism of Nuada of the Dedannan, Nuada of the Silver Hand, a Gaelic divinity of uncertain attributes, but whom some take to be a Celtic Hephaistos. Whether this is any clue I cannot say: or why, since it came, it could not come with more obvious bearing, in a less obscure symbolism. And

157

why, too, should the large round stones on the
shore, the peculiar wind-waved line of old
yews, the stranded fishing-coble, and other
details be so extraordinarily vivid—so vivid
that though I know I have never seen this
headland I could not possibly mistake it were
I some day to come upon its like."

Dreams or visions such as this, are, I fancy,
of a kind that have not necessarily any significance. There are curlews of the imagination
that suddenly go crying through waste places
in the mind.

Of another, I think differently. " In the
middle of a commonplace action of daily life
suddenly I saw a woodland glade in twilight.
A man lay before a fire, but when I looked
closer I saw that what I thought was fire was
a mass of continually revolving leaves, though
no leaf was blown from the maze, which was
like an ever whirling yet never advancing
wheel in that forest silence. He took up a
reed-pipe or something of the kind. He
played, and I saw the stars hang on the
branches of the trees. He played, and I saw
the great boles of the oaks become like amber
filled with moonlight. He played, and then
suddenly I realised that it was a still music,
and had its life for me only in the symbol
of colour. Flowers and plants and tree-

growths of shape and hue such as I had never seen, and have never imagined, arose in the glade, which was now luminous as a vast shell behind which burned torches of honey-coloured flame.

" These changed continually, as the red foliage of fire continually renews itself. Then the player rose, and was a changing flame, and was gone. Another player was in the glade, where all was moveless shadows and old darkness. ' It is I, now, who am God,' he said. Then he in turn was like a shadow of a reed in the wind, that a moment is, and is not. And I looked, and in the heart of the darkness saw a white light continually revolving: and in the silence was a voice . . . ' And I—I am Life.' "

Here, obviously, clear or not, there is the symbolic imagination at work. I do not think an interpreter of dreams need seek here for other than spiritual significance. It is, surely, an effort of the soul to create in symbolic vision a concept of spiritual insight such as the mind cannot adequately realise within its restricted terms, or what is beyond the reach of words. For these, though children of air and fire, have mortal evasive wings, and hands of impalpable dew, and feet wandering and uncertain as the eddying leaf.

Māya

It is less easy to interpret or accept either the rounded and complete dream of sleep—that all too rare visitor in the night of the body—or the waking dream that comes not less mysteriously, unsought, clanless among the tribes of the day's thoughts, an exile from a forbidden land, a prince who will not be commanded in his going or coming, who knows not any law of ours but only his own law.

It is to write of one such vision that I took up my pen and have written these things. It was a dream in sleep, but so potent an image, that, with both body and mind alert in startled wakefulness, I saw it not less clearly, not less vividly, not less overwhelmingly near and present. Its strangeness was in its living nearness in vision, and perhaps neither in aspect nor relation may appeal to others. Perhaps, even, it will seem no more than a luminous phantasy, void of significance. But, to me, it appeared, later, as an effort on the part of the spirit to complete in symbol what I had failed to do in words, while I have been writing these foregoing pages on the children of water—of those in whose hearts is the unresting wave, and whom the tides of happy life lift and leave, and whose longing is idle as foam, and whose dreams are as measureless as all the waters of the world.

Mäya

I saw, suddenly, greenness come out of the
sea, and then the sea pass like a dewdrop in
the heat of the sun. A vast figure stood on
the bare understrand of ocean, and leaned on
his right arm along a mountain-brow so high
that it seemed to me Himalaya or the extreme
Cordillera. As he leaned, I could not see the
face, for the titan stared beyond the rim of
the world. But he leaned negligently, as
though idly watching, idly waiting. There was
nothing of him but was green water, fluent as
the homeless wave yet held in unwavering columnar suspense. Not a limb but was moulded
in strength and beauty, not a muscle of man's
mortal body but was there: yet the white coral
of the depths gleamed through the titanic feet
sculptured as in green jade, and the floating
brown weed of the perpetual tide cast a wavering shadow among the sculptured green
ridges and valleys of that titanic head. But
it was not an image I saw: it was not an image
of life, but life. There was not an ocean withheld in that bended arm, in that lifted shoulder, which could not have yielded in flying
wave and soaring billow, or heaved with a
slow mighty breath sustaining navies and ar-
gosies as drifting shells. When thought stirred
behind the unseen brows, tides moved within
these columnar deeps: and I do not doubt that

the vast heart was a maelstrom where the in-
rush and outrush of tempestuous surges
made a throb that shook the coasts of worlds
beyond our own.

Looking on the greatness of this upbuilded
sea, this titanic statue of silence and water, I
thought I beheld the most ancient of the gods:
the most ancient of the gods, the greatest of
the gods.

Suddenly I heard breaths of music, and a
sound as of a multitude of swift feet around
me and beyond. I turned. There was no
one. But a low voice, that ran through me
like fire, spoke.

" Look, child of water, at your god."

Again I heard breaths of music rise, like
thin spirals of smoke, but I did not see whence
they came.

While the music breathed, I saw the Titan
stand back from the rim of the world. His
face slowly turned. But a whiteness as of
foam was against my eyes, and a sudden intolerable fear bowed my head. When I
looked again I saw only an illimitable sea that
reached from my feet, green as grass: and on
the west of the world the unloosened rains and
dews hung like a veil.

The unseen one beside me stooped, and
lifted a wave, and threw it into my heart.

Mäya

Then I knew that I was made of the kinship of Mânan, and should never know peace, but should have the homeless wave for my heart's brother, and the salt sea as my cup to drink, and the wilderness of waters as the symbol of all vain ungovernable longings and desires.

And I woke, still looking out of time into eternity, and saw a titan figure of living green water sculptured like jade, with feet set in the bed of ancient oceans; leaning, with averted face, on a mountain-brow, vast as Andes, vast as Himalaya.

FOR THE BEAUTY OF
AN IDEA

"The first necessity for peoples, as for man, is to die."—CHATEAUBRIAND, *Mémoires*, pt. xi. bk. iv.

"In the life of cities nothing preserves like early overthrow, nothing destroys like continuous life."—FREEMAN, *Essay on Argos.*

"When a man has attained those things which are necessary to life, there is another alternative than to attain the superfluities; he may adventure on life now."—THOREAU.

For the Beauty of an Idea

I

PRELUDE

The short essay, entitled " Celtic," which forms the second of the three parts of this study in the spiritual history of the Gael, appeared first in *The Contemporary Review*, and a few months later in the volume entitled *The Divine Adventure: Iona: and other Studies in Spiritual History*, and was a signal for divided comment. But for the moment I would recur only to the aspect it wore for many in that country for whose more eager spirits it was above all intended—Ireland being to-day not only the true home of lost causes and a nursery of the heroic powers and influences that go out to conquer and die, but of the passionate and evil powers and influences which seek to conquer and are slow to die.

Although in Ireland, then, this essay towards a worthy peace, where peace may be, and towards a compromise, in nothing ignoble, for the sake of union in a noble destiny, was welcomed by many—there were others, and among them one or two of those deservedly held in honour, who execrated the attempt.[1]

[1] As it has been "authoritatively" stated that no Irish journal has endorsed these views, one out of six or seven of the leading Irish journals representative of all degrees of opinion, which have more or less "endorsed" the views here set forth, may be selected. In the reprinting of so personal a note the author trusts to be absolved of any other intent than to refute in what seems the simplest and most direct way a statement calculated to mislead:

"It seems an unexpected utterance from Miss Macleod. Yet, in point of fact, it only shows the awakening of the same philosophic spirit which we have observed in other parts of this book and in other regions of her thought. Miss Macleod has noticed the narrow separatism of sentiment which has sometimes marked the Celtic literary revival, and sees that it can only keep the Celtic spirit in a hopeless and sterile conflict with fact and truth. . . . In her own words:—

"The Celtic element in our national life has a vital and great part to play. We have a most noble ideal if we will but accept it. And that is, not to perpetuate feuds, not to try to win back what has gone away upon the wind, not to repay ignorance with scorn, or dulness with contempt, or past wrongs with present hatred, but so to live, so to pray, so to hope, so to work, so to achieve, that we, what is left of the Celtic races, of the Celtic genius,

Prelude

I have no ill-will to those who, no doubt in
part through a hurried habit of mind, sought
by somewhat intemperate means to discredit
the plea. I believe—I would say I know, so
sure am I—these had at heart the thought of
Ireland, that passion which is indeed the foremost lamp of the Gael, the passion of nationality; and having this thought and this passion, considered little or for the time ignored
the " sweet reasonableness," the courtesy cherished by minds less sick with hope deferred,
less desperate with defeated dreams. But in
controversy nothing else was revealed than
that enthusiasm can sometimes lead to confused thought and hasty speech, and (it may
well be) that the writer of " Celtic " had failed

may permeate the greater race of which we are a
vital part, so that with this Celtic emotion, Celtic
love of beauty, and Celtic spirituality a nation
greater than any the world has seen may issue, a
nation refined and strengthened by the wise relinquishings and steadfast ideals of Celt and Saxon,
united in a common fatherland, and in singleness of
pride and faith."

    *   *   *   *   *   *

These are great, wise, and courageous words. . . .
When the Irish Celt begins to heed them he will
cease to be the type of self-torturing futility which,
with all his gifts, he so largely is at the present day."
—(From an article, "A Celtic Thinker," in the
Dublin Express.)

to be lucid or adequate on that fundamental
factor in Gaelic union, that essential element
in the continued life and development of the
Gael—the proud preservation of nationality.
I can imagine no worse thing for Ireland than
that, in exchange for a dull peace and a poor
prosperity, it should sink to the vassalage of
a large English shire. In the wise words of
Thoreau, the cost of a thing is the amount of
what may be called life which is required to be
exchanged for it, immediately or in the long
run.

The aim of this essay was to help towards a
workable reconciliation: not between " invet-
erate and irreconcilable foes " (which is but
the rhetoric of those fevered with an epileptic
nationalism), but a reconciliation such as may
be persuaded between two persons, each with
divergent individual aims and ideals, yet able
to unite with decency and courtesy in a league
for the common good, the commonweal. It
seemed, and seems, to the writer that com-
monsense (there is no Celtic word for it)
makes clear that an absolute irreconcilability
is simply a cul-de-sac, down which baffled
dreams and hopes and faiths come at last
upon a blank wall. Strength is built out of
forfeiture as well as of steadfastness, and the
man or woman, cause or race wins, which on

occasion can relinquish or forbear. Merely to be irreconcilable is to prefer the blank wall to the open road.

But when that is said, it does not follow that there are no subjects, no ideals, no aims which stand apart from this debatable ground of reconciliation. On the contrary, I believed, and believe, that there are subjects, ideals, and aims whose continuity lies only in an unswerving steadfastness. Nay, further, with the author of *The Hearts of Men*, I would say with all my faith, " the people that cannot fight shall die." On any such people the shadow of the end is already come. All signs and portents will have borne testimony. Before a nation dies, the soul of that nation is dead; and before the death of the soul of the nation its gods perish: God perishes. For God, who is eternal in the Spirit, is, in the image and in the symbol, as in " omnipotence " as we conceive it, mortal. Unto every nation of man God dies when in the soul of the nation the altars are cold. There are the altars of divine faith, and the altars of spiritual ideals, and the altars of the commonweal. Beware the waning of these fires.

The keynote of " Celtic " is in the sentence, " We have of late heard so much of Celtic beauty and Celtic emotion that we would do well to stand in more surety as to what we mean and what we do not mean."

But I generalised too vaguely, I find, in this merely indicative, merely suggestive paper, when I wrote, " What is a Celtic Writer? . . . It is obvious that if one would write English literature, one must write in English and in the English tradition."

Of course I meant nothing so narrow in claim, so foreign to my conviction, as that one must " be English." There is no " must," in the Academic sense, in literature: the most vivid and original literature has in truth ever been an ignoring or overriding of this strong word of the weak.

Only I can see how some—I am glad to know the few, not the many—misread this sentence. For that, I welcome this opportunity of the open word. There is no need here to recur to the literal meaning of the designation, a " Celtic writer." I would merely add a further word of warning as to the sometimes apt epithet and definitive but often ill-considered use of racial terms in speaking of what are individual qualities and idiosyncrasies rather than the habit of mind or general characteristic of a people. Swedenborg, Blake, and Maurice Maeterlinck do not stand for Scandinavian, and English, and Flemish mysticism, nor is any of these a mystic by virtue of being a Fleming, an Englishman, or a Scandinavian. I recall the considered judgment of an acute French critic, M. Angellier, in his essay on Burns: " The idea of race is fluctuating, ill-established, open to dispute . . . you cannot obtain a conception of the soul of a portion of humanity by merely supplementing certain ethnological labels with a few vague adjectives."

To consider those only, then, who write in English, I would add to my statement that if one would write English literature one must write in English and in the English tradition, the rider that the English language is not the exclusive property of that section of our complex race which is distinctively English, the English nation—any more than it is the exclusive property of the Scots, who speak it; or of the Australians; or of the Canadians; or of the vast and numerically superior American nation. The language is common to all: all share in the heritage shaped by the genius, moulded by the life and thought, and transmitted by the living spirit of the common essential stock—now as likely to be revealed in Massachusetts as in Yorkshire, in Toronto as in Edinburgh, in Sydney or Melbourne or Washington, as in Dublin, Manchester, or

London. An American writes in his native language when he writes in English: so does a Scot, now: so does a Canadian, an Australian, a New Zealander. Therefore the literature of the Australians, the Scots, the Irish, the Americans, must be in English. It is the language that determines, but the thought behind the language may come from any of the several founts of nationality, to reveal, in that language, its signature of the colour and form of distinctive life. It is not the language that compels genius, but genius that compels the language.

Again, literature has laws as inevitable as the laws which mould and determine the destiny of nations. These can be evaded by decay and death: they cannot be overridden. Every literature has its tradition of excellence —that is, the sum of what within its own limits can be achieved in beauty and power and aptitude. This tradition of excellence is what we call the central stream. Of course, if one prefer the tributary, the backwater, the offshoot, there is no reason why one should not be well content with the chosen course. To many it seems, for many it is, the better way; as the backwater for the kingfisher, the offshoot or tributary for the solitary heron. But one must not choose the backwater and declare that it is the main stream, or have the little tributary say that though it travels on the great flow it is not part of the river.

That is what I meant when I said that if one would write English literature one must write in English and in the English tradition. To say that was not to bid the Gael cease to be Gaelic, any more than it would imply that the American should cease to be American. On the contrary, I do most strenuously believe that the sole life of value in literature is in the preservation of the distinct racial genius, temper, colour, and contour. If the poetry of two of the foremost Irish poets of to-day did not conform to the laws and traditions of English poetry—since Mr. Yeats and Mr. George Russell write in their native language, English, the language to which they were born and in which alone they can express themselves—it might be very interesting " Celtic " or any other experimental verse, but it would not be English poetry. The beauty they breathe into their instrument is of themselves ; is individual certainly, and, in one case at least, in spirit and atmosphere is more distinctively Gaelic than English. But the instrument is English : and to summon beauty through it, and to give the phantom a body and spirit of excellence, one must follow in the footsteps of the master-musicians, recognising the same essential limitations, observing the same fundamental needs, fulfilling the like rigorous obligations of mastery.

Since we have to write in English, we must accept the burthen and responsibility. If a Cretan write in the Cretan dialect, he can be estimated by those who know Cretan; but if he is ambitious to have his irregular measures and corrupt speech called Greek poetry, he must write in Greek and conform in what is essential to the Greek tradition, to the laws and limitations of the Greek genius. The Englishman, the Scot, the Irishman, the American, each, if he would write English literature, has of necessity to do likewise.

In a very true sense, therefore, there can be an Irish literature, a Scottish literature, an Anglo-Gaelic literature, as well as an English literature; but in the wider sense it is all English literature—with, as may be, an Irish spirit and Irish ideals and Irish colour, or with a Highland spirit and Highland ideals and Highland colour, or with a Welsh spirit and Welsh ideals and Welsh colour—as Mr. Thomas Hardy's writings are English literature, with an English spirit and English ideals and an English colour.

Prelude

It is the desire and faith of the Irish nation
to mould anew a literature as distinctively its
own as the English nation has a literature that
is distinctively its own: and to do this, in Ireland or the like in Scotland, is possible only
by the cultivation, the persistent preservation
of the national spirit, of the national idiosyn-
crasy, the national ideals. I would see our
peoples reconciled, where reconciliation is just
and therefore wise; believing that in such reconciliation lie the elements of strength and
advance, of noble growth and conquering influence: but I would not have reconciliation at
any price, and would rather we should dwell
isolate and hostile than purchase peace at the
cost of relinquishment of certain things more
precious than all prosperities and triumphs.
The law of love is the nobler way, but there
is also a divine law of hate. I do not advo-
cate, and have never advocated, a reconciliation on any terms. I am not English, and
have not the English mind or the English temper, and in many things do not share the
English ideals; and to possess these would
mean to relinquish my own heritage. But
why should I be irreconcilably hostile to that
mind and that temper and those ideals? Why
should I not do my utmost to understand,
sympathise, fall into line with them so far as

may be, since we have all a common bond
and a common destiny?

To that mind and that temper and those
ideals do we not owe some of the noblest
achievements of the human race, some of the
lordliest conquests over the instincts and forces
of barbarism, some of the loveliest and most
deathless things of the spirit and the imagination?

Let us beware of kneading husks with
Mâyâ's dew, and so—as in the ancient gnome
attributed to Krishna—create but food for
the black doves of decay and death.

As for the Gaelic remnant (and none can
pretend that this means Scotland and Ireland,
but only a portion of Scotland and only a divided Ireland) I am ever but the more con-
vinced that the dream of an outward independence is a perilous illusion—not because it
is impracticable, for that alone is a fascina-
tion to us, but because it does not, cannot alas,
reveal those dominant elements which alone
can control dreams become actualities. Another and greater independence is within our
reach, is ours, to preserve and ennoble.

Strange reversals, strange fulfilments may
lie on the lap of the gods, but we have no
knowledge of these, and hear neither the high
laughter nor the far voices. But we front a

possible because a spiritual greater destiny
than the height of imperial fortunes, and
have that which may send our voices further
than the trumpets of east and west. Through
ages of slow westering, till now we face the
sundown seas, we have learned in continual
vicissitude that there are secret ways whereon
armies cannot march. And this has been
given to us, a more ardent longing, a more
rapt passion in the things of outward beauty
and in the things of spiritual beauty. Nor it
seems to me is there any sadness, or only the
serene sadness of a great day's end, that, to
others, we reveal in our best the genius of a
race whose farewell is in a tragic lighting of
torches of beauty around its grave.

CELTIC

"Search first at home: a fitting glory hast thou got there."—PINDAR.

OED.: *"And where are the young men, thy brothers, at our need?"*

ISMÊNÊ: *"They are . . . where they are: 'tis their dark hour."*

SOPHOCLES: *Oedipus at Kolonos.*

II

CELTIC

"Yea, point thine arrow at a noble spirit, and thou shalt not miss."—SOPHOCLES: *Aias*.

A writer might well be proud to be identified with a movement that is primarily spiritual and eager, a movement of quickened artistic life. I, for one, care less to be identified with any literary movement avowedly partisan. That is not the deliberate view of literature, which carries with it the heat and confused passions of the many. It is not the deliberate view, which confers passions that are fugitive upon that troubled Beauty which knows only a continual excellence. It is not the deliberate view, which would impose the penury of distracted dreams and desires upon those who go up to the treasure house and to white palaces.

But I am somewhat tired of an epithet that, in a certain association, is become jejune, through use and misuse. It has grown fa-

183

miliar wrongly; is often a term of praise or
disdain, in each inept; is applied without mod-
eration; and so now is sometimes unwelcome
even when there is none other so apt and
right.

The " Celtic Movement," in the first place,
is not, as so often confusedly stated, an arbitrary effort to reconstruct the past; though it
is, in part, an effort to discover the past. For
myself (as one imputed to this " movement ")
I would say that I do not seek merely to re-
produce ancient Celtic presentments of tragic
beauty and tragic fate, but do seek in nature
and in life, and in the swimming thought of
timeless imagination, for the kind of beauty
that the old Celtic poets discovered and uttered. There were poets and mythmakers in
those days; and to-day we may be sure that a
new Mythus is being woven, though we may
no longer regard with the old wonder, or in
the old wonder imaginatively shape and colour the forces of Nature and her silent and
secret processes; for the mythopœic faculty is
not only a primitive instinct but a spiritual
need.

I do not suppose our Celtic ancestors—for
all their high civilisation and development, so
much beyond what obtained among the Anglo-
Saxon or Teutonic peoples at the same date—

theorised about their narrative art; but from
what we know of their literature, from the
most ancient bardic chants to the *sgeul* of to-
day, we cannot fail to see that the instinctive
ideal was to represent beautiful life. It is an
ideal that has lain below the spiritual passion
of all great art in every period. Phidias knew
it when he culled a white beauty from the
many Athenian youth, and Leonardo when he
discerned the inexplicable in woman's beauty
and painted Moña Lisa, and Palestrina when
from the sound in the pines and the voice of
the wind in solitudes and the songs of la-
bourers at sundown he wove a solemn music
for cathedral aisles. With instinct, the old
Celtic poets and romancists knew it: there are
no Breton ballads nor Cymric mabinogion nor
Gaelic sgeulan which deal ignobly with petty
life. All the evil passions may obtain there,
but they move against a spiritual background
of pathetic wonder, of tragic beauty and
tragic fate.

The ideal of art should be to represent
beautiful life. If we want a vision of life that
is not beautiful, we can have it otherwise: a
multitude can depict the ignoble; the lens can
replicate the usual.

It should be needless to add that our vision
of the beautiful must be deep and wide and

virile, as well as high and ideal. When we say that art should represent beautiful life, we do not say that it should represent only the beautiful in life, which would be to ignore the roots and the soil and the vivid sap, and account the blossom only. The vision of beautiful life is the vision of life seen not in impossible but in possible relief: of harmonious unity in design as well as in colour. To say that art should represent beautiful life is merely to give formal expression to the one passionate instinct in every poet and painter and musician, in every artist. There is no " art " saved by a moral purpose, though all true art is subtly, informed of the spirit; but I know none, with pen or brush, with chisel or score, which, ignobly depicting the ignoble, survives in excellence.

In this, one cannot well go astray. Nor do I seek an unreal Ideal. In the kingdom of the imagination, says Calvert, one of our forgotten mystics, the ideal must ever be faithful to the general laws of nature—elsewhere adding a truth as immanent: " Man is not alone: the Angel of the Presence of the Infinite is with him." I do not, with Blake, look upon our world as though it were at best a basis for transcendental vision, while in itself " a hindrance and a mistake,' but rather, as a wiser has said, to an Earth spiritualised, not a Heaven naturalised. With Calvert, too, I would say : " I have a fondness for the earth, and rather a Phrygian way of regarding it, despite a deeper yearning to see its glades receding into the Gardens of Heaven."

There is cause for deep regret when any word, that has peculiar associations of beauty or interest, or in which some distinction obtains, is lightly bandied. Its merit is then in convenience of signal rather than in its own significance. It is easy to recall some of these unfortunates; as our Scottish word " gloaming," that is so beautiful, and is now, alas, to be used rarely and with heed; as " haunting," with its implicit kinship with all mysteries of shadow, and its present low estate ; as " melody," that has an outworn air, though it has three secrets of beauty ; as others, that one or two use with inevitableness, and a small number deftly, till the journal has it, and it is come into desuetude.

We have of late heard so much of Celtic beauty and Celtic emotion that we would do well to stand in more surety as to what we mean and what we do not mean.

I do not myself know any beauty that is of art to excel that bequeathed to us by Greece.

Celtic

The marble has outlasted broken dynasties
and lost empires: the word is to-day fresh as
with dews of dawn. But through the heart I
travel into another land. Through the heart
I go to lost gardens, to mossed fountains, to
groves where is no white beauty of still
statue, but only the beauty of an old forgotten day remembered with quickened pulse and
desired with I know not what of longing and
weariness.

Is it remembrance, I wonder often, that
makes many of us of the Celtic peoples turn
to our own past with a longing so great, a
love perfected through forgotten tribulations
and familiar desires of the things we know
to be impossible but so fair? Or do we
but desire in memory what all primitive
races had, and confuse our dreams with
those which have no peace because they are
immortal?

If one can think with surety but a little way
back into the past, one can divine through
both the heart and the mind. I do not think
that our broken people had no other memories
and traditions than other peoples had. I believe they stood more near to ancient forgotten founts of wisdom than others stood: I believe that they are the offspring of a race who
were in a more fraternal communion with the

secret powers of the world. I think their ancient writings show it, their ancient legends,
their subtle and spiritual mythology. I believe
that, in the East, they lit the primitive genius
of their race at unknown and mysterious fires;
that, in the ages, they have not wholly forgotten the ancestral secret; that, in the West,
they may yet turn from the grey wave that
they see, and the grey wave of time that they
do not see, and again, upon new altars, com-
mit that primeval fire.

But to believe is one thing, to convince is
another. Those of us who believe thus have
no warrant to show. It may well be that we
do but create an image made after the desire
and faith of the heart.

It is not the occasion to speak of what I do
believe the peculiar and excelling beauty of
the Celtic genius and Celtic literature to be;
how deep its well-springs, how full of strange
new beauty to us who come upon it that is so
old and remote. What I have just written
will disclose that wherever else I may desire
to worship, there is one beauty that has to me
the light of home upon it; that there is one
beauty from which, above all others now, I
hope for a new revelation; that there is a
love, there is a passion, there is a romance,
which to me calls more suddenly and search-

ingly than any other ancient love or ancient passion or ancient romance.

But having said this, I am the more free to speak what I have in view. Let me say at once, then, that I am not a great believer in " movements," and still less in " renascences "; to be more exact, I hold myself in a suspicion towards these terms; for often, in the one, what we look for is not implicit, and in the other, we are apt rather to find the excrescent and the deciduous.

So far as I understand the " Celtic Movement," it is a natural outcome, the natural expression of a freshly inspired spiritual and artistic energy. That this expression is coloured by racial temperament is its distinction; that it is controlled to novel usage is its opportunity. When we look for its source we find it in the usufruct of an ancient and beautiful treasure of national tradition. One may the more aptly speak thus collectively of a mythology and a literature, and a vast and wonderful legendary folklore, since to us now, it is in great part hidden behind veils of an all but forgotten tongue, and of a system of life and customs, ideals and thought, that no longer obtains.

I am unable, however, to see that it has sustenance in continuity of revolt. A new movement need not be a revolt, but rather a sortie to carry a fresh position. If a movement has any inherent force, it will not destroy itself in forlorn hopes, but, where the need is vital, will fall into line, and so achieve where alone the desired success can be achieved.

There is no racial road to beauty, nor to any excellence. Genius, which leads thither, beckons neither to tribe nor clan, neither to school nor movement, but only to one soul here and to another there; so that the Icelander hears and speaks in Saga, and the brown Malay hears and carves delicately in ivory; and the men in Europe, from the Serb and the Finn to the Basque and the Breton, hear, and each in his kind answers; and what the Englishman says in song and romance and the deep utterance of his complex life, his mountain-kindred say in mabinogi or sgeul.

Even in those characteristics which distinguish Celtic literature—intimate natural vision; a swift emotion that is sometimes a spiritual ecstasy, but sometimes is also a mere intoxication of the senses; a peculiar sensitiveness to the beauty of what is remote and solitary; a rapt pleasure in what is ancient and in the contemplation of what holds an indwelling melancholy; a visionary passion for beauty, which is of the immortal things, beyond the temporal beauty of what is mutable and mortal—even in these characteristics it does not stand alone, and perhaps not preeminent. There is a beauty in the Homeric hymns that I do not find in the most beautiful of Celtic chants; none could cull from the gardens of the Gael what in the Greek anthology has been gathered out of time to be everlasting; perhaps only the love and passion of the stories of the Celtic mythology surpass the love and passion of the stories of the Hellenic mythology. The romance that of old flowered among the Gaelic hills flowered also in English meads, by Danish shores, along Teutonic woods and plains. I think Catullus sang more excellently than Bailè Honeymouth, and that Theocritus loved nature not less than Oisin, and that the ancient makers of the Kalevala were as much children of the wind and wave and the intimate natural world as were the makers of the ancient heroic chronicles of the Gael.

There is no law set upon beauty. It has no geography. It is the domain of the spirit. And if, of those who enter there, peradventure any comes again, he is welcome for what he brings; nor do we demand if he be dark or fair, Latin or Teuton or Celt, or say of him that his tidings are lovelier or the less lovely because he was born in the shadow of Gaelic hills or nurtured by Celtic shores.

It is well that each should learn the mother-song of his land at the cradle-place of his birth. It is well that the people of the isles should love the isles above all else, and the people of the mountains love the mountains above all else, and the people of the plains love the plains above all else. But it is not well that because of the whistling of the wind in the heather one should imagine that no-where else does the wind suddenly stir the reeds and the grasses in its incalculable hour.

When I hear that a new writer is of the Celtic school, I am left in some uncertainty, for I know of many Anglo-Celtic writers but of no " school," or what present elements would form a school. What is a Celtic writer? If the word has any exact acceptance, it must denote an Irish or a Scottish Gael, a Cymric or Breton Celt, who writes in the language of his race. It is obvious that if one would write English literature, one must write in English and in the English tradition.

When I hear, therefore, of this or that writer as a Celtic writer, I wonder if the term is not apt to be misleading. An English writer is meant, who in person happens to be an Irish Gael, or Highland, or Welsh.

I have already suggested what other misuse of the word obtains: Celtic emotion, Celtic love of nature, Celtic visionariness. That, as admitted, there is in the Celtic peoples an emotionalism peculiar in kind and certainly in intensity, is not to be denied; that a love of nature is characteristic is true, but differing only, if at all, in certain intimacies of approach; that visionariness is relatively so common as to be typical, is obvious. But there is English emotion, English love of nature, English visionariness, as there is Dutch, or French, or German, or Russian, or Hindu. There is no exclusive national heritage in these things, save in the accident of racial physiognomy, of the supreme felicity of contour and colour. At a hundred yards a forest is seen to consist of ash and lime, of elms, beeches, oaks, horn-beams; but a mile away it is, simply, a forest.

I do not know any Celtic visionary so rapt and absolute as the Londoner William Blake, or the Scandinavian Swedenborg, or the Flemish Ruysbroek; or any Celtic poet of nature to surpass the Englishman Keats; nor do I think even religious ecstasy is more seen in Ireland than in Italy.

Nothing but harm is done by a protestation that cannot persuade deliberate acceptance.

When I hear that " only a Celt " could have written this or that passage of emotion or description, I am become impatient of these parrot-cries, for I remember that if all Celtic literature were to disappear, the world would not be so impoverished as by the loss of English literature, or French literature, or that of Rome or of Greece.

But above all else it is time that a prevalent pseudo-nationalism should be dissuaded. I am proud to be a Highlander, but I would not side with those who would " set the heather on fire." If I were Irish, I would be proud, but I would not lower my pride by marrying it to a ceaseless ill-will, an irreconcilable hate, for there can be a nobler pride in unvanquished acquiescence than in futile revolt. I would be proud if I were Welsh, but I would not refuse to learn English, or to mix with English as equals. And proud as I might be to be Highland, or Scottish, or Irish, or Welsh, or English, I would be more proud to be British—for, there at last, we have a bond to unite us all, and to give us space for every ideal, whether communal or individual, whether national or spiritual.

As for literature, there is, for us all, only

English literature. All else is provincial or
dialetic.

But gladly I, for one, am willing to be
designated Celtic, if the word signify no
more than that one is an English writer who
by birth, inheritance, and temperament has
an outlook not distinctively English, with
some memories and traditions and ideals
not shared in by one's countrymen of the
South, with a racial instinct that informs
what one writes, and, for the rest, a common heritage.

The Celtic element in our national life has
a vital and great part to play. We have a
most noble ideal if we will but accept it. And
that is, not to perpetuate feuds, not to try to
win back what is gone away upon the wind,
not to repay ignorance with scorn, or dulness
with contempt, or past wrongs with present
hatred, but so to live, so to pray, so to hope,
so to work, so to achieve, that we, what is
left of the Celtic races, of the Celtic genius,
may permeate the greater race of which we
are a vital part, so that with this Celtic emotion, Celtic love of beauty, and Celtic spirituality a nation greater than any the world
has seen may issue, a nation refined and
strengthened by the wise relinquishings and
steadfast ideal of Celt and Saxon, united in a

common fatherland, and in singleness of pride and faith.

As I have said, I am not concerned here with what I think the Celtic genius has done for the world, and for English literature in particular, and, above all, for us of to-day and to-morrow; nor can I dwell upon what of beautiful and mysterious and wonderful it discloses, or upon its bitter-sweet charm. But of a truth, the inward sense and significance of the " Celtic Movement " is, as has been well said by Mr. Yeats, in the opening of a fountain of legends, and, as scholars aver, a more abundant fountain than any in Europe, the great fountain of Gaelic legends. " None can measure of how great importance it may be to coming times, for every new fountain of legends is a new intoxication for the imagination of the world. It comes at a time when the imagination of the world is as ready, as it was at the coming of the tales of Arthur and of the Grail, for a new intoxication. The arts have become religious, and must, as religious thought has always done, utter themselves through legends; and the Gaelic legends have so much of a new beauty that they may well give the opening century its most memorable symbols."

Perhaps the most significant sentence in

M. Renan's remarkable study of the Poetry
of the Celtic Races is that where he speaks of
the Celtic race as having worn itself out in
mistaking dreams for realities. I am not certain that this is true, but it holds so great a
part of the truth that it should make us think
upon how we stand.

I think our people have most truly loved
their land, and their country, and their songs,
and their ancient traditions, and that the word
of bitterest savour is that sad word exile. But
it is also true that in that love we love
vaguely another land, a rainbow-land, and
that our most desired country is not the real
Ireland, the real Scotland, the real Brittany,
but the vague Land of Youth, the shadowy
Land of Heart's Desire. And it is also true,
that deep in the songs we love above all other
songs is a lamentation for what is gone away
from the world, rather than merely from us as
a people, or a sighing of longing for what the
heart desires but no mortal destiny requites.
And true, too, that no tradition from of old
is so compelling as the compelling tradition
that is from within ; and that the long sorrow
of our exile is in part because we ourselves
have driven from us that company of hopes
and dreams which were once realities, but are
now among beautiful idle words.

Celtic

In a word, we dwell overmuch among desired illusions: beautiful, when, like the rainbow, they are the spiritual reflection of certainties; but worthless as the rainbow-gold with which the Shee deceive the unwary, when what is the phantom of a spiritual desire is taken to be the reality of material fact.

And I think that we should be on guard against any abuse of, that we should consider this other side of, our dreams and ideals, wherein awaits weakness as well as abides strength. It is not ill to dream, in a day when there are too few who will withdraw from a continual business, a day when there are fewer dreams. But we shall not greatly gain if we dream only of beautiful abstractions, and not also of actual or imaginative realities and possibilities. In a Highland cottage I heard some time ago a man singing a lament for " Tearlach Og Aluinn," Bonnie Prince Charlie; and when he ceased tears were on the face of each that was there, and in his own throat a sob. I asked him, later, was his heart really so full of the Prionnsa Ban, but he told me that it was not him he was thinking of, but of all the dead men and women of Scotland who had died for his sake, and of Scotland itself, and of the old days that could not come again. I did not ask what old days, for I knew that

in his heart he lamented his own dead hopes
and dreams, and that the prince was but the
image of his lost youth, and that the world
was old and grey because of his own weariness and his own grief.

Sometimes I fear that we who as a people
do so habitually companion ourselves with
dreams may fall into that abyss where the
realities are become shadows, and shadows
alone live and move. And then I remember
that dreamers and visionaries are few; that
we are no such people; that no such people
has ever been; and that of all idle weaving
of sand and foam none is more idle than this,
the strange instinctive dread of the multitude,
that the few whose minds and imaginations
dwell among noble memories and immortal
desires shall supersede the many who are content with lesser memories and ignoble desires.

THE GAELIC HEART

"Beloved and most beautiful, who wearest
The shadow of that soul by which I live."
"Prometheus Unbound."

III

THE GAELIC HEART

One day, on Iona, I met an old woman who had been gathering driftwood in the haven called Port-na-Churaich—the haven of the coracle, for it was there St. Colum landed on the day Christ's hand steered the helm to the Holy Isle. She was weary with her burthen, and had rested on a ledge of granite, and there had fallen asleep. I stood a long time looking at her. I had not seen her for some years, not since the death of her daughter in the Sleat of Skye: but it was not at the way-worn sadness of the old figure I was looking, though that was in my thoughts. I was thinking of what I had heard of her. Long ago a poet of the isles had put song upon song on her, as the saying is: and one known to all of us had made an *oran-ghaoil* about her which is still sung from the Rhinns of Islay to The Seven Hunters. When I was a child I had heard often of the beauty of Mary Macarthur. But sorrow, which had long lain as upon a

rock on the hills, looking at her, had come
suddenly in the twilight, when all was well,
and took her heart in fierce swift hands, and
wrung it, and it was as tide-wrack left by the
ebb on dry sand. She was old, and her beauty
was gone away from her like a rainbow lifted
from a wilderness, long before the last of her
partings came to her in Sleat of Skye.

She too had been known for her songs.
They were pastoral and sweet, or of the sea
and wild and lamenting. One, telling of the
small, shaggy, long-horned kye coming with
a young herd-girl over the braes in mist and
crowding upon a loosened cliff, and so falling
into the surge of the tides a thousand feet below, is well known among the few who remember such things in the old tongue that is
being so swiftly forgotten: another, of the
sea-bulls, is a favourite *iorram* of the boatmen of the middle isles: and Eachan Mac-
Dougall, the blind poet of Skye, used to sing
to women in the twilight, over the kindly tea
or sup of milk and porridge, her seven strange
sad songs that are called "A Day in My
Heart." It was these only I recalled now.
They tell the lives of many women. There is
the dawn-song of wonder and joy, the morn-
ing-song of the proud heart, the noon-song of
the sleeping passions and sleeping thoughts,

the afternoon song of longing and blind anger and pain, the gloaming song of regret and tears and silence, the nightfall song of revolt and the heart aflame, and the midnight song that is not sung, but is smothered in ashes, or drowned in deep water, or burned in the fierceness of fire. In Eachan-Dall's poem, he says her beauty is the beauty of the morning star in June, when it is a white fire in a rose of flame. He says her grace is the grace of the larch in an April wind, of a reed in shaken waters, of a wave tost like a white flower in the blue hair of the sea, of a fawn moving through bracken in the green dusk of old trees. He says men will remember her beauty till they are old; and their sons shall remember it; and their son's sons. He says, " Surely in this fair woman's heart is great joy and pride, for she will be beautiful and glad all the days of her life." And I recall the last of her songs, " Flame on the Wind." I cannot give it aright in English, for its long mournful cadences, lifted on tides of passionate vain regret and old grief, need the language of the old world that has in it so much of the sound of wind in trees and the lamentation of wind and the sighing of waters. I thought of it as I looked at old Mary Macarthur, and of the ending of one verse:

The Gaelic Heart

O burning soul,
Can hills of ice assuage this burning fire?

And then I remembered one of her love-songs,
she who had known so much love, and had
thrown treasures down barren rocks into the
cold seas, and had made a flaming universe
and eternity out of the pale hour of a wintry
noon.

It is dark here, my Love, my Pulse, my Heart, my
    Flame:
Dark the night, dark with wind and cloud, the wind
    without aim
Baffled and blind, the cloud low, broken, dragging,
    lame,
And a stir in the darkness at the end of the room
    sighing my name, whispering my name!

Is that the sea calling, or the hounds of the sea, or
    the wind's hounds?

    *   *   *   *   *   *

Great is that dark noise under the black north wind
Out on the sea to-night: but still it is—still as the
    frosts that bind
The stark inland waters in green depths where ice-
    bergs grind—
In this noise of shaking storm in my heart and this
    blast sweeping my mind!

And now nothing of all this left, nothing but
a tired old woman, sad-eyed and furrowed,
poorly clad, a gatherer of driftwood. Hills of

ice had in truth assuaged this burning fire.
The noise of shaking storm had ebbed from
the troubled heart; no blast now swept the
mind, but only the chill airs of winter froze
dreams and all old sweet thoughts, perhaps
memories even. Poor old woman, how white
and old and withered she looked, so forlorn
in her poor frayed clothes, in the sleep of
weariness, among the yellowing bracken by
the granite rock. Was it all gone, I wondered: all the dream, the wonder, the flame?
Were they all gone, noons of passionate life,
twilights of peace and recaptured hopes, nights
uplifted in dreams or shaken with tears and
longings?

While I was dreaming and wondering, wondering and dreaming, Old Mary stirred, and
opened her eyes. At first sleep was heavy on
her, and I saw she was not yet rightly awake.

" Do not stir," I said, " and I will sit down
here beside you, *Mairi nic Ruaridh Donn.*"
At that, and the familiar name, she knew me,
and was glad to tears, and welcomed me over
and over, as though I had come in some impossible way out of the irrecoverable past.

" Yes, I had the tiredness indeed," she
added after a little, " but what of that? For
I had the good sleep, and a thousand things of
goodness more, for I had a dream of dreams.

Do I remember it? Yes, for sure, I have it as
clear as a cradle. I was lying here, just as I
will be now, with this faggot here too, when a
woman of beauty came up the path and took
the faggot and flung all the sticks an' ends
into the sea. 'What will you be doing,
lady?' I said, but not in anger, only in the
great wonder. ' 'Tis your sorrows I'm throwing away,' she said, with a voice as sweet as
to send the birds to the branches—*chuireadh
e na h'eòin 'an crannaibh.* 'It is glad of that
I am,' I said, 'for it is many of them I
have.' Then she said: 'You'll have peace,
Mary, and great joy, and your songs and
your beauty will never die.' So the tears
were at me at that, an' I cried: 'It is only an
aisling you are . . . a dream and a vision!'
'No,' she said, ' an' by the same token, Mary,
I'll tell you the song that you were singing
below your breath down there on the shore:

> " A Dhe na mara
> Cuir todhar 's an tarruinn
> Chon tachair an talaimh
> Chon bailcidh dhuinn biaidh." '

And sure, an' in truth, these were the very
words I was singing to myself down there on
the shore . . . 'O God of the Sea, fill the
sea-wave with store of the good weed, to feed

the soil that will give us food.' And at that
my heart sank with fear and rose with gladness, for who could this be but . . . an' sure
before I could put word to it, she said *I am
Brighid*. I went on the knees, and cried *gach
la' agus oidche thoir duinn do sheimh*—'each
day and night give us thy peace.' And I was
putting another word to it, for her, fair Foster-Mother of Christ, when she looked at me
and said: 'I am older than Brighid of the
Mantle, Mary, and it is you that should know
that. I put songs and music on the wind before ever the bells of the chapels were rung
in the West or heard in the East. I am
Brighid-nam-Bratta, but I am also Brighid-
Muirghin-na-tuinne, and Brighid-sluagh, Brig-
hid-nan-sitheach seang, Brighid-Binne-Bheul-
lhuchd-nan-trusganan-uaine, and I am older
than Aona and am as old as Luan. And in
Tir-na-h'oige my name is Suibhal-bheann; in
Tir-fo-thuinn it is Cù-gorm; and in Tir-na-
h'oise it is Sireadh-thall. And I have been a
breath in your heart. And the day has its
feet to it that will see me coming into the
hearts of men and women like a flame upon
dry grass, like a flame of wind in a great
wood. For the time of change is at hand,
Mairi nic Ruaridh Donn—though not for you,
old withered leaf on the dry branch, though

for you, too, when you come to us and see all things in the pools of life yonder.'

" And at that I closed my eyes, and said the line of the old poem that you will be knowing well, the Laoidh Fhraoch—*Bu bhinne na farch-chiuil do ghuth*—sweeter thy voice than the sweetest lute.

" And when I opened them she was not there, but I was an old woman on the brae above Port-na-Churaich, and when I looked again it was you I saw and no other." [1]

[1] St. Brighid (in Gaelic pronounced sometimes *Bride*, sometimes *Breed*), St. Bride of the Isles as she is lovingly called in the Hebrides, has no name so dear to the Gael as "Muime-Chriosd," Christ's Foster-Mother, a name bestowed on her by one of the most beautiful of Celtic legends. In the isles of Gaelic Scotland her most familiar name is *Brighid nam Bratta*—St. Briget or St. Bride of the Mantle —from her having wrapt the new-born Babe in her Mantle in Mary's hour of weakness. She did not come into the Gaelic heart with the Cross and Mary, but was there long before as Bride, Brighid or Brithid of the Dedannans, those not immortal but for long ages deathless folk who to the Gael were as the Olympians to the Greeks. That earlier Brighid was goddess of poetry and music, one of the three great divinities of love, goddess of women, the keeper of prophecies and dreams, the watcher of the greater destinies, the guardian of the future. I think she was no other than a Celtic Demeter—that Demeter-Desphœna born of the embrace of Poseidon,

I have thought often of old Mary Macarthur, and of her dream of holy St. Bride, and of that older Brighid of the West, Mother of Songs and Music—she who breathes in the reed, on the wind, in the hearts of women and in the minds of poets. For I too have my

who in turn is no other than Lîr, the Oceanus of the Gael: and instead of Demeter seeking and lamenting Persephone in the underworld, it is Demeter-Brighid seeking her brother (or, it may be, her son) Manan (Manannan), God of the Sea, son of Oceanus, Lir— and finding him at last in Iceland, etc.—as I write here a little further on. Persephone and Manan are symbols of the same Return of Life.

The other names are old Gaelic names: *Brighid-Muirghin-na-tuinne*, Brighid - Conception - of - the - Waves; *Brighid-Sluagh* (or Sloigh), Brighid of the Immortal Host; *Brighid-nan-Sitheachseang*, Bridget of the Slim Fairy Folk; *Brighid-Binne-Bheul-lhuchd-nan-trusganan-uaine*, Song-sweet (lit. melodious mouth'd) Brighid of the Tribe of the Green Mantles. She is also called Brighid of the Harp, Brighid of the Sorrowful, Brighid of Prophecy, Brighid of Pure Love, St. Bride of the Isles, Bride of Joy, and other names. *Aona* is an occasional and ancient form of *Di-Aoin*, Friday; and *Luan*, of *Diluain*, Monday.

Tir-na-h'Oige (commonly anglicised as Tirnanogue) is the Land of (Eternal) Youth; *Tir-fo-thuinn* is the Country of the Waves; and *Tir-na-h'oise* is the Country of Ancient Years. The fairy names *Siubhal-bheann*, *Cù-gorm*, and *Siread-thall* respectively mean Mountain-traveller, Grey Hound, and Seek-Beyond.

211

dream, my memory of one whom as a child
I called Star-Eyes, and whom, later, I called
" Banmorair-na-mara," the Lady of the Sea,
and whom at last I knew to be no other than
the woman that is in the heart of women. I
was not more than seven when one day, by
a well, near a sea-loch in Argyll, just as I
was stooping to drink, my glancing eyes lit on
a tall woman standing among a mist of wild-
hyacinths under three great sycamores. I
stood, looking, as a fawn looks, wide-eyed,
unafraid. She did not speak, but she smiled,
and because of the love and beauty in her eyes
I ran to her. She stooped and lifted blueness
out of the flowers as one might lift foam out
of a pool, and I thought she threw it over me.
When I was found, lying among the hyacinths,
dazed, and, as was thought, ill, I asked eagerly
after the lady in white and with hair " all
shiny-gold like buttercups," but when I found
I was laughed at, or at last, when I passionately persisted, was told I was sun-dazed and
had been dreaming, I said no more. But I
did not forget. And for many days, for
weeks indeed, I stole away to seek or be
found by my white love, though she had gone
away or did not come again. It was years
afterward that I heard a story of a woman of
the divine folk, who was called the Lady of

the Sea, and was a daughter of Lir, and went lamenting upon the earth because she had lost her brother Manan the Beautiful, but came upon him at last among the hills of Iceland and wooed him with songs and flowers and brought him back again, so that all the world of men rejoiced, and ships sailed the seas in safety and nets were filled with the fruit of the wave. And it was years after that before I knew the deeper wisdom, and wrote of the Shepherdess the words that I now say again —" I believe that we are close upon a great and deep spiritual change; I believe a new redemption is even now conceived of the Divine Spirit in the human heart, that is itself as a woman, broken in dreams and yet sustained in faith, patient, long-suffering, looking towards home. I believe that though the Reign of Peace may be yet a long way off, it is drawing near; and that Who shall save us anew shall come divinely as a Woman—but whether through mortal birth, or as an immortal breathing upon our souls, none can yet know. Sometimes I dream of the old prophecy that Christ shall come again upon Iona; and of that later prophecy which foretells, now as the Bride of Christ, now as the Daughter of God, now as the Divine Spirit embodied through mortal birth—the coming of a new

Presence and Power ; and dream that this may
be upon Iona, so that the little Gaelic island
may become as the little Syrian Bethlehem.
But more wise is it to dream, not of hallowed
ground, but of the hallowed gardens of the
soul, wherein She shall appear white and radiant. Or that, upon the hills, where we are
wandered, the Shepherdess shall call us
home."

Yes, I have thought often of Mary Macarthur, that solitary old woman, poor and
desolate, once so beautiful: yet loved by
Brighid, the genius of our people. Was it
not our sorrowful Gaelic world I saw, when
I came upon the poor old woman—that passing world of songs and beauty, of poets'
dreams and of broken hearts, that even now
in forlorn old age is loved again by Brighid
the White—Brighid the White, who even yet
may use the fading voice to lead the wild
trumpets of revelation?

We have in Ross and the Outer Isles a
singular legend, which has a beauty within
and without. A young crofter was unhappy
in love and not fortunate in the hard way of
the hill-life. When bad seasons come on the
back of the black wind, the croft-smoke turns

from blue to brown, as the saying is : and bad
seasons in succession had come to the Strath,
and every one of the scattered clansfolk there
had suffered, but none so much as Fergus
Dhu, who had lost sheep, and crops, and the
youth out of his heart.

One day he went idly across the boggy
moor under Cnoc Glas, mooning among the
loneroid and black heather where the white
tufts of canna were like blown foam of the
sea. A single tree grew on that waste, a
thorn that on a forgotten Beltane had been
withered into a Grey Woman, the Fairy Thorn
or The Singing Tree or Tree of Bad Music.
At many a winter *ceilidh* by the peat-glow
tales were passed of what had been seen or
heard there : but they were all at one in this,
that only the happy and fortunate were in
peril there, that only the unhappy and un-
fortunate might go that way, and, indifferent,
see the tall swift woman in grey, or hear the
thin music.

Likely that was why Fergus—Fergus Dhu
as he was called, because of his black hair,
and black eyes, and the dark hours into which
he so often fell—wandered that day along the
sodden bracken-covered sheep-ways. When
he came to the thorn he saw no grey woman,
perhaps because there was no room in his

dreaming mind for any but one woman who
now would never warm to him but be a kindly stranger always; and heard no thin air, gay
or wild, perhaps because the sad lift and fall
in his heart was a daylong sound that dulled
his ears.   But while he was staring idly into
the withered thorn he saw a short stem break
into little green leaves. He could not believe
what his eyes showed him, but when he saw
also pink and white blossoms run in and out
among the leaves and break into a fall of
snow, and felt the sudden sweetness in the
air about him, he believed. He went closer,
and his wonder grew when he saw that the
stem had seven holes in it. He put his hand
on the stem, and it came away. There was a
hole at each end, and the thorn-reed was like
any *feadan*. So he put it to his mouth, and
ran his familiar fingers up and down the
holes, for Fergus Dhu was the cunningest
player in the Strath. He played till the whole
thorn went into a wave of green. He played
till a snow of blossom came all over the green
of the sea. Although it was November, and
wet, and the hill-wind moaned searching the
corries, by the thorn it was like a May noon.
Fergus looked at the sky, and saw that it was
blue: at the long moor, and saw that it was
covered with April yellow and with a shim-

mer of the wings of little birds. He looked at
the grey hills to the east, and they were rose-
red and a star was above them: he looked at
the grey hills to the west, and they were blue
as peat-smoke and a rainbow leaned against
them. Then his heart filled with joy, and he
said to himself, "I have found my desire."
So he played his joy. As he played, the rainbow leaned away from the grey hills of the
west, and took their sadness, and was no
more: the star sank behind the grey mountains of the east: the long moor faded into
the old silence: the white foam and the green
wave ebbed from the thorn.

Fergus looked at the thorn-pipe, and it was
only a black cloud-wet *feadan* with seven
mossy holes in it.

He "went away" in that hour. No one
saw him that night, or the next day, or the
next: and months and years passed, and no
one saw him, and his body was never seen,
though his bonnet was found near the withered thorn.

In the seventh year after that a strange
thing happened. A new life quickened the
thorn. A thousand small green buds shook
out little fluttering green leaves, and, from
these, white moths of blossom continually
rose. Linnets sang on the branches.

One day Fergus Dhu came strolling that way. He had no memory of the years that had gone, or with whom he had been, and the sweet fatal accent was out of his ears. But when he saw the thorn he remembered his *feadan*, and took it from his coat-fold, and played because of his gladness. The tears fell from his eyes when he saw the grey rain come down and blot out the new life from the thorn, so that it was old and withered again: and at the wet hill-wind calling again its old mournful cry, wheeling like a tired hawk above the far lamentation of the sheep. "Why is this?" he said. "When I saw this lonely place in its sorrow I played it into joy. And now when I come upon it in its beauty, I have played it back into the old sorrow. Grief to my heart, that it is so."

One man of the Strath saw Fergus Dhu that day, and he spoke of Fergus as a thin worn leaf that one sees through when it hangs in the wind. Certainly no other saw him, nor has seen him since.

This tale of Fergus, who was fēy, and went down the west with strangers, is it not also a symbol, even as Mary Macarthur, old and poor but treasured and loved and cared for by the Genius of our race . . . is it not also a

symbol of the Gaelic heart, of the Gaelic
muse let me say? For the Gaelic muse seems
to me the beautiful and sad and waywardly
joyous spirit of whom poor Fergus was but
the troubled image. Does she, too, not go to
and fro in a land where rainbows bloom and
fade above desolate places and where a star
hangs above the holy hills of the east, seeking her desire: going in sorrow, but, suddenly
beholding the world radiant, breaking into
songs of joy and laughter: coming again,
after an evil time, and finding the grey thorn
of the world full of the green leaf, blossom,
and undying youth, and, so finding, turning
suddenly to tears, and to the old sorrow, and
to the longing whose thirst is not to be
quenched, to the cry of the curlew for the
waste, of the heart going a long way from
shadow to shadow?

One must with this lanthorn of the spirit
look into the dark troubled water of the
Gaelic heart, too, I think, if one would understand. How else can one understand the
joy that is so near to sorrow, the sorrow that
like a wave of the sea can break in a moment
into light and beauty? I have heard often in
effect, " This is no deep heart that in one
hour weeps and in the next laughs." But I
know a deeper heart that in one hour weeps

and in the next laughs, so deep that light dies away within it, and silence and the beginning and the end are one: the heart of the sea. And there is another heart that is deep, and weeps one hour and in the next laughs: the heart of Night . . . where Oblivion smiles, and it is day; sighs, and the darkness is come. And there is another heart that is deep, and weeps in one hour and in the next laughs: the soul of man: where tears and laughter are the fans that blow the rose-white flame of life. And I am well content that the Gaelic heart, that in one hour weeps and in the next laughs, though it be so sad and worn among smiling nations, is in accord with the great spirits of the world and with immortal things.

ANIMA CELTICA

". . . *le rêve de la vie vue en beauté* . . ."—RENAN.

"*To see things in their beauty is to see them in their truth.*"

MATTHEW ARNOLD.

Anima Celtica

THE GAEL AND HIS HERITAGE [1]

"He who moves about happy in dreams, he is the Self, this is the immortal, the fearless."—*Khanda x. of the 8th Prapâthka of the Khandogya-Upanishads.*

The last tragedy for broken nations is not the loss of power and distinction, nor even the loss of that independence which is so vital to the commonweal. It is not, perhaps, even the loss of country, though there is no harder thing than to see the smoke of the stranger, or to hear upon the wind the forlorn business of the going of those who are dispossessed and the coming of those new in possession. The last tragedy, and the saddest, is when the treasured language dies slowly out, when winter falls upon the leg-

[1] Reprinted from *The Nineteenth Century*, Nov., 1900, where it appeared as an article upon *"Carmina Gadelica;* Hymns and incantations, etc. In 2 vols. large 4to. Orally collected in the Highlands and islands of Scotland, and translated into English by Alexander Carmichael."

223

endary remembrance of a people. Sometimes
a bitter destiny descends suddenly upon a
nation, as when Russia all but strangles Fin-
land, permitting that broken people, when
it gasps for life, to live, but on condition that
it relinquishes freedom, language, tradition,
hope, pride, and honour. The wrong is not
the blind wrong of a barbaric people too savage to know the sacredness of pledge and
solemn oath, but is the open wrong of a
cynical Government, scorning the most sacred pledge and the most solemn oath. Then
again the destiny that comes upon a crushed
nation may be only retributive and regenera-
tive, as with Spain. Such nations are bent,
not broken: they have no tragic sunset. They
have not lost the irrecoverable, and they have
hope. Another destiny there is, that which
awaits a people which has never been a sov-
ereign power, but has had national greatness;
which has never striven to extend its dominion, but has seen its own frontiers, liberties,
possibilities, and at last even its language and
cherished national inheritance of legend and
gathered incalculable beauty shrink from age
to age, from generation to generation, from
decade to decade, from year to year. Such a
people is the Gaelic people. When I speak
of the Gaelic people of Ireland and Scot-

land, I speak, alas! only of the small Gaelic
remnant in the Scottish Highlands and in the
Isles, and of the remnant in Ireland. This
people is unable or unwilling to accept the
bitter solace of absorption in the language,
the written thought, the active, omnipresent,
and variegated energy of the dominant race.
It has to keep silence more and more, and
soon it too will be silent.

It is a strange thing: that a nation can hold
within itself an ancient race, standing for the
lost, beautiful, mysterious ancient world, can
see it fading through its dim twilight, without
heed to preserve that which might yet be
preserved, without interest even in that which
once gone cannot come again. The old
Gaelic race is in its twilight indeed; but now,
alas! it is the hastening twilight after the
feast of Samhain, when winter is come at last,
out of the hills, down the glens, on the four
winds of the world.

There are some, however, who do care.
There are some whose hearts ache to see the
last pathetic stand of a retreating people, and
who would gladly do what yet may be done
to preserve awhile the beautiful old-world
language and the still more beautiful and
significant thought and legend and subtle
genius enshrined in that language; who are

truly loth to let die and become legendary
and literary that which had once so glorious
a noon, and has now a sunset beauty, is even
yet a living aspect, is still the coloured
thought of life and not of the curious imagination only.

Those who think thus and desire thus must
ever be grateful to Mr. Alexander Carmichael, who, after so many years of prepara-
tion through a long life of loving and sympathetic heed for the beautiful things of the
past as seen and heard in the Hebrides, but
now, alas! hardly to be seen and rarely to be
heard, has given us the invaluable record of
his life-work. It is not too much to say that
Mr. Carmichael is the last great chronicler of
the Gael. Even before the late John Campbell of Islay died, having won a European
reputation for his collection and translation
of Gaelic folklore, he feared that the day was
over when much more was to be gleaned.
He knew that when Mr. Carmichael left the
Hebrides, and went to Edinburgh to prepare
the life-work of forty years, he would have
no like successor. This not because there
are no willing workers now (one of the foremost of these, John Gregorson Campbell of
the island of Tiree, is our latest loss); but
because it is too late. Even in the Gaelic-

speaking Irish west, from Donegal to Clare, the native collector finds more and more difficulty; for the old are proud, and the middle-aged have forgotten or are silent, and the young do not know and do not care. Dr. Douglas Hyde, the late William Larminie, and others have done what they could, but the gleaners now have a small aftermath for their gain, because of the narrowing pastures of a once vast and fruitful national heritage. Most of the folk-lore and folk-tales now got in Gaelic Scotland and Ireland are at third-hand, got by the person who tells them from some other, who had them from this man or that woman, but in English, and too often with a perplexing dual light on them as of noon and moonlight, and even at the best without the determining savour and unalloyed colour and unique accent of the Gaelic original.

By a singular irony the students of Gaelic literature and Gaelic language are increasing: of ancient Gaelic, indeed, there are many scholars to whom we owe much and shall owe more—Dr. Whiteley Stokes, Dr. Keneo Meyer and Dr. George Henderson among them, in Ireland Dr. Douglas Hyde, Mr. T. W. Rolleston, and others. Soon there will be only a few old peasants and a few learned

men (mostly Germans) who will be able to
speak in the old language.

Now that Mr. Carmichael has given us so
much of his life-work (let us trust not all,
and that he has yet much accumulated lore
to give us from remembrance and translation), and that advanced years will prevent
him from again relinquishing time and means
in his enthusiastic quest, there are few who
can take up his work. What is sadder is that
there are fewer and fewer among the islanders and the Highlanders of the remoter dis-
tricts of the mainland who can or will repeat
the desired old wisdom, beauty, and strangeness of ancient faiths and customs. The
Gaelic-speaking islesman or Highlander has
an all but unconquerable reticence now, and
will seldom speak of the hidden things that
were once common and beautiful with the
commonness and beauty of sunlight and
wind. Many causes have led to this. When
a people is forced by circumstances to speak
two tongues the native speech naturally remains that of the inward life, the inward remembrance, the spirit. The English-speaking
Gael is apt to be silent and morose in English if he does not know it well or is not at
ease in its use, and naturally is not found
communicative by those who would hear him

speak of the things they wish to hear. He is proud and sensitive too, and does not appreciate the superior smile and the ill-bred laugh with which his interrogator so frequently punctuates his curiosity. When things sacred to his forefathers, and to him too for that very association as for others, are broached—as when one would ask about the potato blight or the herring failure—it is surely only natural that he should be irresponsive, or, if he answer, be evasive, or take refuge in a seeming boorish dulness. But how much greater a gulf exists between these Scottish or English foreigners and those Gaels who practically have no language but their own, so little English have they, and in that isolation are so remote from the confusedly coloured verbiage of modern speech, and our modern ways of thought, and, above all, our modern ways of life. It is a gulf that few can realise, except those few who perforce live much with both peoples, and speak readily the speech of both, and understand what is in each that here repels and there attracts the other. I have known many instances of Gaelic crofters and fishermen who have not only refused to be drawn into confidence but have wilfully misled their interrogators. I remember on one occasion crossing the

Sound of Eriskay, between the island of that
name and South Uist: when two men were in
the ferry, and with them was a man whom
they had hired to go with them on their
fishing excursion in Uist and Benbecula.
They asked many questions of the boatmen,
and learned little, the men for one thing
having their work to see to, and their daily
needs to bear in mind, and not caring for the
idle curiosity of strangers. The latter seemed
aggrieved, and spoke heedlessly concerning
the stupidity of " these Highlanders," and
how ignorant they were. A week or two
later I met the man who had gone with them
to fish. " Well, Pòl M'Phail," I said, " and
how did you get on with your English
friends? Did you tell them what they wanted
to know about what we do, and what we
think on this and that? " " At first I told
them nothing," he said, " and then when
they bothered me every hour I told them a
little that was nothing at all, and they were
pleased; and at last when they wanted more,
and spoke of things I did not wish to speak
about, I told them a fathom o' nonsense,
and the older man he put a net into my
words and took out what he fancied, and
told his friend to write them down as he
said them over. I laughed at that for sure,

for it was all foam and forgetfulness. And
on the last night, when he brought out a
book with nothing but white paper in it, and
said he wanted to take down some things
from me, and for me to put my name and
place at the end of it, I said then I could not,
for being only a Barra man I had no more
English, having used all I knew in telling the
fine tales I had told. And at that he seemed
surprised, and I don't know yet if he has
thought it out, and sees that a man can tell
tales only with the words he has, and that
when these are used up he can tell no more
tales."

I recall this little anecdote as significant.
One other, equally significant, will suffice as
commentary on what I have said. I was
staying with friends who had taken a farmer's
house in Glen Usinish, under the shoulder
of mighty Hecla, in South Uist, and heard
from a crofter of a foreign gentleman who
had the Gaelic like the *sruthmara* (the flowing tide), though it was not the Gaelic of the
isles ; and this gentleman was asking, asking
everywhere, and writing down whenever he
could get what he wanted. " No," added the
crofter, " it was not old tales or old songs
he wanted, like good Father Allan of Eriskay,
but if we did this or if we did that, and the

why of it, and who did it now, and did we
believe in it, and could we give names? So
we just all had a heavy silence like mist on
us. For we knew that though he had the
Gaelic tongue he had not the Gaelic heart.
For sure it was not for love and kinship, but
just to find out and to speak scornfully to
others about our ways, that he asked. So
he got little, and what little he got would not
be a good catch for any one but an *âmitan*
(a fool)." The next day one of our company
was fishing on Loch Druidibeg, and there
met the folklore hunter, who was fishing there
also, and learned from him that he had got
much unexpected information, though confusedly told, and that he found the people
strange and quite unlike what he had read
about them, with nothing of that peculiar
imagination and Celtic beauty of speech and
thought of which he had heard so much and
found in books both old and new, and that,
far from being a spiritual and poetic race, he
found the highlander and still more the islander dull and prosaic, and with interests
wholly commonplace and selfish. In the following winter I heard from a friend that this
gentleman had lectured on " The Gael as he
is to-day " (I give, not the title, but the sub-
ject of his lecture), and though I had merely

the vaguest report of it, I can well believe, as my correspondent said, that the lecturer betrayed not only a radical ignorance of the actual manners, customs, and thought, the outward and inward life of the Gael of to-day, but constantly misapprehended and misinterpreted what little he had been able to gather. We have an old saying that it takes three years to get into a man's mind, and twice three years to get to what is secret in a man's mind, and thrice three years to get a man to speak of the secret things that are in his mind.

This, then, is one of the obvious reasons why it is so difficult for those of foreign speech and manners and ways of thought and life to reach into the true life of the Gael, by whom, of course, I mean not the Anglicised or Scoticised persons of Highland parentage who live in Glasgow or in Edinburgh, for example, but the remoter Gael who speaks his ancient tongue, and to a great extent lives the life lived by his ancestors for many generations.

Of the relatively small number capable of this sympathetic understanding and this adequate interpretation only for a very few it is possible to do anything even approximating the great service done by Mr. Alexander

Carmichael. Dr. George Henderson, for instance, a Gaelic-speaking Gael and one of the most learned Celtic students living, is fitted for the congenial work; but his labours in Oxford and elsewhere render a task of the kind practically impossible. Even the greatest enthusiast, and a clansman, cannot get into the life of the people in the sense of intimate comradeship in a few holiday weeks; and, as all of us who are of the north know, there are interclan or local suspicions and jealousies which, superficial and removable as they commonly are, yet perforce have to be considered. Indeed, I know of only one man who can do for us anything equivalent to the great task which Mr. Alexander Carmichael has now triumphantly brought to the long-desired end. I allude to Father Allan Macdonald, of Eriskay in South Uist, a priest who is not only beloved of his people, and truly a father to them, but is an enthusiast in Gaelic lore and literature, who in his many years' ministration has collected what, if ever translated, will be almost as invaluable a treasure-trove as these "Ortha nan Gaidheal," the *Carmina Gadelica* of Mr. Carmichael.

Incidentally may I be excused the personality and say with what eagerness those of us

234

who love and cherish the beautiful oral literature and legendary lore and folk-songs of
the Gael wish that there were more priests
and ministers like Father Allan Macdonald,
and the late Gregorson Campbell of Tiree?
I do not think any one who has not lived
intimately in the Highlands can realise the
extent to which the blight of Calvinism has
fallen upon the people, clouding the spirit,
stultifying the mind, taking away all joyousness and light-hearted gaiety, laying a ban
upon music even, upon songs, making
laughter as rare as a clansman landlord, caus-
ing a sad gloom as common as a ruined croft.
And even where matters are no longer so
bitter as they were a generation ago, even
where to-day a certain half-hearted turning
towards a truer conception of human life is
evident, it is too late—too late for the
recovery of that which is gone away upon
the wind.

But as this is a matter on which (when I
have written to a like effect) I have been held
unjustifiably prejudiced either from the Gaelic
or sectarian standpoint or both, I will give
without comment an episode incidentally
cited by Mr. Carmichael in his Introduction,
and give it with the more propriety as it will
reveal to many readers the splendid native

material which has been so piteously per-
verted.

During my quest I went into a house near Ness.
The house was clean and comfortable, if plain and
unpretending, most things in it being home-made.
There were three girls in the house, young, comely,
and shy, and four women, middle-aged, handsome,
and picturesque in their homespun gowns and high-
crowned mutches. Three of the women had been
to the moorland pastures with their cattle, and had
turned in here to rest on their way home.

"Hail to the house and the household," said I,
greeting the inmates in the salutation of our fathers.
"Hail to you, kindly stranger," replied the housewife. "Come forward and take this seat. If it be
not ill-mannered may we ask whence you have come
this day? You are tired and travel-stained, and
probably hungry?" "I have come from Gress," I
said, "round by Tolasta to the south and Tolasta
to the north, taking a look at the ruins of the Church
of St. Aula at Gress, and at the ruins of the fort of
Dunothail, and then across the moorland." "May
the Possessor keep you in His own keeping, good
man. You left early and have travelled far, and
must be hungry."

With this the woman raised her eyes towards her
daughters, standing demurely silent and motionless
as Greek statues in the background. In a moment
the three fair girls became active and animated.
One ran to the stack and brought in an armful of
hard, black peats; another ran to the well and
brought in a pail of clear spring water, while a third
quickly spread a cloth, white as snow, upon the table

in the inner room. The three neighbours rose to leave, and I rose to do the same. "Where are you going, good man?" asked the housewife in injured surprise, moving between me and the door. "You must not go till you eat a bit and drink a sip. That indeed would be a reproach to us that we would not soon get over. These slips of lassies and I would not hear the end of it from the men at the sea, were we to allow a wayfarer to go from our door hungry, thirsty, and weary. No! no! you must not go till you eat a bite. Food will be ready presently, and in the meantime you will bathe your feet and dry your stockings, which are wet after coming through the marshes of the moorland."

Then the woman went down upon her knees, and washed and dried the feet of the stranger as gently and tenderly as a mother would those of her child. "We have no stockings to suit the kilt," said the woman, in a tone of evident regret, "but here's a pair of stockings of the houseman's which he has never had on, and perhaps you would put them on till your own are dry."

One of the girls had already washed out my stockings, and they were presently drying before the bright fire on the middle of the floor. I deprecated all this trouble, but to no purpose. In an incredibly short time I was asked to go "ben" and break bread.

Through the pressure of the housewife and of myself the other three women had resumed their seats, uneasily, it is true; but immediately before food was announced the three women rose together and quietly walked away, no urging detaining them.

The table was laden with wholesome food sufficient for several persons. There were fried herrings and boiled turbot fresh from the sea, and eggs fresh from the yard. There were fresh butter and salt butter, wheaten scones, barley bannocks, and oat cakes, with excellent tea and cream The woman apologised that she had no "aran coinnich" (moss bread—that is, loaf bread) and no biscuits, they being simple crofter people far away from the big town [Stornoway].

"This," said I, taking my seat, "looks like the table for a 'reiteach' (betrothal) rather than for one man. Have you betrothals in Lews?" I asked, turning my eyes towards the other room where we had left the three comely maidens. "Oh, indeed, yes, the Lews people are very good at marrying. Foolish young creatures, they often marry before they know their responsibilities or realise their difficulties," and her eyes followed mine in the direction of her own young daughters. "I suppose there is much fun and rejoicing at your marriages—music, dancing, singing, and merry-makings of many kinds?" "Oh, indeed, no; our weddings are now quiet and becoming, not the foolish things they were in my young days. In my memory weddings were great events, with singing and piping, dancing and amusements all night through, and generally for two or three nights in succession. Indeed, the feast of the "bord breid" (kertch table) was almost as great as the feast of the marriage table, all the young men and maidens struggling to get it. On the morning after the marriage the mother of the bride, and, failing her, the mother of the bridegroom, placed the "breid tri chearnach" (three-cornered kertch) on the head of the bride before she rose from her bed. And the mother did this ("an ainm na Tri Beannaichte" (in the name of the Sacred Three), under whose guidance the young wife was to walk. Then the bride arose and the maidens dressed her, and the bards sang songs to her, and recited "rannagail mhora" (great rigmaroles), and there was much rejoicing and merry-making all day long and all night through. "Gu dearbh mar a b'e fleagh na bord breid a b'fhearr, cha'ne hearr bu mheasa" (indeed, if the feast of the kertch table was not better it was not a whit worse).

"There were many sad things done then, for those were the days of foolish doings and foolish people. Perhaps, on the day of the Lord, when they came out of church—indeed, if they went into church—the young men would go to throw the stone, or to toss the caber, or to play shinty, or to run races, or to race horses on the strand, the young maidens looking on the while, ay, and the old men and women." "And have you no music, no singing, no dancing now at your marriages?" "May the Possessor keep you! I see that you are a stranger to Lews, or you would not ask such a question," the woman exclaimed, with grief and surprise in her tone. "It is long since we abandoned those foolish ways in Ness, and, indeed, throughout Lews. In my young days there was hardly a house in Ness in which there was not one or two or three who could play the pipe or the fiddle or the trump. And I have heard it said there were men, and women too, who could play things they called harps, and lyres, and bellow-pipes, but I do not know what those things were." "And why were those discontinued?" "A blessed change came over the place and the people," the woman replied in earnestness, "and the good men and the good ministers who arose did away with the songs and the stories, the dancing and the

239

music, the sports and the games, that were pervert-
ing the minds and ruining the souls of the people,
leading them to folly and stumbling." "But how
did the people themselves come to discard their
sports and pastimes?" "Oh, the good ministers
and the good elders preached against them, and
went among the people, and besought them to forsake their follies and return to wisdom. They made
the people break their pipes and fiddles. If there
were foolish men here and there who demurred the
good minister and the good elders themselves broke
and burnt their instruments, saying:

" 'Is fearr an teine beag a gharas la beag na sithe
Na'n teine mor a loisgeas la mor na feirge'

(Better is the small fire that warms on the little day
    of peace
Than the big fire that burns on the great day of
    wrath.)

The people have forsaken their follies and their
Sabbath-breaking, and there is no pipe, no fiddle
here now," said the woman, in evident satisfaction.
"And what have you now instead of the racing,
the stone-throwing, and the caber-tossing, the song,
the pipe, and the dance?" "Oh, we have now the
blessed Bible preached and explained to us faith-
fully and earnestly, if we sinful people would only
walk in the right path and use our opportuni-
ties."

    "But what have you at your weddings? How do
you pass the time?"

    "Oh, the carles are on one side of the house, talk-
ing of their crops and their nowt, and mayhap of the

days when they were young and when things were different; and the young men are on the other side of the house, talking about boats, and sailing, and militia, and naval reserve, perhaps of their own strength, and of many foolish matters besides."

"And the girls, what are they doing?" "Oh, they, silly things, are in the 'culaist' (back-house), perhaps trying to croon over some foolish song under their breath, perhaps trying to amble through some awkward steps of dancing on the points of their toes; or, shame to tell, perhaps speaking of what dress this or that girl had on at this or that marriage, or, worse still, what hat this girl or that had on the Day of the Lord, perhaps even on the day of the Holy Communion, showing that their minds were on the vain things of the world instead of on the wise things of salvation."

"But why are the girls in the 'culaist'? What do they fear?" "May the Good Being keep you, good man. They are in the 'culaist' for concealment, and the fear of their life and of their death upon them that they may be heard or seen should the good elder happen to be passing the way." "And should he what then?" "Oh, the elder will tell the minister, and the good minister will scold them from the pulpit, mentioning the girls by name. But the girls have a blanket on the door and another blanket on the window to deafen the sounds and to obscure the light."

"Do the young maidens allow the young men to join them in the 'culaist'?" "Indeed, truth to tell, the maidens would be glad enough to admit the young men were it not the fear of exposure. But the young men are so loud of voice and heavy of foot, and make so much noise, that they would betray the retreat of the girls, who would get rebuked, while the young men would escape. The girls would then be ashamed and cast down, and would not lift a head for a year and a day after their well-deserved scolding. They suffer most, for, sad to say, the young men are becoming less afraid of being admonished than they used to be."

"And do the people have spirits at their marriages?" "Oh yes; the minister is not so hard upon them at all. He does not interfere with them in that way unless they take too much and talk loudly and quarrel. Then he is grieved and angry, and scolds them severely. Occasionally, indeed, the carles have a nice 'frogan' (liveliness) upon them, and are very happy together. But, oh, they never quarrel nor fight, nor get angry with one another. They are always nice to one another and civil to all around them."

"Perhaps were the minister to allow the people less drink and more music and dancing and merry-making they would enjoy it as much. I am sure the young girls would sing better, and dance better, with the help of the young men. And the young men themselves would be less loud of voice and less heavy of heel among the maidens. Perhaps the happiness of the old people too would be none the less real nor less lasting at seeing the joyousness of the young people."

To this the woman promptly and loyally replied: "The man of the Lord is untiring in work and unfailing in example for our good, and in guiding us to our heavenly home, constantly reminding us of the littleness of time and the greatness of eternity, and he knows best, and we must do our best to follow his counsel and to imitate his example."

Mr. Carmichael speaks also of a famous
violin-player, who died a few years ago in the
island of Eigg, a good man celebrated for his
knowledge of old-world airs and for his old-
style playing. One day at divine service a
preacher denounced him, saying, " Tha thu
shios an sin cul na comhla," etc. (in effect,
" You that are down there behind the door,
miserable grey-haired man with that old fiddle beside you, that you play with a cold hand
without and the devil's fire in your heart ").
After that public admonition the old man's
family pressed him to play no more of his
sinful airs and old songs and to burn his
fiddle. In vain this last minstrel pleaded that
his violin was a valuable one, as indeed it
was, and famed for its tone and as the handi-
work of a pupil of Stradivarius. At last he
was forced to part with it to a passing pedlar
for a few shillings. " It was not the wretched
thing that was got for it," he exclaimed afterwards, " that grieved my heart so sorely, but
the parting with it! the parting with it! . . .
and I to that gave the best cow in my father's
fold for it when I was young." The voice of
the old man faltered, and tears ran down his
face. He was never again seen to smile.

One other instance and I have done. A
lady, still youthful, related to Mr. Carmichael

what follows: "When we came to Islay I was sent to the parish school to obtain a proper grounding in arithmetic. I was charmed with the schoolgirls and their Gaelic songs. But the schoolmaster (a Lowlander) denounced Gaelic speech and Gaelic songs. On getting out of school one evening the girls resumed a song they had been singing the previous evening. The schoolmaster heard us, however, and called us back. He punished us till the blood trickled from our fingers, although we were big girls with the dawn of womanhood upon us. The thought of that scene thrills me with indignation."

I think the thought of that scene, and of a crowd of incidents of a kindred nature, must fill with bitter resentment and indignation every man and woman who has a drop of Gaelic blood in his or or her veins, all men and women who have any ancestral pride, any love for the things of beauty and honour that their fathers and mothers loved and their forebears for generations loved.

For forty years Mr. Carmichael collected a vast mass of oral lore, written down from the recital of men and women throughout the Highlands and Islands, from Arran to Caithness, from Perth to St. Kilda, but the greater

part in the outer Hebrides. The present collection, long announced as *Òr agus Òb* (Gold
and Dross), and now more adequately and
fitly called *Carmina Gadelica*, is a selection
from this mass. *Ortha nan Gaidheal*, runs
the Gaelic title; and the setting forth, " Ur-
nan agus Ubagan, le solus air facla gnatha
agus cleachdana a chaidh air chul crussaichte
bho bhialachas feadh Gaidhealtachd na H-
Alba: agus tionndaichte bho Ghaidhlig gu
Beurla, le Alastair Macgillemhicheil," which,
being interpreted, means in effect ·that this
collection of ancient hymns and incantations, and records of old rites and old customs, has been gathered in the Highlands
and Islands of Scotland (the Gaeldom of
Alba . . . *Gaidhealtachd na H-Alba*) and translated from Gaelic into English by Alexander
Carmichael. Of the people who to this day,
at the winter *ceilidh* or in the boats on summer nights, still repeat the legendary tales
Mr. Carmichael gives several interesting
sketches. In every crofting townland there
are several story-tellers who recite the oral
lore of their predecessors. These story-tellers
of the Highlands, says Mr. Carmichael, " are
as varied in their subjects as are literary men
and women elsewhere: one is a historian,
narrating events simply and concisely; an-

other is a historian with a bias, colouring his narrative according to his leanings. One is an inventor, building fiction upon fact, mingling his materials, and investing the whole with the charm of novelty and the halo of romance. Another is a reciter of heroic poems and ballads, bringing the different characters before the mind as clearly as the sculptor brings the figure before the eye. One gives the songs of the chief poets, with interesting accounts of their authors, while another, generally a woman, sings, to weird airs, beautiful old songs, some of them Arthurian. There are various other narrators, singers, and speakers, but I have never heard aught that should not be said nor sung."

There is no people in the world so well bred in this beautiful reticence as the Gaelic peasant. He has an innate refinement which makes him unique among the races of the north. It is this people which is now but a remnant, and soon will be a memory.

And what stores of old wisdom and legend and song they had as their common heritage, that a few (alas a small and ever diminishing few!) still have. Here are two types in instance, Hector Macisaac and his wife. This old couple lived alone (their daughter having gone into service to help her parents) in a turf-walled hut thatched with reeds; and their life, like that of so many of the crofters, was one of utmost penury and often of actual privation. Mr. Carmichael knew both well: from the woman he heard many secular runes, sacred hymns, and fairy songs; from the husband numerous heroic tales, poems, and ballads. Indeed so many were the stories and poems which the old islander recited at different times that Mr. Carmichael says they would fill several volumes; and many books, he adds, could have been filled with the stories and poems recited by two others alone, out of the many score of like-gifted islanders he knew—an old blind cottar, Hector Macleod of Lianacuithe, in South Uist, and another old cottar, Roderick Macneill of Miunghlaidh, in Barra. Yet neither of them told more than a small part of what he knew. None of the three men knew any letters, nor any language but Gaelic, nor had ever been out of his native island. All expressed regret in well-chosen words that they had not a better place in which to receive their visitors (Mr. Carmichael and Campbell of Islay), and all thanked them in polite terms for coming to see them and for taking an interest in their decried and derided old lore. All were in all things courteous.

247

Some idea of the way in which the continuity of oral lore is maintained is given by Mr. Carmichael in an account such as that of his friend Kenneth Morrison, an old, blind, and poor man of Trithion, in Skye. He knew many stories and poems, but mentioned the names of many old men in the extensive but now desolate parish of Minnhnis who had been famous story-tellers in his boyhood— men who had been born in the first decade of the century. Several of these, he said, could recite stories and poems during many nights in succession, some of the tales requiring several nights to relate. Kenneth repeated fragments of many of these, identical with poems and stories or with parts of poems and stories published by Macpherson, Smith, the Stewarts, the MacCallums, the Campbells, and others.

Of the treasure of old songs, hymns, and folk-lore of incalculable interest brought together in these two beautiful volumes, the greater number have been rescued from oblivion in the islands and among the Roman Catholic population. Broadly speaking, the northern Hebrides are Protestant, the southern Catholic. At the same time, it should be added, many of these treasure-trove have been equally common on the mainland, and a

248

large proportion among Protestants also. Nor was the collector content with a single version only. From one to ten have been taken down, differing more or less; and it must often have been no easy matter to select. In some instances Mr. Carmichael has given variants. Even this selection, however, could not be used as it stood, and the collector adds that several poems and many notes are wholly withheld, while a few of the poems and all the notes have been abbreviated.

The collection comprises *Achaine* (Invocations, Blessings, and Prayers); *Aimsire* (Hymns of the Seasons); *Oibre* (Songs and Hymns of Labour); and, in the second volume, *Uibe* (Incantations, Charms, Spells) and *Measgain* (Miscellaneous).

Every one of these *Achaine*, *Aimsire*, and *Oibre* has a singular beauty of thought and generally of expression also, and often that beauty is made more excellent for us by the note that goes with the *rann, achanaidh,* or *urnuigh* (rune, invocation, or blessing). Take, for example, the "Rann Romh Urnuigh," or Rune before Prayer. "Old people in the isles sing this or some other short hymn before prayer. Sometimes the hymn and the prayer are intoned in low, tremulous, unmeasured cadences, like the moving and moaning, the soughing and the sighing of the ever murmuring sea on their own wild shores. They generally retire, perhaps to an outhouse, to the lee of a knoll, or to the shelter of a dell, that they may not be seen or heard of men. I have known men and women of eighty, ninety, and a hundred years of age continue the practice of their lives in going from one to two miles to the seashore to join their voices in the voicing of the waves and their praises with the praises of the ceaseless sea."

This " Rune before Prayer " is as follows in English:

I am bending my knee
In the eye of the Father who created me,
In the eye of the Son who purchased me,
In the eye of the Spirit who cleansed me,
    In friendship and affection.
Through Thine own Anointed One, O God,
Bestow upon us fulness in our need,
    Love towards God,
    The affection of God,
    The smile of God,
    The wisdom of God,
    The grace of God,
    The fear of God,
    And the will of God,
To do on the world of the Three
As angels and saints
Do in heaven.

Each shade and light,
Each day and night,
Each time in kindness,
Give Thou us Thy Spirit.

Can we imagine an English peasant or a peasant of any other country repeating nightly, alone and solemnly, this poem or one of the hundreds like it; or an aged English or any other peasant going habitually from one to two miles to the seashore "to join his voice with the voicings of the waves and his praises with the praises of the ceaseless sea"?

The very names of many of these rescued songs and hymns are beautiful. Some of the songs are very ancient, with their meanings obscure or lost now, as *Duan na Mathairn.*

Thou King of the moon,
Thou King of the sun,
Thou King of the planets,
Thou King of the stars,
Thou King of the globe,
Thou King of the sky,
Oh! lively thy countenance,
Thou beauteous Beam.

Two loops of silk
Down by thy limbs,
Smooth-skinned;
Yellow jewels,
And a handful
Out of every stock of them.

251

Very likely this is but a fragment, remembered perhaps with some dim recollection of when and how it should be said, and to what end. "The Guiding Light of Eternity," "The Light'ner of the Stars," "The Soul Plaint," the several Sleep Prayers and Resting Blessings and Consecrations, of Peace and "The Soul Peace," are among the most beautiful names. Sometimes, in a relatively modern poem some old-world wisdom will suddenly appear, as in this quatrain in a singular "Ora Boisilidh," or Bathing Prayer:

> A chuid nach fas 's a chumhanaich,
>   Gum fas 's an dubha-thrath;
> A chuid nach fas 's an oidhche dhiot.
>   Air dhruim a mheadhon la.

(The part of thee that does not grow at dawn, may it grow at eventide; the part of thee that does not grow at night, may it grow at ridge of middle-day.)

Sometimes too a peculiarly Celtic symbolism occurs even in the most unlikely place, as in an "Invocation for Justice" for an intending litigant, where the wronged man says he will go forth in the likeness of a deer, in likeness of a horse, in likeness of a serpent, and at last as a king, meaning that he will be wary, strong, wise, and dignified.

252

The Gael and His Heritage

A beautiful and touching poem called *Eosai Bu Choir a Mholadh* (Jesu, who ought to be praised) is made the more wonderful for us by the knowledge that it was composed by a poor illiterate woman of Harris, and a leper. She had to leave the upland community and dwell alone on a desolate tract of seashore, and live on herbs and shell-fish. After a time she became cured, and made this touching song, remembered with affection to this day. In some of the good-wishing poems there are not only lovely lines but others which enshrine old names and legendary associations once familiar to the ancient Gael of a now forgotten day. Thus the *Ora nam Buadh*, or Invocation of the Graces, opens in these lines:

> I bathe thy palms
> In showers of wine,
> In the lustral fire,
> In the seven elements,
> In the juice of rasps,
> In the milk of honey,
> And I place the nine pure choice graces
> In thy fair dear face,
> > The grace of form,
> > The grace of voice,
> > The grace of fortune,
> > The grace of goodness,
> > The grace of wisdom,

253

> The grace of charity,
> The grace of maidenliness,
> The grace of whole-souled loveliness,
> The grace of goodly speech.

This *ora* is one of the longest poems in Mr. Carmichael's collection. In it is one of those survivals to which I have alluded, as in the verse beginning, " Is tu gleus na Mnatha Sithe ":

> Thine is the skill of the Fairy Woman,
> Thine is the virtue of Bride (Bridget) the calm,
> Thine is the faith of Mary the mild,
> Thine is the tact of the woman of Greece,
> Thine is the beauty of Emer the lovely,
> Thine is the tenderness of Darthula delightful,
> Thine is the courage of Maebh the strong,
>   Thine is the charm of Honey-Mouth.

How typically Gaelic this is, with its mixture of Christian and old Celtic and pagan lore, the Virgin Mary and St. Bride *Muime Chriosd* (Christ's Foster-Mother) alternating with the Fairy Woman and with some dim legend of Helen of Troy,[1] and she again with the fair wife of Cuchulain, the great champion of Gaeldom, and with Deirdrê (Darthula—Deardhuil—*Dearshul* as in this Gaelic text),

[1] At least I take it that *Is tu gniomh na mnatha Greuig* is an allusion to Helen.

the Helen of the Gael, and with Maeve, the
Dark Queen whose name and personality
loom so vast and terrible in ancient Gaelic
history, and " Honey-Mouth " (*Binne-bheul*),
whom I take to be Angus, the God of Love.

Of a singular and touching beauty also is
the strange " farewell " or death poem called
An Treoraich Anama, The Soul-Leading—or
sometimes *Fois Anama*, Soul Peace. This is
slowly intoned over the dying person by some
dear and intimate friend, and all present join
in his strain. During the prayer, the *anama
charu*, or soul friend, makes the sign of the
cross with the right thumb over the lips of
the dying. A strange scene, truly, and fit
for a Gaelic Rembrandt, that of the smoke-
begrimed turf cottage of a poor crofter, with
the soul friend and others near and dear
intoning this invocation to " strong Michael,
high king of the angels," and the dying man
with his feet already *abhuinn dubh a bhais* (in
the black river of death), and his soul about
to go on its long wayfaring across the *bean-
ntaibh na bithbhuantachd* (the mountains of
eternity).

The whole second section consisting of the
Aimsire, or Seasons Chants, is fascinating and
valuable to an extraordinary degree, and in
no part of the two volumes is there such a

wealth of valuable commentary, particularly
in the long sections devoted to St. Michael
and to *Sloinntireachd Bhride*, the genealogy
of St. Bride, the Mary of the Gael, the beloved Muime Chriosd, Christ's foster-mother,
the dearest of all the great dead to the heart
of every true Gael. Michael is the Poseidon
of the Gael, is indeed no other than Manannan, perhaps the greatest of the Celtic
gods. From Mounts St. Michael in Brittany
and in Cornwall to Ard-Micheil in far North
Uist there were temples to his honour, and
to-day the scattered names keep him in remembrance, and many places have remains.
His legendary tomb, though Mr. Carmichael
does not allude to this, is at Kilmicheil, in
the Kyles of Bute; but perhaps this was not
the *brian Micheil*, the god, but some good
saint from Columba's brotherhood on Iona.
To this day on the 29th of September the
Feast of St. Michael is still celebrated in the
Hebrides, and perhaps elsewhere; but the
ceremonies are much curtailed, and are rap-
idly being ignored and forgotten. In the invaluable pages which Mr. Carmichael has
devoted to " Michael nam Buadh " and to
St. Bride there is a treasure of legendary lore
and beauty, a profoundly significant record
of now forgotten customs.

256

The Gael and His Heritage

In lovely and primitive beauty the third section, that of the *Oibre*, or Chants of Labour, stands unique. These kindling blessings and smooring-of-the-peats blessings, these herding croons and milking croons, these shepherd songs and reaping chants, these beautiful lamb-marking chants and quaint waulking or warping songs and loom blessings, these hunting blessings and sea prayers, and solemn ocean blessing, for sure there is not in any country in the world so beautiful a heritage.

What would the sportsman of to-day think of the young Gaelic huntsman, who was consecrated before he began his experiences? Oil was put on his head, a bow placed in his hand, and he was required to stand with bare feet on the bare grassless ground, and to take a solemn oath as to what not to do —not to kill a bird sitting, nor a beast lying down, nor the mother of a brood, nor the swimming duck (*i.e.* because of her young), and so forth.

> The white swan of the sweet gurgle,
> The speckled dun of the brown tuft

are to be held free. The *Beannachadh Seilg* ends quaintly with—

[And with you for guidance be]
The fairy swan of Bride of flocks,
The fairy duck of Mary of peace.

Fascinating as is the second volume its appeal is to the folklorist primarily. Here are scores of strange and often in their inconsequence bewildering examples of the *eolas* and *sian*, the charm or spell. These range from the beautiful " Charm of the Lasting Life " to various spells of the evil eye and to mysterious and weird maledictions. In the Miscellaneous section are some singular poems, notably *Bantighearna Bhinn*, the Melodious Lady-Lord, and the *Duan nan Daol*, or Poem of the Beetles, with interesting notes by the translator dealing with this ancient and peculiar Christian superstition. The great collection ends with a strange and apt little song, a fragment of a sea chant perhaps.

Mar a bha,	As it was,
Mar a tha,	As it is,
Mar a bhitheas	As it shall be
Gu brath.	Evermore.
Ri tragadh,	With the ebb,
'S ri lionadh.	With the flow.

There is an appendix of the names of the reciters to whom Mr. Carmichael was indebted, their occupation, place of residence,

258

and district. Many of his informants were women—as Ciorsdai Macleod, who had much lore about the *sluagh*, the fairy hosts, and the second sight; or Morag Mackay, who had her isolated cot among the green, grassy mounds of the ruined nunnery on the lovely little island of Heisgeir-nan-Cailleach; or Oighrig Maccriomthain (Macrimmon), " who had many beautiful songs "; or Isebeal Chisholm, a wandering tinker of North Uist, who knew innumerable incantations and incantation formulæ; or Fionnaghal Macleod, of Clachanreamhar, in South Uist, " who was full of occult lore and old beliefs of many kinds."

There was another woman, Mary Macrae of Harris, from whom Mr. Carmichael learned much, including the beautiful prayer and invocation, *Dia Liom A Laighe,* " God with me lying down," given in vol. i. In her youth this woman came to the Hebrides from Kintail with her father, Alexander, whose mother was one of the celebrated ten daughters of Macleod of Rarasay, mentioned by Dr. Johnson and Boswell. Let me finish this article by quoting what Mr. Carmichael has to say of her, for indeed I think she also is a type of the half forlorn and weird, half wildly gay and young spirit of her ancient, disappearing race, ever ready to dance to its own shadow

if nothing else be available, yet so sad with
a sadness that must live and pass in silence.

She often walked with companions, after the work
of the day was done, distances of ten and fifteen
miles to a dance, and after dancing all night walked
back again to the work of the morning fresh and
vigorous as if nothing unusual had occurred. She
was a faithful servant and an admirable worker,
and danced at her leisure and carolled at her work
like "Fosgay Mhoire," our Lady's lark, above her.
The people of Harris had been greatly given to old
lore and to the old ways of their fathers, reciting and
singing and dancing and merry-making; but a re-
action occurred, and Mary Macrae's old-world ways
were adjured and condemned. But Mary Macrae
heeded not, and went on in her own way, singing
her songs and ballads, intoning her hymns and incantations, and chanting her own "port-a-bial"
(mouth-music), and dancing to her own shadow
when nothing better was available.

Truly Mary Macrae stands for her people,
who, poor and ignored remnant as they are,
heed little the loud ways of a world that is
not for them, but go their own way, singing
their songs and ballads, intoning hymns or
incantations, chanting their own wild, sea-
smitten music, and dancing to their own
shadow, to the shadow of their ancestral
thought and dream, whether in blithe waywardness or in an unforgetting sorrow.

SEUMAS: A MEMORY

"A ghraidhean mo chridhe,"
A ghaoilean mo dhaoine.

(Thou dear one of my heart,
Thou beloved one of my people.)

I have again and again, since my first
book, *Pharais*, alluded to Seumas Macleod:
and as I have shown in the sketch called
"Barabal" and in the dedication of the volume entitled *The Divine Adventure*, it is to
this old Highlander, as well as to my Hebridean nurse Barabal, that I owe more than to
any other early influences.

Let me tell one other story of him, which
I have meant often to tell, but have as often
forgotten.

He had gone once to the Long Island, with
three fishermen, in their herring-coble. The
fish had been sold, and the boat had sailed
southward to a Lews haven where Seumas
had a relative. The younger men had " han-
selled " their good bargain overwell, and were
laughing and talking freely as they walked

up the white road from the haven. Something was said that displeased Seumas greatly, and he might have spoken swiftly in re-
proof; but just then a little naked child ran
laughing from a cottage, chased by his smiling mother. Seumas caught up the child,
who was but an infant, and set him in their
midst, and then kneeled and said the few
words of a Hebridean hymn beginning:

> "Even as a little child
> Most holy, pure. . . ."

No more was said, but the young men understood; and he who long afterward told me
of this episode added that though he had
often since acted weakly and spoken foolishly,
he had never, since that day, uttered foul
words. Another like characteristic anecdote
of Seumas (as the skipper who made his men
cease mocking a " fool ") I have told in the
tale called " The Amadan " in *The Dominion
of Dreams*.

I remember asking him once—as simply as
one might ask about the tides, or the weather
—what he thought of the elements. And he
answered as simply. " Fire is God's touch,"
he said: " and light is God Himself: and
water is the mother of life." I asked him if
he thought all the old gods were dead. He

262

asked why. I said that he had just spoken
of water as the mother of life, and yet that
he had often told me legends of Mânan, the
god of the sea.

" No," he answered, " they are not all
dead. They think *we* are. They do not
change. They are very patient, the old ancient gods. Perhaps it is because they do
not care at all, no, not a whistle of the wind,
for what we think or what we do."

" But," he added, " some have died. And
some are very old, and are sleeping, till they
get their youth again."

" And Mânan . . . does *he* live? "

" Ay, for sure. He was here before Christ
came. He will see the end of all endings.
They say he sleeps in the hollows of great
oceans, and sits on mountain-bergs of ice at
the Pole, chanting an old ancient chant."

Another time I asked him why he had
never married. " There is only one love," he
said simply, " and that I gave to the woman
of my love. But she died of a fever when I
was down with it too. That was in Skye.
When I got up, my heart was in her grave.
I would be very young, then: but I had too
much life put away. And then," he added,
with a smile half whimsical, half wistful, " to

marry a woman for comfort or for peace is
only for those who haven't the way of the
one or the power to make the other." I am
glad to know that another is hardly less indebted to old Seumas Macleod. I am not
permitted to mention his name, but a friend
and kinsman allows me to tell this: that when
he was about sixteen he was on the remote
island where Seumas lived, and on the morrow of his visit came at sunrise upon the old
man, standing looking seaward with his bonnet removed from his long white locks; and
upon his speaking to Seumas (when he saw
he was not " at his prayers ") was answered,
in Gaelic of course, " Every morning like this
I take off my hat to the beauty of the world."

The untaught islander who could say this had
learned an ancient wisdom, of more account
than wise books, than many philosophies.

I could write much of this revered friend—
so shrewd and genial and wordly-wise, for all
his lonely life; so blithe in spirit and swiftly
humorous; himself a poet, and remembering
countless songs and tales of old; strong and
daring, on occasion; good with the pipes, as
with the nets; seldom angered, but then with
a fierce anger, barbaric in its vehemence; a
loyal clansman; in all things, good and not so
good, a Gael of the Isles.

AILEEN: A MEMORY

(The Soul of a Story)

"But to what headland of a strange shore, O my soul, art thou steering the course of my ship?"—
PINDAR, Nem. iii.

This is not a story, in truth: it is a memory and a speculation.

One day many things fell away from her, or became unreal. A friend had said to her: "You cannot understand the thing I speak of, because you have all happiness and all fortune, and above all because you have no sorrow."

She had said that surely this life was enough: why did the mind crave so passionately for more life, for life to be taken up again? It troubled her. Thought was meshed in a net of dreams. Had she put her hand secretly upon sorrow, she wondered. She remembered an old tale of a mother, young too, and beautiful, who had all things of desire, and yet never saw the white flame of

her heart's desire: to whom treasures of the
world were as dust by the highway, blossom
on the grass, foam on the shore. Below her
gladness lay an incalculable sorrow, as below
her beauty lay the enchantment of a beauty
greater than hers. " You have all things,"
said those who loved her: and one added,
" You of all people must long to live again,
to taste life anew."

To live again—to taste life anew—Aileen
wondered. Did she? No: in that thought
her soul shook like a flame in wind. Could
she not love Beauty, and yet be no bondager;
reflect it, and yet be free of it, as a small
pool reflects the mysterious march of the
stars? It was a revelation to her that she
had, unaware, nourished a pain that was with
her every day, as the shadow of a mountain
over a lake will lie in that lake from dawn
to dayset, though wind and sunlight weave
traceries from hour to hour.

And this pain—it was an irremediable
loneliness. She suffered the more because
this companion was unguessed by others.
She strove to overcome, to ignore, to hide
this phantom, which so often came on the
breath of a rose or the vibration of a lovely
sound, unexpectedly, subtly, as though wilfully clothing itself in the extreme essence

of beautiful things, finding even the most
delicate beauty too obvious.

One day she knew that fear had been born
in her heart, and was a watcher there beside the other dweller. This fear was of life.
It was a fear that life might not, after all,
be laid away with the suspended breath. It
was the fear of immortality. No, she thought,
not that perhaps. She did not know. It was
not the vague immortal life she feared: the
" future " so long taught as a surety and out-
held as a goal. It was the fear that life might
have to be taken up again, here: that the
soul had lives to go through, as, in the old
tale, the King of Ireland's son had to live
and die in the seven kingdoms of his inheritance before he should at last be free and
let forth to be a wandering beggar. But the
soul has little concern in our happiness or
unhappiness. That silent watcher has her
own inexplicable sorrow and her own inexplicable joy. All the rest is of hazard; and
we may be happy and fortunate, and yet
inwardly bow down before entranced sorrow
—as we may have ills and misfortunes and
gathered griefs, and yet inwardly rejoice with
the pulse of life and the inextinguishable
hope of that strong passion to be taken up
again and lived anew.

And I wonder—I wonder—how often I
have wondered if so beautiful and vivid a
soul could really pass and be as dust upon
the wind that is blown now this way and now
that, and in the end is gathered to the wilderness of lifeless things.   There is an old wisdom, that what the soul itself desires, that
it shall surely have.   And among the people
to whom Aileen belonged there is a mysterious saying, " It is not every one, happy or
unhappy, or good or bad, who has a living
soul."   Is there any wave upon the sea or
leaf before the wind more feeble than the
aimless will?—or is there any disaster of the
spirit worse than that by which a winged
destiny becomes a wingless and obscure fate?
But who is to know how fatality is measured
or how fulfilled—who is to know that behind
the broken will there is not a heroic spirit
upon whom has fallen the mystery of untimely sleep?

THE FOUR WINDS OF EIRINN

FOREWORD

"Belles et puissantes sont les harmonies nouvelles des gens de Thulé."—MELCHIOR DE VOGÜÉ.

This essay originally appeared in *The Fortnightly Review* (February 1903), on the publication of the volumes entitled *Cuchulain of Muirthemne Arranged and Retold by Lady Gregory,* and *The Four Winds of Eirinn: Poems by the late Ethna Carbery (Anna Macmanus).* Since its appearance, and just as the contents of the present volume had been completed for printing, two books reached me, which, coming out of the heart of Ireland, should be mentioned under a title so distinctive as that which heads this page. *The Divine Vision,* the new volume of poetry of Mr. George Russell (" A. E."), has the spiritual intensity, the rapt ecstasy of his most characteristic verse. It is the poetry of a mystic who is caught in the heavenly nets. But though it is lifted at times on the Gaelic

269

spirit and has allusions to what is intimate in
the spiritual life of the Gael, it is not Gaelic
in the sense in which either of the two books
discussed in the following essay is Gaelic.
Ethna Carbery's poems are the poems of the
Irish heart, and Miss Hull's and Lady Gregory's retold saga-tales are the mirror of the
ancient Irish genius, as Mr. Yeats's poetry is
preëminently the poetry of the Irish spirit:
but the poems of " A. E." are the poems of a
strayed visionary, of a visionary strayed into
Ireland, and in love with that imagination
and with that dream, but obviously in himself
of no country set within known frontiers, of
no land withheld by familiar shores. Sur-
charged with the intensest spirit of Ireland in
the less mystical and poetic sense, is the slim
volume of a handful of prose papers by Miss
Ethel Goddard, entitled *Dreams for Ireland.*
This book is uplifted with a radiant hope and
with an ecstasy of spiritual conviction that
make the heart young to contemplate: and
would God that its glad faith and untroubled
prophecies could be fulfilled in our time, or
that in our time even the shadows of the
great things to come could lighten the twilight road. If I am too sad to share in full
the radiant faith, too sad to see with such
glad eyes or to be so joyously dissuaded by

lovely phantoms from the bitterness of things that are, I am sure-set enough in the hope that great things are yet to be accomplished, that a great destiny is yet possible of achievement, an achievement greater than the shaping of proud kingdoms and empires. But of that I will say no more here, having already said what I have to say in this paper and in the first part of the section called " For the Beauty of an Idea." Only, to the little volume of *Dreams for Ireland*, and to all who write and strive in a like spirit, the spirit that brings victory or transforms defeat, I would give this word of the great Pindar, noblest of poets: *But sowing in the fair flower of this spirit . . . be not too careful for the cost: loose free like a mariner thy sail unto the wind.*

If, with two books before me on which I have something to say, I have chosen the title of the lesser, that is because of its peculiar fitness. The four winds of Eirinn breathe through each, if with a stronger sound and more primitive voice in that which deals with a spiritual and material order long ago remote from us, with the heroic passions and beauty of a world that ceased before English was grown a language. Even in the order of importance I am not prepared to admit

271

that the small posthumous book of verse by
Ethna Carbery is so far behind the admirable compilation we owe to Lady Gregory.
But by that I do not mean literary importance. The poems of *The Four Winds of
Eirinn* have already appeared in Nationalist
papers and circulated throughout Ireland,
and are loved and treasured in innumerable
hill-crofts and moorside cabins. A thousand
readers knew the author's name who had no
idea whether she was of the small band of
living singers or of that great Irish company
whose songs are the treasure of a whole people. Only a few knew that Ethna Carbery
was the wife of a Donegal patriot and writer
of distinction, Seumas Macmanus; but long
before her recent premature death she had
become a familiar presence at many hearths.
Her slender posthumous volume may now
be had at a sum which is within the reach
of all save the poorest of her own land.
That, however, need not trouble any. There
is not a poem in her book unknown to hundreds who could not purchase the little volume or could read it were it possessed. One
copy of a book such as *The Four Winds of
Eirinn* is enough to light many unseen fires.
Few readers out of touch with the Gaelic
peasant have any idea of the power of a

single enthusiast ; of how one man, speaking
in a barn at harvest-time, or by the croftside,
or on the long road, or by the fireside at the
winter *ceilidh*, or at the rising of the moon
in the dusks of summer, can spread from
one to one, to a little group, to a gathering
clan, to countless unknown brothers and
sisters, tidings that are sprung from a
living heart and march in music and are
clothed in the speech of beauty. For there
is perhaps no people so susceptible to the
charm of verbal rhythm as the Gaelic Irish.
To put a sorrow or a joy into mournful or
dancing music is as natural to them as, to
the English temperament, it is natural to se-
crete sorrow and to veil joy.

It would be uncritical to say that the poetry
of Ethna Carbery is compelling because of
its art.

Poetry may express itself subtly in the
" signature of symbol," or immediately in the
utterance of unveiled emotion. The one
method is not necessarily superior to the
other. But only the artist may dare to move
beyond elemental emotion. He who would
pass from the cries and tumult of the unloosened passions, and create anew in symbol
those ancient cries and that unresting tumult,
must be as Orpheus descending into the in-

ferno of defeated dreams, to come again, in
the serene mystery of song, with lovelier
music and more far-seeing eyes. "I tell
you," says Nietzsche, "one must have chaos
within to enable one to give birth to a dancing star."

In each there is one perfection: simplicity.
In art, whose controlling spirit is delibera-
tion, there is nothing so deliberate as simplicity. It may be an innate quality, a habit of
the mind; it is more often, perhaps, the disdain of the imagination for artifice, the pride
of the imagination in a noble economy.

In itself, poetry is, to put an old definition
in a new way, the emotion of life rhythmically
remembering beauty: as pictorial art and the
art of verbal romance are the vision of life
seen in beauty and in beauty revealed: and as
music is the echo of life heard in beauty.
But the poet, in emotion rhythmically remembering beauty, must, in the purging fire
of creation, be not less the artist than the
poet—he who knows how to shape and control, what to enhance, above all what to forgo,
for supreme art is the irreducible economy
of the imagination accepting the last austere
law of beauty. Emotion is not enough, nor,
even, is the passage of emotion into rhythmic utterance enough. The thyme and mar-

joram are not yet honey, as Emerson said
beautifully of the poetry of Thoreau. In the
rarest lyric verse there must be unseen lightning—" the fiery lightning that goeth with all
victory," as Pindar has it in one of his great
odes. There are few poets in a generation
to whom the " fiery lightning " is a reality.
That generation is fortunate, indeed, which
produces wrestlers in song worthy of an
Olympian wreath of wild olive, or a Pythian
wreath of bay, or Isthmian pine-garland, or
the wild parsley of Nemea.

Ethna Carbery had not time to become a
rare artist, for she died in those early years
when emotion does not readily come under
the yoke of that severe discipline which is the
first commandment of art. She is not a poet
to compare with Mr. Yeats, for example. In
technical quality she has not the metrical
facility of Nora Hopper or Katharine Tynan.
Her lyrics lack the precision and distinction
of the verse of Moira O'Neill. But in essential poetic faculty she stands high among the
Irish poets of to-day; in this respect indeed
she falls behind none save Mr. Yeats and
" A. E."; and as an Irish writer for an Irish
public I doubt if any of those just named has
more intimately reached the heart of the
people. The poetry of Mr. Yeats is a poetry

275

that appeals to those for whom the charm of
beauty is beyond any other charm, and to
whom beauty means a trained and ordered
loveliness, and in whom is a more or less
trained and ordered sense of that loveliness.
The poetry of " A. E." is a poetry that appeals to those to whom the charm of spiritual
ecstasy is beyond any other charm. The
poetry of writers such as Katharine Tynan
and Nora Hopper, and in a less degree of
Moira O'Neill, is a poetry written rather for
the delight of those in sympathy with the
keen and warm life of the people than for
the people themselves. Their poetry is rarely
in the signature of interpretation; they are
minnesingers of charm and distinction. There
are not many of their verses which would
come naturally to the lips of an Irish peasant,
as would come one or two of Moira O'Neill's
Songs of the Glens of Antrim; for, to mention
only the most significant reason, they are
commonly shaped in the English and not in
the Gaelic form of thought—and the form of
thought is a still subtler thing than the form
of literary style. True, most of Mr. Yeats's
poetry is Gaelic in its inward life, partaking
of the Gaelic colour and shaped in the Gaelic
mould; but he has the esoteric manner of
those ancient poetic ancestors of his who

were renowned for their obscurity. In one
of the old Irish tales a bard is alluded to with
great praise, for after he had spoken before
the king and the assembled warriors, priests,
and other bards, it was admitted that no other
showed so great wisdom or so irrefutably cut
away the ground from the matter in debate,
because neither king nor any other could
understand him, "so great was his high,
noble, beautiful obscurity." And in another
episode, that Dr. Whiteley Stokes has translated for us in the *Irische Texte*, we learn
how one Senchan went on a circuit into Scotland, and how there "the Spirit of Poetry
met him on the road in the shape of a loathly
monster, and conversed with him in the obscurity of poetry." Truly, the chronicler of
Senchan must have suffered much ere he
committed himself to that "loathly monster!"

Well, I am sure that if Irish peasants were
to hear *The Shadowy Waters*, or even the
greater number of the poems of *The Wind
Among the Reeds*, they would, while respon-
sive to the music and the charm of atmosphere, rank the author as the greatest of living bards by virtue of his " high, noble, beautiful obscurity." That they could really follow *The Shadowy Waters*, as they have proved

they can follow with sympathy and delight *The Countess Cathleen*—or as they could follow the stories of Hanrahan the Red in *The Secret Rose*, or the episodical essays in *The Celtic Twilight*—is hardly to be believed. This is not to disparage one side of Mr. Yeats's genius, nor is it to disparage a poem of great beauty that I for one account among the excelling things he has done. It is merely to state what seems to be a fact, and to emphasise the difference of approach in the work of a poet like Ethna Carbery, a writer not less saturated with the Gaelic atmosphere but with a simplicity of thought and diction foreign to the most subtle of contemporary poets, who is never more subtle than when he creates a verbal simplicity as a veil for occult thought and remote allusion.

We hardly need the tribute of proud love paid to Anna Macmanus, in the pathetic little memoir contributed by Mr. Macmanus to this posthumous edition of the poems of " Ethna Carbery." In these poems we find everything that the husband says of the wife and the friend of the friend. No reader, surely, could fail to recognise how " before the tabernacle of poor Ireland's hopes a perpetual flame burned in her bosom "; how that from childhood even, " every fibre of her

frame vibrated with the love of Ireland ";
how that her love went out to the hills of
Tir-Chonaill long before her joy quickened
among the Donegal mountains, because of
the passion come to her upon the Hills of
her Heart!

> *"Hills o' my heart!*
> For sake of the yellow head that drew me wandering
>   over
>   Your misty crests from my own home where sor-
>   row bided then,
> I set my seven blessings on your kindly heather
>   cover,
>   On every starry moorland loch, and every sha-
>   dowy glen,
> *Hills o' my heart!"*

Her earliest as her latest verse has the
quality of song and the vibration of poetry.
And from first to last there is in it the Gaelic
note—so distinctive from any other note.
Here Ethna Carbery is Irish in a sense in
which the other women poets of her hour and
nation cannot claim to be: for there is no
reason why much of the poetry of Katharine
Tynan, for example, might not be written by
one who had lived away from Ireland and
permitted a foreign colour to be the colour
of her songs of life, or why much of the
poetry of Norah Hopper might not be written

by one who had never lived in Ireland and
knew the Ireland of the heart only imaginatively and as one among many dreams in the
secret gardens of the imagination. But with
Ethna Carbery Ireland is always the Motherland, and she the child that will not be put
away from her, no, not by any wandering of
longing nor by any chance of accident. How
unmistakable the note in the very first lines
of this little collection of some seventy poems
—only two-thirds of which had been revised
by the author before her early death:

"There's a sweet sleep for my love by yon glimmer-
        ing blue wave,
    But alas! it is a cold sleep in a green-happed narrow
        grave.
            O shadowy Finn, move slowly,
            Break not her peace so holy,
    Stir not her slumber in the grass your restless
        ripples lave."

And what an added pathos to this poem
of " The Cold Sleep of Brighidin " that it
was the singer's own death-lament as well as
that of the " Breedyeen " of her song; and
that she too lies in sleep by the " glimmering blue wave " of Loch Finn!

Again, in the second poem, " Shiela Ní
Gara ":

The Four Winds of Eirinn

"Shiel Ní Gara, is it lonesome where you bide,
With the plover circling over and the sagans
spreading wide?

.   .   .   .   .

"Is it a sail ye wait, Shiela? 'Yea, from the westering sun.'
Shall it bring joy or sorrow? 'Oh joy, sadly won.'
Shall it bring peace or conflict? 'The pibroch in
the glen,
And the flash and crash of battle where my banner
shines again.'

"Green shears of Hope rise round you like grass-
blades after drouth,
And there blows a red wind from the East, a white
wind from the South,
A brown wind from the West, _gràdh_, a brown wind
from the West—
But the black, black wind from Northern hills,
how can you love it best?"

"Said Shiela Ní Gara, ''Tis a kind wind and a true,
For it rustled soft through Aileach's halls and
stirred the hair of Hugh:
Then blow, wind! and snow, wind! What matters
storm to me,
Now I know the fairy sleep must break and let the
sleepers free?'

"But, Shiela Ní Gara, why rouse the stony dead,
Since at your call a living host will circle you instead?
Long is our hunger for your voice, the hour is drawing near—
_Oh, Dark Rose of our Passion—call, and our hearts
shall hear!_"

Again, in the third, " In Tír-Na'n-Og ":

> "*In Tír-na'n-Og,*
> *In Tír-na'n-Og,*

Summer and spring go hand in hand, and in the
radiant weather
Brown autumn leaves and winter snow come floating
down together.

> "*In Tír-na'n-Og,*
> *In Tír-na'n-Og,*

All in a drift of apple-blooms my true love there is
roaming,
He will not come although I pray from dawning
until gloaming.

> "*In Tír-na'n-Og,*
> *In Tír-na'n-Og,*

The *Sidhe* desired my Heart's Delight, they lured
him from my keeping.
He stepped within a fairy ring while all the world
was sleeping.

> "*In Tír-na'n-Og,*
> *In Tír-na'n-Og,*

He hath forgotten hill and glen where misty shadows
gather,
The bleating of the mountain sheep, the cabin of his
father.

> "*In Tír-na'n-Og,*
> *In Tír-na'n-Og,*

No memory hath he of my face, no sorrow for my
sorrow,
My flax is spun, my wheel is husht, and so I wait the
morrow."

But, in truth, one might quote from each poem in the book. All are Gaelic in mould of thought and colour of art. Of the sixty-eight there are at least sixty whose very names have a cradle-song for some of us, but must be strangely foreign to many. "Shiela Ní Gara," "The Song of Ciabhan," "Mo Chraoibhín Cno," "Páistín Fionn," "Niamh," "The Brown Wind of Connaught," "Mo Bhuachaill Cael-Dubh," "I-Breasil," "To the Comely Four of Aran," "Vein o' my Heart," "Nial Glondubh to Gormlai," "The Shadow-House of Lugh," and the like.

These poems of the *Four Winds of Eirinn* fall into four groups, though (and wisely) not so arranged—poems of the Gaelic past, poems of love, poems of national longing and a burning patriotism, and poems of the Gaelic imagination and of the unquenchable longing and desire of the heart for an Avalon of which it dreams, but whose foam-white coasts it cannot see—for the "Well o' the World's End" which it cannot reach:

"Beyond the four seas of Eri, beyond the sunset's rim,
It lies half forgot, in a valley deep and dim,
Like a star of fire from the skies' gold tire,
And whoso drinks the nine drops shall win his
heart's desire—
At the Well o' the World's End.

283

"What go ye seeking, seeking, seeking,
  O girl white-bosomed, O girl fair and young?"—
"I seek the well-water, the cool well water,
  That my love may have love for me ever on his
    tongue."

      .   .   .   .   .

    Perhaps the poems which longest will lie close to the Irish heart are those which show the shadow of Irish sorrow and the rainbow-gleam of Irish hope—that sorrow and that hope which from the grey glens of Donegal to Kerry of the Kings inspire all the songs that are sung, and all that is imperishable in the nation's heart. Of these a typical example is " Mo Chraoibhin Cno " (*Mo chree-veen no*—literally " My cluster of nuts," figuratively " My brown-haired girl " — here used by the poet as an analogue of Ireland, one of her many secret names of love):

Mo Chraoibhín Cno!

"A sword of light hath pierced the dark, our eyes
  have seen the star.
O Mother, leave the ways of sleep now days of
  promise are;
The rusty spears upon your walls are stirring to
  and fro,
In dreams they front uplifted shields—Then wake,
  Mo Chraoibhín Cno!

The Four Winds of Eirinn

"The little waves keep whispering where sedges fold
    you in,
  And round you are the barrows of your buried kith
    and kin;
  O famine-wasted, fever-burnt, they faded like the
    snow
  Or set their hearts to meet the steel—for you,
      Mo Chraoibhín Cno!

"Their names are blest, their *caoine* sung, our bitter
    tears are dried;
  We bury sorrow in their graves, Patience we cast
    aside;
  Within the gloom we heard a voice that once was
    ours to know—
  It was Freedom—Freedom calling loud, Arise!
      Mo Chraoibhín Cno!

"Afar beyond that empty sea, on many a battle-
    place,
  Your sons have stretched brave hands to death
    before our foeman's face—
  Down the sad silence of your rest their war-notes
    faintly blow,
  And they bear an echo of your name—of yours,
      Mo Chraoibhín Cno!

"Then wake, *a gradh!* we yet shall win a gold crown
    for your head,
  Strong wine to make a royal feast—the white wine
    and the red—
  And in your oaken mether the yellow mead shall
    flow,
  What day you rise, in all men's eyes—a Queen,
      Mo Chraoibhín Cno!

"The silver speech our fathers knew shall once again
  be heard;
The fire-lit story, crooning song, sweeter than lilt
  of bird;
The quicken-tree shall break in flower, its ruddy
  fruit shall glow,
And the gentle people dance beneath its shade—
    Mo Chraoibhín Cno!

"There shall be peace and plenty—the kindly open
  door,
Blessings on all who come and go—the prosperous
  or the poor—
The misty glens and purple hills a fairer tint shall
  show,
When your splendid Sun shall ride the skies again—
    Mo Chraoibhín Cno!"

Alas! 'tis but the old sweet impossible
dream for what is gone away upon the wind.
Not now, never again in this little world
that is *our* world, as we know it to-day, can
come this golden age, heralded by our re-
turning prayers. For us, the Gentle People
have no longer a life common with our own.
They have gone beyond grey unvisited hills.
They dwell in far islands perhaps, where the
rains of Heaven and the foam of the sea
guard their fading secrecies. Not here, in
any Avalon betwixt the last beaches of the
Hebrides and the stones of Carnac, shall that
glen be found, that shore be touched, where

the old Gaelic world shall live anew. An
evil has fallen upon us, that may or may not
have been inevitable; that may or may not
be from within ourselves as well as from without. It is inevitable now.

> "*In Tír-na'n-Og,*
> *In Tír-na'n-Og,*
> The blackbird lilts, the robin chirps, the linnet
> wearies never,
> They pipe to dancing feet of *Sidhe* and thus shall
> pipe for ever."

Yes, but that is in Tír-na'n-Og, the land of
the ever-young. That is in I-Breasil, the Isle
of Youth. That is in Flatheanas, where the
strong of soul are. It has no shores, that
land; no boat's prow cleaves the surf around
that isle; we do not hear the laughing voices
yonder. Alas! yes—in Tír-na'n-Og. But now
we front new ways. The spirit has changed
within us; and with the changing of the
spirit in the soul of a nation all that was its
treasure must be lost too, all that cannot be
preserved against Time and the bitter moth.
And indeed we lament often for what never
was: only the same old desire of the heart,
the same old longing, that a thousand years
ago dreamed against to-day, and that to-day
re-dreams the dream of the world a thousand
years ago.

The happy years may come. Who shall
dare say No? But they cannot come, as
things are: not for us, at least, longing in
our own way. For we long for what is gone,
and going, and we are caught in the great
net which has swept in our kindred, and all
the nations. Can any Gael honestly say that
Ireland, that the Highlands, that the Isles are
in the deep sense nearer true wellbeing now
than they were half a century ago, twenty
years ago, ten years ago? Depopulation, the
decay of the old language, the ceaseless
pressure of what in bitter unconscious irony
is called the civilising factor; the deadening
of a new and dull ideal of prosperity, not
a blithe weal but a restless discontent; the
cancer of racial hate in Ireland, the levelling
and crushing curse of a growing materialism
in Scotland; the paralysing selfishness of both
native and alien landowners; and, with these,
and much else, the losing of old virtues in
the half-eager, half-sullen assumption of other
ways and manners—all this has made, and
is making, the passing of the old order bitter
and tragic for those whose hearts are bound
up in it, whose life is part of it, whose souls
are the offspring of its soul.

If I and others of my generation feel this,
how much more must those feel it whose

memories go far back; who remember the
homeless glens, when the smoke of many
hearths rose in peace; the deer-forests, where
the hillside crofts held a contented people;
the islands where now the flocks of the capi-
talist sheep-farmer are the only inhabitants?
A few days ago I met a grey-haired Highland gentleman on his way back to the far
Isles, to take farewell of the last of his clan
who upheld the old ways and kept to the
old traditions and used the ancient speech.
" For it is all going," he said; " no, it is all
gone. Soon I will be the last, there. They
have no Gaelic now, the young people. They
and the others have forgotten all that our
fathers had of tale and song. Our old world
is passed away. It is a new world we are in
now. For them that like it, it may be well;
it is not well for us who do not like it. For
me, as with Donnacha' Bàn:

> " ' 'S mithich teàrnadh do na gleannaibh
>   O'n tha gruaimich air na beannaibh,
>   'S ceathach dùinte mu na meallaibh
>   A' cur dallaidh air ar léirsinn.' "

" It is time now to go down into the glens,
for gloom is fallen on the mountains, and
mists shroud the hills, darkening our vision."
There are still many of us who are of this

broken clan. We have not wholly lost heart; there is much left to fight for; there is still one inspiring hope: but we know that nearly all of what we would see stay must go, that nothing of what we see going shall turn back, that nothing of what we know gone shall come again.

The secret of the Celtic muse is veiled in tears. The poetry of the Gael is the poetry of sorrow. It is not impossible that one day a new triumphal pæan may be heard, the clarions of joy. That, indeed, would be a divine ministry of the patient and watching gods.

Years ago, when writing went with drifting thought and not with thought rising from the depths, I wrote this: without pain as a memory, and without despair as a will-o'-the-wisp, there would be no lyric beauty of enduring worth.

But now I do not think this, though up to a point its truth is obvious. For joy can be, and ought to be, the supreme torch of the mind; and hope can be and ought to be the inspiration of that grave ecstasy which is art become religious, that is . . . art expressing an august verity, with the emotion of the life that is mortal deepened by the passion of the soul that is immortal.

"So simple is the heart of man,
  So ready for new hope and joy;
Ten thousand years since it began
  Have left it younger than a boy."

Nevertheless it is true that pain is a wind that
goes deep into the obscure wood, and stirs
many whispers and lamentations among the
hidden leaves, and sends threnodies on long
waves from the swaying green shores of oak
and pine and beech. " It is that which gives
artists the strongest power of expression,"
wrote one who for himself knew the truth
of what he said, the great Millet. But despair . . . that is a quality of the mind, while
pain is an elemental condition of life. It is
in nature for all that lives to know pain: it
is not natural for anything that lives to know
despair. So while despair may have its beauty,
as a desolate polar sea has its own desolate
beauty, or as a barren hillside without green
of grass or song of bird may have a wild
and barren beauty, it is the beauty of what
redeems—light and cloud, mist and shadow
and air—not a beauty inherent, not the
beauty of those things which fundamentally
are elemental and eternal. The clouds of
man's hopes and dreams which drift through
the human sky, and the wind of the spirit that
shepherds them, belong to the higher regions.

Here, by some subtlety of association, I recall those beautiful lines in *The Last Adventure of Balaustion:*

"Why should despair be?   Since, distinct above
  Man's wickedness and folly, flies the wind
  And floats the cloud. . . ."

And this poor girl, with her heart of song
and her frail reed of life, who died so young
among the mountains of Donegal, she, too,
knew it.   What a *caoine* of world-old sadness
in that poem she wrote not long before her
death, " The Passing of the Gael ":

"The whip of hunger scourged them from the glens
      and quiet moors,
   But there's a hunger of the heart that plenty
      never cures;
   And they shall pine to walk again the rough road
      that is yours.

"They are going, going, going, and we cannot bid
      them stay;
   The fields are now the strangers', where the
      strangers' cattle stray.
   *Oh! Kathaleen Ni Hoolihan, your way's a thorny
      way!*"

But pain wearies even the sense of pain,
and it is a relief to turn to this dead young
singer's poetry of fantasy.   How fine much

of this is, whether simple as " The King of
Ireland's Cairn ":

> "Blow softly down the valley,
>   O wind, and stir the fern
> That waves its green fronds over
>   The King of Ireland's cairn.
>
> .   .   .   .   .   .
>
> "Say, down those halls of Quiet
>   Doth he cry upon his Queen?
> Or doth he sleep contented
>   To dream of what has been?"

Or of more sutble thought and remoter expression in poems such as that (" Angus the
Lover ") which begins:

"I follow the silver spears flung from the hands of
   dawn"—

or as " The Green Plover," or as " The
Shadow-House of Lugh ":

"Dream-fair beside dream waters, it stands alone:
   A winging thought of Lugh made its corner stone:
   A desire of his heart raised its walls on high.

   .   .   .   .   .   .

"He hath no vexing memory of blood in slanting
   rain,
   Of green spears in hedges on a battle plain;
   But through the haunted quiet his love's silver
   words
   Blew round him swift as wing-beats of enchanted
   birds.

   .   .   .   .   .   .

"He plays for her pleasure on his harp's gold wire
    The laughter-tune that leaps alone in trills of fire;
    She hears the dancing feet of *Sidhe* where a white
        moon gleams,
    And all her world is joy in the House of Dreams.

"His days glide to night, and his nights glide to day:
    With circling of the amber mead, and feasting gay:
    In the yellow of her hair his dreams lie curled,
    And her arms make the rim of his rainbow world."

Or in poems of the longing of love, as
" Feithfailge ":

> "*The blue lake of Devenish!*
> I vex the purple dark with sighs—
>   (*The blue lake of Devenish*)
> Across the world my sorrow flies,
> A-hunger for the grey and wistful
> Beauty of Feithfailge's eyes."

Or as " At the Well of the Branchy Trees,"
or " Hills o' My Heart," or " Mo Bhuachaill
Cael-Dubh," or " The Sad Song of Finian,"
with its true Gaelic hyperbole of lament in—

> "I am adrift on the waves of the world—
>   Ochon! Ochon!
> Tossed by the storm, by the green seas whirled,
> All for the sake of the yellow-curled
> Slender girl that I wished my own"—

or a half-score more as fine.

The Four Winds of Eirinn

There is a legend common throughout
the Highlands and Isles, and current in
many parts of Ireland, about the Lennan-Shee
(*Leannain-Sidhe*), or Fairy Lover. Only the
other day I heard a striking variant of the
usual tale, and at the same time a good
answer. One of the hearers objected that all
these stories of the Lennan-Shee were untrue,
for he had lived many years in the Highlands
and had never heard of any who had met or
seen or known of a fairy lover, and that what
one was not aware of in a country would not
be existing in that country. "As for that,"
said the narrator, " *'s iomadh rud a bhios am
measg an t' sluaigh air nach bi fios agaibh-sa* "
("There's many a thing among the people
of which you are left in ignorance"), a re-
mark greeted all round with "*Tha sin fìor*"
("That is true"). And of the many who in
one way or another have dealt with this
legend, I recall none who has done so more
subtly than Ethna Carbery in "The Love-
Talker":

"I know not what way he came, no shadow fell
    behind,
  But all the sighing rushes swayed beneath a fairy
    wind:
  The thrush ceased its singing, a mist crept about,
  We two clung together—with the world shut out.

295

"Beyond the ghostly mist I could hear my cattle
    low,
The little cow from Ballina, clean as driven snow,
The dun cow from Kerry, the roan from Inisheer,
Oh, pitiful their calling—and his whispers in my
    ear!

"His eyes were a-fire; his words were a snare;
    I cried my mother's name, but no help was there;
    I made the blessed Sign: then he gave a dreary
    moan,
    A wisp of cloud went floating by, and I stood
    alone."

How natural it seems to turn from this
Gaelic singer of to-day to the unknown
shenachies who told the primitive Gaelic
legends of the Cuchulain cycle at a time when
the Angels had not troubled the fens of England—to that largely lost and much confused
cycle of legendary lore from which, in *Cuchulain of Muirthemne* (Coohoolin of Mŭr-ĕv-na,
as pronounced), Lady Gregory has with
much skill and no little beauty evolved a
sequent narrative! For the two worlds meet,
thus: or rather, they are one. Time makes
no division when the mental outlook, the
mental life, remains unchanged save in what
is unessential in manner and method. The
Gael who believes in the fairy lover can also
well believe in the story of the love of Angus,

son of the Dagda, for Caer Ormaith, daughter of Ethel Anbual; and how for one year Caer would be a beautiful woman and for the next year be a white swan on a mountain loch, and how Angus, because of the longing of his love, took swan-shape upon him by the loch-side, so that the lovers spread their wings and rose from the loch, in their going their wings making a music so sweet that all who heard it fell asleep for three days and three nights. Or in that tale of how Cathbad the Druid told the childless Fedlimid that his wife would bear a daughter for whom many great heroes and bright candles of the Gael would lose their lives; and of how the girl was born, she for whom heroes would fight and kings go seeking; and how Cathbad said: "Let Dêirdrê be her name, sweet menace that she is": and how he chanted to her:

"Many will be jealous of your face, O flame of beauty; for your sake heroes shall go to exile. For there is harm in your face: it will bring banishment and death on the sons of kings. In your fate, O beautiful child, are wounds and ill-doings, and shedding of blood.

"You will have a little grave apart to yourself; you will be a tale of wonder for ever, Dêirdrê."

Or in that tale of how Fedelm of the Sidhe —the young girl of the mouth of red berries,

with voice sweeter than the strings of a
curved harp, and skin showing through her
clothes like the snow of a single night—was
of a sudden seen by Maeve, the Warrior-
Queen, sitting on a shaft of her chariot, and
had no word to say to the Queen about her
hosts of Cruachan gathered for battle against
Cuchulain and the Ultonians, but only, over
and over, " I see crimson on them, I see red."
And how true that foretelling was, when that
great army of Ireland was swept away, " wandering and going astray like a mare among
her foals that goes astray in a strange place,
not knowing what path to take "; and how
the remnant crossed the ford of the Sionnan
at Athluain, notwithstanding that in Maeve's
company were unvanquishable heroes and
three princes of the Sidhe in shining armour,
Delbaeth, and Cermat Honey-mouth, and
Angus Õg, son of the Dagda—for even the
gods do not always prevail against the souls
of the greatest.

Or in that tale of how the harpers of Cain-
bile came to Maeve's camp, and played on
magic harps; but how they were driven forth
as spies, and followed with spears till they
reached the great stone of Lecmore, when
the harpers took on themselves the shape of
wild deer and went away. Or in that tale of

the Wedding of Maine, son of Ailell and
Maeve, where beauty and death are as subtly
interwoven as in the familiar Gaelic *sgeul* of
the love of Bailê the Sweet-Spoken and Ail-
linn, when, after death, grave-wood grew into
grave-wood and green branches from the
North and the South became one overhang-
ing branch under which the four winds
moved. Or in that tale of how, after the
heavy wound of Fraech, " boy darling of the
King of the Sidhe of Ireland," a sorrowful
crying was heard on Cruachan, and strange
women in beautiful raiment were seen on the
hill, and how Fraech in his sickness called
suddenly, " Lift me out of this, for that is
the cry of my mother and of the women of
Boann "; and how he was carried to Cruachan, and left upon the hill, and how thrice
fifty queens bore him to the secret gates,
crying a sorrowful cry; and how it is from
this cry that the musicians of Ireland learned
the sorrowful cry of the women of the Sidhe.

Or in a hundred tales akin to these tales,
in this book and in other books, and in many
minds, might belief as well be.

To come under the enchantment of a book
such as this legendary lore—gathered by
Lady Gregory from many sources, with constant excellence in choice, retold with care-

ful art of simplicity, and not rarely in that
spellbound prose which is born of the enchanted mind—one must be, as Mr. Yeats
says in his finely persuasive rather than critical preface to this book, as were the people
of old-time, who were in love with a story
and gave themselves up to imagination as if
to a lover. Not otherwise can this sea of
troubling winds and troubled waters, and of
bewildering currents and rising and falling
tides, be rightfully enjoyed. To change the
image, the book must be approached as one
approaches a forest, dense with intricate by-
ways, proud with wide glades, given over to
the wilderness at times, and to enter which
with the dews of dawn means that one need
not look to emerge till the stars are come.
The paths may be difficult, sometimes the
way seem trackless. But "delight will always overtake one in the end."

Cuchulain of Muirthemne is no mere book of
pleasure for the eager or the weary reader.
It is the initial part of a work which, possibly,
may ultimately be considered worthy to rank
with the Arthurian chronicle of Malory and
with the *Mabinogion* which Lady Charlotte
Guest (in some such manner as Lady Gregory
has now done) gave to the world. Had Macpherson been profoundly intimate with Gaelic

life, and had he been a Gaelic scholar—had
he been free from the ideals of a Lowland
bourgeois, and not caught in the intellectual
sentimentality of the eighteenth century of
his day—he might have achieved a triumph
as great, I think greater, perhaps, than any
of these. For with all my appreciation of
Lady Gregory's achievement, I cannot think
with Mr. Yeats that it is so great a book as
he maintains. This is not to disparage a
work which calls for gratitude. But Lady
Gregory's *Cuchulain* is not the shapen triumph of imagination; it is—and how different this is, while so fine—the skilful and in
the main satisfying relation of many imaginations by an enthusiast, and an enthusiast who
shows that she is also an artist in the use of
words.

Surely one need not mistake the editorial
faculty for the creative faculty. A year or
two ago Miss Eleanor Hull summarised the
Cuchulain Saga, achieving therein a work of
great value as well as of interest. Without
it, it is very doubtful if Lady Gregory's book
would be as nearly excellent as it is. For
students of Gaelic legend and literature, moreover, Miss Hull's "Saga" is much the more
valuable work: and I am glad of this opportunity to draw attention to its unfair neglect

since the appearance of its more literary but
in one or two vital respects much less satisfying rival. *Cuchulain of Muirthemne* is the
ordered and artistic narration: the *Cuchulain
Saga* is the careful analysis, or, to put it another way, the crude architectural structure
from which a symmetrical edifice was to
emerge. But one knows that there is another and greater way: the way that a Gaelic
poet of the first order might take—the way
that would give us all the beauty and wonder
gathered out of the past, with a new beauty,
a new wonder, gathered somehow, we know
not how, out of the present—and yet, when
we look curiously, neither the floating wonder
nor the rising and falling beauty being dis-
sociate in time, but one wonder, and one
beauty. A new and greater Macpherson,
working from deep knowledge truly in a
true way; a new Villemarqué, with more
scrupulous heed and with a familiarity as
great and a power greater than that of Briz-
ieux; a Celtic William Morris—what might
such an one make of the Cuchulain Cycle,
the Fionn Cycle, of Oisin of the Deer?

Sir Samuel Ferguson might have done it,
but he was never on the crest, only alone for
a time on the uplift of the great wave, and
he lacked the supreme gift of the Celt, the

gift of an incommunicable charm. Mr. Yeats
might do it: the *Wanderings of Oisin* uphold
the chance. But I fear the work is for one
far less preoccupied than he with the many
subtle problems of art and of the shaken
mind and of life turning for ever among her
revolving mirrors. It will have to be the life-
work of a single-minded dreamer and maker,
as, with all its insincerities and banalities,
Ossian was the life-work of that perplexing
genius, at once so high and so small, so uni-
versal and so provincial, James Macpherson.

For I feel this about *Cuchulain of Muirthemne*, that it is a fine ideal finely fulfilled
(and how much that is in a day of few ideals
and few fulfillings!), but that it is—I know
not what?—over-scholarly in its unwavering
heed to be consciously the thing it sets out
to be: over-cold in its strange sameness of
emotion: a little chill with the chill of studi-
ous handicraft. Once, with two-thirds of the
book read, and somewhat weary of its even
waters, I turned to the earlier and fragmentary and in every way cruder telling of Stan-
dish O'Grady. It was like leaving the banks
of a still loch for the slippery heather slopes
of a mountain torrent—but the sudden fresh-
ness, the leap, the vigour, the cry in the ears,
the stir, the rush! In a word, it seems to me

that the literary flaw in Lady Gregory's
version is its monotonous passionlessness.
Rightly or wrongly, I have the idea that her
mind may have quickened continually when
she was writing this book, but that her pulse
never quickened. " It is not the book for
the beating of my heart to be heard in," the
author might reply. But can that plea be
averred of any book of the imagination,
whether primary or reflected? It is here that
style—that subtle revealer—brings to the
test. And to me the style of this book, simple and gracious as it is, reveals rather an
enamoured mind than an enthralled heart.
Perhaps, however, one less familiar than the
present writer with the themes and legends
which Lady Gregory has woven in sequence
could better estimate the general value of
this book. That I am indeed ready to admit. For I miss, too often, a wilder but a
native note that she has purposefully ignored;
sometimes wisely perhaps, sometimes inevitably I suppose, sometimes I cannot but feel
to the weakening of her tale and the adum-
brating of that tale's features for those whose
approach is new. Again and again I have
felt her rendering to be, from this standpoint,
disastrous. The wind was out of the leaves,
the fires had faded, the authentic voices were

the dim echoes of phantoms. And though, again, I feel with others the charm and re-cognise the art of Lady Gregory's style, I find in it, constantly, a lack of virility that is at times almost prettiness—as, to take the first instance I can come upon at random, the fatal vulgarism (one indulged in not once only but again and again) of the misuse of "nice" in the story of Aileel's treachery upon Fraech—"So he went and broke a branch off the tree . . . and it is beautiful he looked over the black water, his body without fault and his face so nice," etc.

But lapses of the kind are perhaps inevitable. In the main the fine and quiet art of the telling is the justification of the aim the writer had in view—to write an English as nearly as possible the vernacular of those who now have the foreign language as their own language, but still retain the Gaelic mind.

To say that every lover of Celtic literature should obtain, should become familiar with this book, is to say what is obvious. But surely others also may read it with pleasure: as, a century ago, readers knowing nothing of the mabinogi of Bronwen, or the mabinogi of Pwyll, or the mabinogi of Manwyddan, turned with curiosity, and then with interest,

and then with delight to these and other
mabinogion in the beautiful English retelling
of Lady Charlotte Guest; as, later, readers
turned to the Arthurian romances under the
compelling spell of a great poet; as, later,
readers ignorant of Scandinavian poetry and
mythology turned to a new world, led by the
chanting voice of the poet of Sigurd the
Volsung. One does not need knowledge of
Celtic myth and legend in order to find charm
and delight in *Cuchulain*, though the wider
the knowledge and the deeper the intimacy
the greater that charm and the greater that
delight. If one love the tale of Homeric war,
if one quicken at the name of Achilles, or at
the doom of the house of Agamemnon, or at
the wanderings of Odysseus, or at mention
of the place where Kronos is the silent King,
or at the tale of Danaë imprisoned in her
tower, or at the tale of Penelope, or at the
tale of Helen, surely he can turn also to like
ancestral tales of the mighty warfare of Moytura, of the Titanic conflict by the Ford of the
two champions of the Gael, of that terrible
battle at Muirthemne, of Cuchulain that peer-
less lord, of the doom of the House of Usna,
of the Odyssey of the sons of Turenn, of
Conann's Tower of Death, of Ethne in the
rock-set Dûn of Balor, of Emer the lovely

and noble wife of Cuchulain, and of Deirdrê, whose beauty is undying legend in the songs and memories of the Gael to this day.[1]

Not in the *Mabinogion*, not in the Scandinavian Sagas, not even in the Arthurian romances are there women who hold us more enthralled than Emer holds us, than Dêirdrê holds us, than wild Maeve holds us as with a spear, than Findabair, that frail reed shaken in the wind, that Fand of the Sidhe. How beautiful this Fand—" And the meaning of the name Fand is, a tear that passes over the fire of the eye: it was for her purity she was

---

[1] The greatest living Celticist, M. d'Arbois de Jubainville, reminds the general reader, what to the specialist is obvious, that Celtic mythology is not copied from Greek mythology. "It is based," he says, "upon conceptions originally identical with those from which Greek mythology is derived, but has developed the fundamental elements of the myth in a manner of its own, which is as independent as it is original." As again, in an earlier chapter, he writes: "The characteristics common to Gaelic and to Greek mythology come from an old foundation of Græco-Celtic legends anterior to the separation of the two races, at that unknown period when the Hellenes, or Greeks, abandoning to the Celts the cold valley of the Danube and the mist-laden regions of Western Europe, settled down to the warm plains and the splendid coasts of the peninsula lying to the south of the Balkans."

called that, and for her beauty: for there **was**
nothing in life with which she could be compared beside it." How beautiful this queenly
Emer, in girlhood and womanhood, and beautiful the manner of her death beyond that of
any other, I think. And is there any pathos
of great love in sight of the House of Sorrow greater than that renouncing bitterness
of Emer when she bids Cuchulain go with
Niamh, since he says that she only can save
him? . . . " And after that Emer bade Conall
to make a wide, very deep grave for Cuchulain: and she laid herself down beside her
gentle comrade, and she put her mouth to
his mouth, and she said: ' Love of my life,
my friend, my sweetheart, my one choice of
the men of the earth, many is the woman,
wed or unwed, envied me until to-day; and
now I will not stay living after you.' " If
there is any loveliness of pathos beyond this
loveliness, in any literature, I do not know
it. And the last words of this saga, how fitting are they:

" And her life went out from her, and she
herself and Cuchulain were laid in the one
grave by Conall. And he raised the one stone
over them, and he wrote their names in Og-
ham, and he himself and all the men of Ulster
keened them.

" But the three times fifty queens that loved Cuchulain saw him appear in his Druid chariot, going through Emain Macha; and they could hear him singing the music of Sidhe."

TWO OLD SONGS OF MAY

(From the Gaelic)

One of the most beautiful of old Gaelic poems is an Ecstasy of Spring composed no one knows how many generations before the lyric voices of Elizabeth's day. The name of the poet a thousand years ago went away like a blossom on that swift river which fills the pools of oblivion. Perhaps even then it was hardly remembered, for the singer is often but the fleeting shadow who sang of a star, while the star remains. This Ecstasy of Spring is known as the May Day Song, and it is recorded in an old Gaelic MS. of the later part of the ninth or beginning of the tenth century, though how much older it is than this MS. none knows. The MS. is called " Macgnimartha Finn," and recounts the Boyish Exploits of Finn, the great warrior-king of the Gael, the Gaelic Nimrod. This narrative in Middle-Irish has been translated by Dr. Keneo Meyer in " Eriu," vol. i. Pt. 2, who gives there also a portion of the

May Song. It is to be found intact in the
" Four Songs " translated by this indefati-
gable Celtic student, who brings the light of
poetry into his most severely difficult work . . .
and how difficult old Gaelic is to translate
few can realise. If any present reader knows
modern Gaelic, with its confusing complex-
ity, its puzzling spelling, its singular inver-
sions and habitual pleonasms, let him see
what he could make of ancient Gaelic so
crudely concise as

> "*Tānic sam(h) slān sōer,*
> *dīa mbi clōen caill cīar,*
> *lingid ag sing snéid*
> *dīa mbi rēid rōn rīan.*"

He will almost certainly find it incomprehensible. The other day I read slowly to a
Gaelic islesman the following two quatrains
(from another old-Irish poem):

> "*Maidid glass for cach lus,*
> *bilech doss daire glaiss:*
> *tānic sam(h), rofāith gaim*
> *gonit coin ciulinn caiss.*

> "*Canaid lon dron dord*
> *dīa mbi forbb caill cerb,*
> *sūanaid ler lonn līac(h)*
> *foling īach brec bedc.*"

311

On a second and slower reading, dwelling on each word, he got nothing more from the first quatrain than what he had already got —"there will be something about a flower (*lus*) and a dog (*coin*) and maybe holly (*cuilinn*)." In the second, *lon* was easily recognisable as a blackbird: but he did not even guess at any more except to make a mistake in *brec*, first thinking it the familiar Gaelic name for a trout (*breac*) and then thinking it might be the old word for a wolf (also *breac*, for one of the meanings of the word is "brindled"), where as here it is the adjective "speckled" qualifying "salmon" (*iach*), a name which naturally he did not know. And what this islesman, a Gael with very little English, and in a sense learned, for he could read Gaelic well and even that with old-fashioned spelling and obsolete words, could not do, I do not think even a specialist in modern Gaelic could do. But the crude jerky quatrains are full of poetic feeling, as word by word unfolded for us out of the past by Dr. Keneo Meyer:

> "Green bursts out on every herb,
> The top of the green oakwood is bushy,
> Summer is come, winter has gone,
> Twisted hollies wound the hound.

"The blackbird sings a loud strain,
 To him the live wood is a heritage;
 The sad excited sea sleeps,
 The speckled salmon leaps."

Literally, and Dr. Meyer might as well have
so rendered his translation: "Breaks greenness on every herb" . . . "arrived is summer, gone is winter" . . . "Sings the blackbird a strain loudly" . . . "sleeps the sea,
sad, heaving"—for *líac* may mean that rather
than "excited," which does not go with
súanaid, "sleeps.")

In this old poetry the observation is always
very close, and what we should call uncon-
ventional, as "*Forbrit brain, tānic sam(h)*"
. . . "Ravens flourish, summer has come"
—which is every whit as true, and in the
northlands of the Gael even more true, than
the identification of May-tide with the often
refraining cuckoo, the often tardy swallow.
But of the cuckoo, also, the old poetry can
speak revealingly; for if, as seems likely, the
word *mbind* can be rendered "drowsy" (or
"softly tender"), the line "*canaid cūi cēol
mbind mbláith*," "singeth the cuckoo a drowsy
sweet music," is full of the heat of the summer days that come in May.

In giving my version, as concisely and in
as brief a metre as practicable, of this old-

world Song of May, after the redaction of
Keneo Meyer, I am aware of how much is
missed even though I have tried to retain the
most distinctive phrases, as that lovely phrase
in the seventh quatrain " where the talk of the
rushes is come."   I cannot improve upon
Dr. Meyer's version, but mine is an effort
to translate into rhymed quatrains the old
Gaelic song in a metre as succinct as that of
the original, to keep to the sense always, and
to the actual words where practicable.   When
I have changed these, it has been to the
loss of the old poet; *e.g*, his dust-coloured
cuckoo does not personify summer, and call
her a queen.   It says: " Welcome, splendid
summer."   But in the main I have tried to
keep to the original.

> "May, clad in cloth of gold,
>   Cometh this way:
> The fluting of blackbirds
>   Heralds the day.
>
> "The dust-coloured cuckoo
>   Cries 'Welcome, O Queen!'
> For winter has vanished,
>   The thickets are green.
>
> "Soon the trampling of cattle
>   Where the river runs low!
> The long hair of the heather,
>   The canna like snow!

Two Old Songs of May

"Wild waters are sleeping,
    Foam of blossom is here:
Peace, save the panic
    In the heart of the deer.

"The wild-bee is busy,
    The ant honey spills,
The wandering kine
    Are abroad on the hills.

"The harp of the forest
    Sounds low, sounds sweet:
Soft bloom on the heights;
    On the loch, haze of heat.

"The waterfall dreams:
    Snipe, corncrakes, drum
By the pool where the talk
    Of the rushes is come.

"The swallow is swooping;
    Song swings from each brae:
(?) Rich harvest of mast falls;
    The swamp shimmers gay.

"Happy the heart of man,
    Eager each maid:
Lovely the forest,
    The wild plane, the green glade.

"Truly winter is gone,
    Come the time of delight,
The summer-truce joyous,
    May, blossom-white.

"In the heart of the meadows
    The lapwings are quiet:
A winding stream
    Makes drowsy riot.

Two Old Songs of May

"Race horses, sail, run,
    Rejoice and be bold!
See, the shaft of the sun
    Makes the water-flag gold.

"Loud, clear, the blackcap;
    The lark trills his voice—
Hail, May of delicate colours!
    'Tis May-Day—Rejoice!"

The other old Gaelic May-poem is not ancient, but is certainly over a hundred and thirty, and may be about two hundred years old. I came upon it the other day through the courtesy of an unknown correspondent in America. This gentleman caught sight of a little leather-bound volume in a second-hand book shop in New York, and was puzzled at the language in which the poems it contained appeared. Well he might be at first, he not having the Gaelic, for the title runs " Comh-Chruinneachidh Orannaigh Gaidhealach," and how was he to know that the imprint at the bottom of the page " Dun-eidiunn M.DCC.LXXVI.," is merely Edinburgh? He was good enough to ascertain an address to which he could forward the book to me, and in his letter said that he thought it only right that this forlorn exile should return to its own land. And right

316

glad was I to have it so. This little volume
of Gaelic minstrelsy is " Le Raonuill Mac-
domhnuill, ann 'N Eilean Eigg," *i.e.*, by Ron-
ald Macdonald of the Isle of Eigg, that beautiful precipitous island of the Inner Hebrides
which so many years ago Hugh Miller made
famous in his geological " Cruise of the
Betsy." Or, rather, it was compiled by him;
for the poets of the songs and poems in this
volume are for the most part as nameless, as
well as tameless and rude and wild, as the
makers of the border-ballads. The contents
are diversified too: now one comes on a
Iorram, or boat-chant, now on a *Marbh-rann*
or threnody, now on a love-song such as the
" Oran gaòil le Mac Cailein d'inghein Mhic
Dhonuill Ilea," or a feudal song so well
known as the " Oran le Inghin Alastair
ruaigh do Mac Lèoid " (" Song by the
Daughter of Alexander the Red—*i.e.*, the
famous Mary Macleod—to the Macleod ").
The book is a delight if only for its quaint
wild-swanlike primitive refrains or chorus ef-
fects, *e.g.*:

> "*Holibh o iriag o ilil o,*
>   *Holibh o iriag o ro thi,*
>   *Holibh o iriag o ilil o,*
>   *Smeorach le clann*
> *Raonuil mi,*"

317

whi●h may well have been caught from the *smeorach* (thrush) itself: or this other *luinneag:*

> "*Hi il u il agus o,*
>   *Hi il o ho ri nan,*
>   *Hi il u il agus o*
>
> *Fa lil o hu lil o*
>   *Ho ri ghealladh hi il an.*"

But to the Maytide poem! It is nameless, as to author; and is entitled simply " Oran an 't Samhraidh." It is, however, too long, and in its metrical skill too involved and continuously alliterate to be rendered into English here. So I do no more than give the drift of it, for in the opening stanzas is to be found the essential part of the whole poem. I may add that in the first stanza here " son o' the wind " is a poetic simile for the bagpipes (or here, perhaps, the *feadan,* the whistle or flute of the pipes): and that, in the third, May is, Gaelic fashion, personified as a youth.

> "At break of day when all the woods are wet,
>   When every bush is shining white,
>   When in a silver maze the grass is set,
>   And the sun's golden light
>   Floods the green vale,
>   Lift, lift along the dewy grassy trail
>   The cheerful music of the son o' the wind,
>   Till, in the forest, floating voices sail,
> And vanishing echoes haunt the old rocks stern
>   and blind.

318

"Let the fresh windy birch her odours breathe,
  Her shimmering leaves ablaze:
Let the wide branchy beech with sunbeams seethe
  While clustered cattle gaze,
  The sunshine on them too:
Let yonder thrush that flew
  Carry the tidings of the golden day
Till not a glen or copse heart-turning to the blue
But thrills with the green rapturous loveliness of
  May.

"When evening falls, what bell is't rings so
    clear? . . .
  The cuckoo tolling down day's ebbing tide.
And what is that glad call, so near? . . .
  The Mavis with his rain
  Of song thrown far and wide.
And what these blooms May gathers to his side,
  And with his sweet warm breath doth redly
    stain? . . .
Roses, red roses, culled from hill and plain,
Roses, white roses dipt in dew, for May's awaiting
  bride."

"THE SHADOWY WATERS"

"I have flown out of the sorrowful eary wheel."—
PYTHAGORAS, *The Golden Verses.*

It is hardly a decade since the rise of a new Gaelic or Anglo-Celtic "school" in literature was looked at as the idle dream of an enthusiast here, a visionary there. As for a Celtic Drama—a drama that would have nothing in common with the accepted Irish melodrama so popular in England, but would have everything in common with the dreams of Irish poets and the tragic history of Ireland; a drama that would not set itself to please through a facile laughter and an easy pathos, but through the magic of legendary associations and the spell of a timeless imagination working within a passionate nationalism of mind and spirit—for a Celtic drama such as this, there was not even derision. The idea was too remote.

To ignore, now, the Anglo-Celtic school—I prefer to say the Anglo-Celtic group—would be too parochial even for a London

320

critic trained in the narrowest academical and literary conventions. One may ignore this or that writer: all cannot be ignored, for they are now many, and some have that distinction which rebukes the sullen. One may deprecate the movement, may decry it, may more insolently patronise it—as some French critics patronise Aubanel, Mistral, and the Provençal school, or as they patronise the poets and romancists of the Breton people: but one can no longer say it is not present, or is not to be reckoned with. There are, of course, faults on both sides. On each are wrong claims as well as wrong refusals, wrong assertions as well as wrong denials. In time, these adverse influences will combine in understanding, and, later, in sympathy and amity. If on the one side there has been, and still is, obtuseness (to speak of a sullen ill-will on the part of England towards Gaelic Ireland and Gaelic Scotland is now untrue), there is on the other a worse quality than obtuseness, a cultivated hate. It is almost inconceivable to what lengths this cult of revenge or hatred, this blind irreconcilability, will go. Not only the ignorant and idly passionate yield to its facile contamination, but those who would be spiritual guides and leaders pin to it all their hopes. These influences

321

and blind advocates, of course, must exist, so
that out of evil good may come: but mean-
while they are the subtlest foes of Ireland
and of that whole Anglo-Gaelic world which
is now gathering itself for a last effort to
resist extinction.

At present, however, there is, of the Irish
group, one writer who stands apart. Whether
one care for or dispute " the Celtic movement," none denies that Mr. Yeats is of the
very few writers of the younger generation
who can persuade us to the use of that sadly
abused word " genius." As essayist, roman-
cist, dramatist, but above all as poet, he has
a unique place.

The colour of his style is the colour of his
thought, and the colour of his thought is the
colour of a genius larger than his own, the
genius of a race.

With the romances of " The Secret Rose,"
the fantasies and episodes of " The Celtic
Twilight," or the several fascinating and suggestive essays in which, I think, is to be found
Mr. Yeats's finest work in prose, I do not
now attempt to concern myself. Nor, indeed,
do I wish at present to consider his poetry as
a whole: for his work in verse is familiar to
most of us, and has been widely considered
by others. But I would say a few words

concerning his latest book of verse, and his
" Shadowy Waters " and other dramatic work.

In a small book of verse, " The Wind
among the Reeds," recently given us by Mr.
Yeats, I think a note is touched which is
significant. It is the beginning of a new
music, and of a new motive. It is not often,
I imagine, that titles are so apt as that chosen
for this little book. These fewer than two-
score poems, most of them within the bound-
ary of a page, are small and slight as reeds;
and the wind which moves in them a delicate
music is as invisible, as mysterious, as elemental as that " strong creature, without flesh,
without bone, that neither sees nor is seen,"
of which long ago Taliesin sang. To understand its intimate music, certainly to feel that
music translate itself into the rhythm of
dream, one must go to this book as to a
solitary place where reeds rise in the moonshine. To know intimately the mystery of
these solitudes, it must be when the wind is
the only traveller, and sunlight and shadow,
the stars and darkness and the wandering
plover are the sole visitants. How else is one
(though, indeed, the blind bird in the heart
must have sung the same song) to feel as
Hanrahan felt, with the curlew wailing overhead, and an old memory beating with

bewildered wind against a sense of further sorrow yet to come:

"O, Curlew, cry no more in the air,
Or only to waters in the West;
Because your crying brings to my mind
Passion-dimmed eyes and long heavy hair
That was shaken out over my breast;
There is enough evil in the crying of wind."

This little book has the remoteness, the melancholy, of all poetry inspired by spiritual passion. It has, too, that other melancholy of which one of the subtlest of modern poets wrote in a forgotten early tale: "*Les rêves du poète et de l'amant—rêves qui, par une loi inexplicable de notre nature, ont toujours une teinte de mélancolie, même dans leurs plus splendides rayonnements, et qui ne sont les plus délicieux des rêves que grâce à cette même mélancolie.*" Here we are aware of the stillness of things that are past or are not again to be:

"I bring you with reverent hands
The book of my numberless dreams;
White woman that passion has worn
As the tide wears the dove-grey sands,
And with heart more old than the horn
That is brimmed from the pale fire of time,
White woman with numberless dreams,
I bring you my passionate rhyme."

This note of loss, of regret, finds constant expression.

> "I hear the shadowy Horses, their long manes
>   a-shake,
> Their hoofs heavy with tumult, their eyes glim-
>   mering white;
> The North unfolds above them clinging, creeping
>   night,
> The East her hidden joy before the morning break,
> The West weeps in pale dew, and sighs passing
>   away,
> The South is pouring down roses of crimson fire.
> O vanity of Sleep, Hope, Dream, endless Desire,
> The Horses of Disaster plunge in the heavy clay.
> Beloved, let your eyes half close, and your heart
>   beat
> Over my heart, and your hair fall over my breast
> Drowning love's lonely hour in deep twilight of
>   rest,
> And hiding their tossing manes and their tumul-
>   tuous feet."

Mr. Yeats is assuredly of that small band of poets and dreamers who write from no other impulse than because they see and dream in a reality so vivid that it is called imagination. With him the imagination is in truth the second-sight of the mind. Thus it is that he lives with symbols, as unimaginative natures live with facts.

Of his work might be said what in effect an

eminent critic said of François Millet, that he
is so intent upon the expression of poetry that
sometimes he prefers his ideas to his material,
that sometimes he dematerialises his ideas,
and suggests mystery instead of realising
beauty.

A symbolist stands in some danger here.
The obvious peril is a confusion of the spiritual beauty behind the symbol with the arbitrary expression of that spiritual beauty
through that particular symbol. There are
blind alleys and lost roads in symbolism, and
few of those who follow that loveliest trail
into " the undiscovered Edens " of Beauty
but sometimes lose themselves, and go after
shadows, and idly name the stars, and inhabit
planets with their own desires, putting their
vain dreams upon these unheeding children
of eternity.

Perhaps a truer wisdom is that which would
see the symbols in the facts, and the facts
translated from their material body to their
spiritual significance. It is the constant
reminder of the man who breaks stones to the
man who measures the stars, that he concerns
himself with remote speculations; but the
star-gazer is also apt to forget that without
broken stones no road would be paven. And
I cannot but think that Mr. Yeats is a star-

gazer too reluctant to listen to the plaint of
those who break stones or are spiritually
dumb hewers of wood and drawers of water.
He does not always sing of things of beauty
and mystery as the things of beauty and mystery are best sung, so that the least may understand; but rather as those priests of Isis
who, when bidden to chant the Sun-Hymn to
the people, sang, beautifully, incomprehensible algebraical formulæ.

"The Powers whose name and shape no living
    creature knows
  Have pulled the Immortal Rose:
  And though the Seven Lights bowed in their
    dance and wept,
  The Polar Dragon slept,
  His heavy rings uncoiled from glimmering deep
    to deep:
  When will he wake from sleep?"

Or, again:

"We who still labour by the cromlech on the shore,
  The grey cairn on the hill, when day sinks drowned
    in dew,
  Being weary of the world's empires, bow down to
    you,
  Master of the still stars and of the flaming door."

Or that strange poem of love with its fantastic dream-beauty, beginning:

"Do you not hear me calling, white deer with no
    horns?
I have been changed to a hound with one red ear."

To some there is no need to explain " the
white deer with no horns," " the hound with
one red ear," " the boar without bristles, out
of the West "; to some of the symbols of the
" Polar Dragon " and the " Immortal Rose "
stand evident. But these must be few: and
though in a sense all excelling poetry is
mystical, in the wider and not less true sense
it should be as water is, or as air is, or as
flame is. For it too is an elemental, being in
the spiritual life what wind is in the natural
life.

When the reader, unfamiliar with " the signature of symbol," shall read these and kindred lines, will he not feel that this new priest
of the Sun should translate to a more human
key his too transcendental vision? What, he
will ask, is the Immortal Rose, and what the
Polar Dragon? Who is the guardian of the
flaming door, and of what is it the portal?
If a Gael, he may have heard of the white
fawn that is Love, of the white hound that
is Death. Is it this symbol that lives anew
in the hound with one red ear, in the white
deer without horns?

328

"The Shadowy Waters"

For all who may not be able readily to
follow his honey of old wisdom, Mr. Yeats
has added notes. It would be more exact to
say that one-half of the book comprises the
prose equivalent of the verse. If all notes
afforded reading such as one may read here!
Mr. Yeats turns round mentally and shows us
the other side, where the roots grow and the
fibres fill with sap, and how they grow to that
blossom we have already seen, and what the
sap is. In their kind, these notes have something of the charm of the poems which they
illuminate. Yet they should be superfluous.
It is not their presence that one objects to,
but their need. Poetry is an art which should
be as rigorously aloof from the explicative as
the art of painting is, or as sculpture is, or
music. When Mr. Yeats gives us work on a
larger scale, with a greater sweep, he will, let
us hope, remember that every purely esoteric
symbol is a vague image—and vagueness is
the inevitable defect against which the symbolist has to contend.

But, when all is said that criticism is called
upon to say, what a lovely gift of music and
spiritual intensity and beauty is here. I have
an incalculable pleasure in this subtle magic
which creates so much loveliness out of a few
words. If, at times, the motive has triumphed

at the expense of the manner, it is rare that music and meaning do not go in delectable harmony. What lover of perfect verse but could take keen pleasure in a little poem so rose-like in its intricate symmetry as this:

"Had I the heavens' embroidered cloths,
    Enwrought with golden and silver light;
The blue and the dim and the dark cloths
    Of night and light and the half light;

" I would spread the cloths under your feet;
    But I, being poor, have only my dreams;
I have spread my dreams under your feet,
    Tread softly because you tread on my dreams."

The nobler use of symbolism—which is but an analogue of the soul's speech—gives a strange spiritual intensity to these poems. All do indeed live with an intense life, though of conventional actuality they have little or nothing. Some seem to be written in accordance with " the magical tradition "; some conform to the complex legend of Celtic mythology; some have no other shape or aspect than their own, as they issued like moths out of twilight, from the twilight of the poetic imagination. All come

"from a more dream-heavy land,
A more dream-heavy hour than this";

and it is the infinite, because never wholly
to be overtaken, charm of these breaths—
breaths of the reeds of the spirit shaken in
that wind which comes out of the past of time
and the past of the heart—that, in them, we
too, as the poet himself, may hear " white
Beauty sighing." In no descriptive sense, but
in a deeper sense, this book is one of a small
company that are pioneers in that intimate
return to nature from which we may and do
expect so profound and beautiful a revelation.
For a few come with new vision, to reveal
what is so old, what is younger than all else,
and new always.

It is a return, that in some sense, if only
for solace and strength, all of us who feel life
acutely must make.

I remember an old Highland fisherman saying to me once, when asked if he thought
God could ever tire: " I think He has the sea
in His right hand, and all the moors and hills
of the world in His left, and when He is
tired o' lookin' at the wickedness o' man, He
washes it out in the sea, an' then watches His
mercy like a soft shadow creepin' across the
moors an' hills." I do not profess to give
the exact words, for the old islander spoke in
Gaelic; but this is the drift of them. " It's all
obair an doill, the work of the blind," he

331

added—meaning the vanity of the human
heart. And, recalling this, I think that true
poets and all the silent kindred of poets must
often seek remote places, the loneliness of
hill or moor, must often listen to the desert
wind, to the whispering reeds, as a refuge
from the dull trouble of the habitual life;
that so they, too, may take comfort from
the stealing forth of soft and kindly shadow — symbol of natural rest and spiritual
re-birth.

A larger note is struck in " The Shadowy
Waters." In this dramatic poem—in this
poetic vision, told in verse cast in a dramatic
form—Mr. Yeats has forsaken the acute
emotion become lyrical for the lyrical thought
become continuous. It is not a drama, because it is a symbolical reflection of what is in
the poet's mind, rather than the architectonic
revelation of what his imagination has defi-
nitely shaped. It is not, strictly, a poetical
drama, even structurally, for action and
speech are subservient to the writer's entranced vision of the symbolism of the action
and of the speech. It is one of those new
and strange utterances, so perplexing to many
minds, wherewith conventional methods are
used for novel, perturbing, sometimes bewildering, at times bewildered, thought: one of

those dramas of the mind, best seen against
imagined tapestries, which reveal so much
more to us than do the common or familiar tapestries, the dramas of the obvious, of
merely spectacular life.

I wonder how many who read this short
drama of a score pages understood straight-
way what they read? The personages are
mythical: even the famous name of Dectora
(or Dectera) does not indicate that lovely
queen with whose beauty old legend is fragrant: indeed, the poet has but taken the
anglicised name of Cuchulain's mother and
given it to an imaginary crowned woman out
of Lochlann. This Dechtire is not a king's
bride seeking a new kingdom, but the symbol
or image of the Desire in the poet's heart, in
the hearts of poets. And Forgael, what is he?
A Gaelic prince, weary of songs and women
and war, a lost king with a forgotten kingdom? Yes, but more: is he not the inappeasable Ideal that calls to the Desire that is
in our heart; but, having won it, and led it
from shadowy lands across shadowy waters
till the grey wave is all that is left of the
visible world, will not lift it up nor wed it
unless it will relinquish its own flame—unless,
in a word, the beautiful mortal shall put on
immortality, shall leave the warmth and the

333

dream for a perhaps too stellar radiance, a
certitude too divinely impassive?

Many an one, besides Dectora, who has
relinquished all for the divine dream of imperishable and perfect love, has, at the last,
cried out in the extreme bitterness of a new
dismay:

> "Where are these bought? Where are the holy
>   woods
> That can change love to imperishable fire?
> O! I would break this net the gods have woven
> Of voices and of dreams."

It is the cry, not of Dectora only, but of all
women, nay, of all who through dream and
passion love to the extreme:

>   "Beloved,
> We will . . . . escape
> The nets the gods have woven and our own hearts,
> And will find out valleys and woods and meadows
>   To wander in";

and it is the answer of that inexorable Ideal
which echoes in:

> "All that know love among the winds of the world
> Have found it like the froth upon the ale."

Not the plea of one shaken heart but of all
the troubled hearts of mortal love is uttered,

when Dectora suddenly cries passionately to
Forgael:

"Love was not made for darkness and the winds
   That blow when heaven and earth are withering,
   For love is kind and happy. O come with me!
   Look on this body and this heavy hair;
   A stream has told me they are beautiful.
   The gods hate happiness and weave their nets
   Out of their hatred";

and when her mysterious lover abruptly bids
her farewell, and tells her to seek Aibric, who
loves her also, and with him go back to her
lost and regretted land, it is not Forgael only
that speaks, but again that inexorable Ideal
which will not temporise, which offers but
wind and shadow and yet demands all that
clinging hands and turning feet are loth to
leave. And the tragic pity of that final word
is, that it always comes too late for the man
or woman who would turn again to the beloved and mortal:

             "I should wander
   Amid the darkness, now that all my stars
   Have fallen and my sun and moon gone out."

Shall we have this visionary love, with its
terrible renunciations, or the light in loved
eyes, the touch of hands, the whisper in the

shadow? Dectora is a woman and knows but one love:

> "The love I know is hidden in these hands
>   That I would mix with yours, and in this
>   hair
>   That I would shed like twilight over you."

Forgael is not a man but a spirit, for to him love is idle as the unfolding of a rainbow, the colour of a moment on the grey eternities:

> "The love of all under the light of the sun
>   Is but brief longing, and deceiving hope,
>   And bodily tenderness";

and he adds (alas, the cold radiance of precious stones after the glow and flame of that little infinite trouble in the dark, the human heart)

> "but love is made
> Imperishable fire under the boughs
> Of chrysoberyl and beryl and chrysolite
> And chrysoprase and ruby and sardonyx."

It is lovely rhetoric, but the heart's silence is more eloquent. "The Shadowy Waters" has a continual loveliness. Many lines dwell with one:

> "already
> The cloudy waters and the glimmering winds
> Have covered them."

"The Shadowy Waters"

Many passages sink into the mind as dews
sink through the dusk:

> "The pale hound and the deer wander forever
> Among the winds and waters; and when they pass
> The mountain of the gods, the unappeasable gods
> Cover their faces with their hair and weep.
> They lure us to the streams where the world
>   ends"—

Or:

>   "Crumbled away
> The grass and the blue shadow on the stream
> And the pale blossom"—
>   "With a sound
> I had woven of the sleep that is in pools,
> Among great trees, and in the wings of owls"—

Or:

> " . . . . he who longs
> For happier love but finds unhappiness,
> And falls among the dreams the drowsy gods
> Breathe on the burnished mirror of the world,
> And then smooth out with ivory hands and sigh."

In his symbolical and mythological allusions, Mr. Yeats is again, as in " The Wind
among the Reeds," at times too esoteric, at
times too vague. One may speak the tongue
of angels, but the accent must be human and
familiar. Nor will the critical reader be blind

337

to the overuse of certain words: " winds and waters," " the pale hound," " heart's desire," and others, come too readily from Mr. Yeats's generally so heedful art. Mannerism begets disillusion when it becomes a common use, as when in close conjunction Mr. Yeats thrice uses a favourite, but at best dubious epithet, druid, uses it as an adjective for " mystic " or kindred word: " a druid vapour," " druid moons," " with druid applewood." It has contagion, for a day or two ago I saw in a paper an allusion to " the druid spell of Mr. Yeats's poetry, its druid lights and shadows." I can understand a druid spell, though " druidic " is the fit word: but not druid lights and shadows.

" The Shadowy Waters " does not yield all its beauty at once. It is like that flower which Moan, a dark queen of the Hidden People, showed to Cuchulain in his madness: a flower of a pale hue and faint fragrance, which every day disclosed a richer hue, the colour of a moment, or that loosed, passing as a moth's wing, a new fragrance. It is the story of a dream, of a symbolic vision; but its enchantment lies in its subtly beautiful interpretation of a dream that is not of one mind but of many minds, of a vision that has not sustained one heart's desire only but the desire of many

338

hearts in the troubled congregation of men
and women.

The miscarriage which awaits the pioneer
lurks in the probable failure between theory
and fulfilment. Mr. Yeats has written carefully concerning dramatic ideals and the Celtic Theatre: but he has not yet seemed explicit to the reader eager to sympathise with
both, nor has his published dramatic work
fulfilled the desired end. Like so many of us,
he mistakes sometimes the gossamer drama
woven inwardly of the wind of the spirit and
the light of the imagination, for the tangible
drama woven to represent adequately the
things of the imagination and the spirit. He
thinks in light and dreams in shadow, but
forgets that the translation of these into
thought made visible must be as explicit as
the translation of the wind's cry on the wave
or murmur among the leaves, when through
a formal and exact notation the musician
would convey the mystery of the one and the
troubled deeps of the other. Hitherto, he has
stood overmuch by the inner sureties of the
loom of thought: now, if he has to achieve
what he has in aim, he must study the outward weaving of the web, the external aspect of the woven dream, with not less careful heed, with careful, careful art. In " The

339

Land of Heart's Desire," in " Countess Cathleen," in " The Shadowy Waters," he does
not convince dramatically. In these he per-
suades. It may be the finer way for the
imagination: to persuade by the thing seen,
rather than by the thing shown. But it is
not the way accepted of Drama, which has
to be achieved by methods of illusion other
than those of cadence and colour. Mr. Yeats
seems to ignore that the particular method of
illusion demanded by the Drama necessitates
both an acceptance of certain conventions,
and an avoidance of certain scenic imaginative realities inept as visible scenic actualities.
" The Countess Cathleen " ranks first in what
he has done in dramatic form, a play of great
beauty, and whose repeated public perform-
ance delighted those who saw it. Yet it is
impossible not to feel that something is want-
ing. This want is not of the obvious: we do
not mean that it should be longer or shorter,
swifter or slower, more humorous or more
tragic, more wrought in poetry or sustained
in prose. We take it as it is, and judge it
for its shape and colour, its own life, its spirit,
its aim. It is, then, that below the charm of
the verse we are aware of a lack. It is not
that the thought is slight, though it is not
strenuous or deep; or that the phrase is in-

adequate in suggestion; or that unrealities wave conflicting plumes among the ordered march of the words, though insurgent unrealities there are at moments, and rebel insincerities, unconscious traitors no doubt. But something is lacking; as in a still, breathless wood we miss the lifting airs that are the wind. And the wind whose airs Mr. Yeats does not yet command is the wind of the dramatic spirit. He does not think, shape, reveal dramatically. This is as obvious in his dramatic poems as in his tales. A dramatic conception of an event or a linked sequence of events is not enough: there must be a dramatic vision of the coherent and actual congregation of the symbols in which that conception is to be made unique and visible: there must, further, be that faculty of mental economy which can use the few words only, the slight detail, which can relinquish the literary idea for the visible actuality: and there must be the power to distinguish between the method of illusion that lies with reverie and inward vision, and the method of illusion that lies with concentrated thought and its immediate expression, with their demonstration in the visible.

The flaw in Mr. Yeats's dramatic work seems to me to be just this, that he is not

primarily a dramatist. That he can write a
beautiful dramatic poem is evident in " The
Shadowy Waters ": that he can write a beautiful poetic drama is evident in " The Countess Cathleen ": that he can transmute into
dramatic form the essential spirit of poetry
is evident in " The Land of Heart's Desire."
But these are not dramas in the sense that
they are the outward and actual representation, through men and women and the actual
world, of the dreams and thoughts and ideas
of which men and women and the actual
world are the shadows and vivid phantoms.
It is not the visible, the dramatic interpretation that Mr. Yeats gives us, but the woven
shape and colour of his dreams. " The Shadowy Waters " is a vision related as a dramatic poem: it could have been related in
dramatic prose, or in the continuous linked
prose of reverie, or in the deftly entangled
prose of dialogue, or in the mirroring lucidi-
ties of the prose of narrative. We are glad
of it as it stands: we may consider that it
could not appeal to us more finely in another form. But it has not inevitableness.
Even in the one drama more nearly suited for
external representation which Mr. Yeats has
written, there are spiritual truths, symbols,
images which are as foreign voices crying for

interpretation: images, symbols, and truths which, in their reality to him, he has forgotten are, to others, unrelated voices, wandering shapes, the idle loveliness of stars falling from abyss to abyss.

And yet since I have re-read " The Shadowy Waters " I believe that Mr. Yeats may give us, may at least lead us towards a signal compromise that shall be almost a new art; a new art perhaps. He may find the way where the dreaming spirit and the shaping mind are not two companions but one traveller: he may stoop by a well we have not seen, and hear the forgotten voice of Connla, and out of old wisdom fashion newly a new thing. In words already quoted,

> " dramas of the mind there are,
> Best seen against imagined tapestries,"

and it may well be that, in a day of outworn conventions, many of us may turn gladly from the scenic illusions of the stage-carpenter, and the palpable illusions of the playwright, to the ever-new illusions of the dreaming mind, woven in a new intense dramatic reality against " imagined tapestries " as real, and as near, as the crude symbols of painted boards and stereotyped phrase in which we still have a receding pleasure.

343

NOTE

This essay was published before the issue of Mr. Yeats's recent dramatic ventures, "The King's Threshold," "On Baile's Strand," and other short Irish dramas of old and of to-day, of unchanging Ireland. My commentary on his work must be read as applying to what, at the time of its writing, Mr. Yeats had published.

STRANGER. *"And what help can there be from one who sees not?"*

ŒDIPUS. *"In all that I speak there shall be sight."*
—*Œdipus at Kolonos.*

"But . . . have you asked for that teaching through which the unheard is heard, the unthought is thought, the unknown is known?"—*The Chandogya Upanishad,* vi.

A TRIAD

In the thirty-second Triad of the " Mystery of the Bards " it is said that when the soul inherits Gwynnfyd, that is to say, Happiness, three supreme gifts—once, long ago, its crown, but long, long ago, lost—will be restored to it. And these three things are, we are told in this Triad, primitive genius, primitive love, and primitive memory.

No doubt there have been many interpretations of these triads. It is not easy to say of one quality what it is; nor what another may stand for; nor what the third may indicate. What is meant by genius, and what by primitive genius? And what love is primitive love, and between whom, and at what altar lit, and under what star a creature of joyous or malign life? And what is primitive memory, and of what is it the energy; of the mind, called into brief life, like a match lit in the wind; or of the racial spirit, that lives upon the nerves as the aërial spirits of old legend live upon the beauty and fragrance of flowers and grasses; or of the soul, that has so much

347

to recollect in its single transient passage before it can gather again the sound and colour of its earlier migrations, and so far to travel along this dim road of vicissitude before it can meet the shining brows of the forgotten children of beauty and wonder, who were with us, once?

In the " Roman de Merlin," when that son of earth and fire is wooed in spiritual ecstasy by the mysterious Radiance, this Triad is recalled in the words: " J'éclaire la partie immortelle de ton ame . . . je serai ta Force, ta Muse, et ton Génie."

But I think the unknown Druid meant more than this. I think more is meant than an original possessing spirit, a dæmon or genius; than a first love, burning with the white flame of purity and inspiration; than a divinity born of the passion that desires and the will that achieves.

For I think that nowhere, in any age, in any faith, is there a finer spiritual promise than what this Triad holds. If we be sure of these things, we need not trouble about any other. To remember, with the remembrance of the soul; to love, in the ecstasy of the morning of the world; to enter into the genius of the earth, to be at one with every breath of life, to share every separate rapture; to

see thought like flame, and life like clear
water, and death like the shifting shadows of
clouds; to *be* an eddy in that clear, swift flowing water; to *be* a flame of thought, shaken
like a plume of fire before the mirrors of a
myriad minds, or to descend like fiery snow
into their hills and valleys—and yet never to
be lost, never to be drowned in light or fire,
eternally errant yet ever at the call of the
Herdsman—that, indeed, is to live back into
the life that was, and to live on into life
that is.

To be possessed by primitive genius. That
would be to arise each morning with the wonder of a child awaking, for the first time, by
the sea, or among great mountains, or in a
forest roofed with wandering cloud and inhabited by a whispering wind. It would be
to arise, too, with the heart of a woman
suddenly knowing all things because of her
shaken heart. It would be to arise with the
spirit of youth, proud as a young eagle staring across the dominions of the sun or upon
the green lands and grey seas far below. It
would be to arise with the thrill and longing
of the poet, with the ecstasy of the seer, with
the uplifted silence of the visionary. It would
be to arise with the instinctive gladness of
every child of the bushes, of every little one

of the grass; of the salmon leaping in the
sunlit linn; of the swallow and the wild bee,
of the lark in the blue pastures of the air. Do
not the creatures of an hour rejoice in wheeling their grey mazes in the green shadows of
boughs? It would be to share the rapture.
We have forgotten that; we have forgotten
rapture. The communion of life! To breathe
once more in a common joy! To feel the
brotherhood of life, from the blossom on the
bough to the grey silence of old hills; from
the least of the blind offspring of the earth to
the greatest of the winged children of the four
winds; from the wild lives that lurk and are
afraid to the fearless lives that openly rejoice; from the stilled lives that do not move,
the hill-rock and the sea-caverned coral, to
the wild swan of the arctic wave or the swallows that with white breast and purple wing
thrid an ever-moving maze from the Hebrid
Isles to where the Nile narrows in tufted
reed and floating nenuphar. To feel thus,
with the thrill of conscious oneness, rejoic-
ingly; as children of one mother, nestlings of
one brood; and, thus feeling, to perceive and
be at one with the secret springs of the inward life, in caverned thought and image-
building dream, and of the life made visible
in motion, colour, and form—this would be

to know the primitive genius, to be possessed by it, to be of the genii of the morning.

But without love, rapture would be a cold flame. Lovely are the fires of the sea, and lovelier the fainting opal and pale rose of the shaken aurora; but the red warmth of a hearth-side is even more near to the soul as well as dearer to the body. This is an old wisdom, indeed, but the Druid of the Triad had thought and dreamed deeply before he placed this white greatness of love second in the trinity of the beatitudes. It was not of the commoner loves he dreamed; but of love. The cushat loves his mate of the cedar branch and the greenness, and the wolf leaping in the starlight answers the howl of the she-wolf, and even the scattered clan of the lapwing and the seamew have their faithful companionships by the moor-orchis and where the wrack-flower swims. But these are loves, not love. It is so great a thing that the wings of sunrise and sunset do not enclose it, and the stars are eddies of dust behind its feet; and yet this immortal can be claspt between the shaken flames of two hearts, and meshed in the subtle nets of dreams. It has many raiments, many faces. The mother bends low and kisses it, the friend clasps its hand, husband and wife uplift it, lovers worship it, the just

351

uphold it, great minds and deep natures
breathe it as a common air, the pure of heart
inhabit it. And, of old, it was even now as
with the pure of heart. It was a habitation.
The soul dwelled in it, as light in water, as
rhythm in light, as vibration in sound. Primitive genius beheld the world in wonder; when
it was wedded to primitive love, it looked
through the rainbow of a new passion and a
new joy, and knew that beyond the rapture of
things seen with the eye was the throbbing
world of things not seen but known, of things
not held but felt, of things not measured in
surety but treasured in hope. With love,
coming to one and all with each new dawn as
wind and light come, the heavens were opened
and the world stood disclosed in a new beauty.
To the enchantment had come music.

To recapture these — primitive genius,
primitive love! Might not the Druid of yesterday or to-day think there was no further
crown for the rejoicing spirit? And yet, assuredly, it was from the unplumed depth of
knowledge which we call intuition that the
seer of the Triad placed primitive memory as
the third and chief of the stars in the spiritual
crown. For Genius, which is the rejoicing
spirit of the world, could not see beyond its
own radiance of life; and Love, which is at

once the little shaken flame in a single heart
and the shoreless fire of immortality, could
not with its mortal eyes see beyond death;
but Memory—mother of all art, overlord of
destiny, the Word of humanity—she sits
apart. She looks down upon the whirling of
the wheels of chance and the dust of empires;
she remembers the Sons of the Morning; she
holds the clues of all interpretation. Sitting
at the throne of Life, she has seen the passage of the divine multitude; many gods have
gone by her; she has stood by the starry
graves of great deities. Like love, she is an
Eternal, and incommensurable, and yet can
whisper in a sleeper's ear or lie tranced in a
dreamer's mind. She has all songs on her
lips, all music in the touch of her hands, all
desires in her eyes, all hopes in her breath, all
joys and all sorrows, all faiths and all des-
pairs. It is she who gives joy to genius, and
a pulse to love; she knows the secret roads;
wisdom is the star upon her brows.

Primitive genius, primitive love, primitive
memory; what are these phantoms of the
dreaming mind?

So will many say. For, they will add,
where, in any age, in any record of any age,
in any dream, even, of the estates of man, did
the soul rejoice in this genius, travail in this

sacred love, crown itself as a god with this
diadem of omniscient light?

I do not know. I have not read of any.
But I think the soul knows. I think the soul
remembers. I think that intuition is divine
and unshakable. I think, if we can fill the
ruined palaces of the mind with the wind of
immortality and the light of the eternal—not
forgetting that the symbol is but the shadow
of the reality, and that into no symbol can
the inconceivable be translated—that we may
doubt these unstable temples served by blind
votaries rather than the spirit which Eternity
breathes and Immortality bestows.

I think we have travelled a long way, and
have forgotten much, and continually forget
more and more. The secret road of the soul
is a long road. When, at last, we turn, looking backward so as at last to go forward, we
shall see a long way off the forsaken homes
of joy, and above these our inheritance be-
hold the stars of our spiritual youth.

THE ANCIENT BEAUTY

"Sogna, sogna, mia cara anima! Tutto
Tutto sarà come al tempo lontano."
Poema Paradisaco.

Little girl, when you grow to maidhood and
womanhood, it is a hope of mine that you
will love these old legendary tales, of which
the tale of Deirdrè and the Sons of Usna is
one. Before you read this time-sweet story
of great love you will come to the story of
Fionnula and her brothers, because the Tale
of the Children of Lir, or the Tale of the
Four Swans as it is sometimes called, is first
among the old beautiful stories for the delight
of those standing in or passing beyond childhood. For a thousand years Gaelic youth has
loved and wept over it. By many fires, by
lonely seas, in hill-glens . . . in the great
straths where of old was no change but the
changing colour of season following season
and where no strangers came save birth and

Dedicatory introduction for an American reprint
of my versions of the old Gaelic tales of *Deirdrè and
the Sons of Usna* and *The Children of Lir.*

355

death, but where the deer now have their
wilderness or vast flocks browse where the
smoke of crofts and homesteads rose . . .
from generation to generation children, and
maids and youths keeping children's hearts,
have had their lives deepened in love and de-
votion, because of this tale of endurance noble to the end, and of patience so great that
the heart aches at the thought of it. You will
hear much of the other virtues, dear: but do
not forget these, which are so great, the stars
of Christ . . . endurance and patience. It
may help you to remember if you read of
them in verse, as has been written in beauty:

"Endurance is the noblest quality
And Patience all the passion of great hearts."

But, when you are older, I think there will
be no tale on the high lift of love, of heroic
love, to move you more than that now retold
for you here, out of the dim beautiful past
whose shadows sleep, in lengthening fans of
twilight, across the sunset-lands of the imagination.

In all the regions of the Gael throughout
Scotland, and in every isle, from Arran and
Islay in the south to Iona in the west and
Tiree in mid-sea and the Outer Hebrides,
there is no story of the old far-off days so

well known as that of Deirdrê. In some
places she is called Darthool, or Dartuil, or
Darthray, or Darrathray (the last I have
heard once only), but Deirdrê is the one name
common to all the Gaels; and in Ireland to
this day there is not a cowherd who has not
heard of that queenly name.

Her beauty filled the old world of the Gael
with a sweet, wonderful, and abiding rumour.
The name of Deirdrê has been as a lamp to
a thousand poets. In a land of heroes and
brave and beautiful women, how shall one
name survive? Yet to this day and for ever,
men will remember Deirdrê, the torch of
men's thoughts, and Grainne whom Diarmid
loved and died for, and Maev who ruled
mightily, and Fand whose white feet trod
faery dew, and many another. For Beauty
is the most unforgettable thing in the world,
and though of it a few perish, and the myriad
dies unknowing and uncaring, beneath it the
nations of men move as beneath their pilgrim
star. Therefore he who adds to the beauty
of the world is of the sons of God. He who
destroys or debases beauty is of the darkness,
and shall have darkness for his reward.

The day will come when you will find a
subtle enchantment in these names. They
will bring you a lost music, a lost world, and

imperishable beauty. You will dwell with
them, till you love Deirdrè as did the sons of
Usna, and would die for her, or live to see
her starry eyes; till you look longingly upon
the Grainne of your dreams, and cry as
Diarmid did, when he asked her, as death
menaced them, if even yet she would go
back, and she answered that she would not:
" Then go forward, O Grainne!"

Empires become drifted sand, and the
queens of great loveliness are dust on the
wind. They shall not come again, towered
cities of sand, palaces built upon the sea, roses
of beauty that blossomed for an hour on the
wind that is ever silently and swiftly moving
out of darkness and turning a sunlit wing
and then silently and swiftly moving into
darkness again. But the wind is changeless
in divine continual advent, and the sunlit
wing is that immortal radiance we call Beauty,
which we see as the mirage hung upon the
brows of Life. In that mirage Death is but
a beautiful phantom walking among rainbows
and white flowers; and the poets of the world
—who have ever been in love with Love and
Death, which in the deep sense are one—look
into that lovely mystery and see again the
towers and palaces of white nameless cities,
and hear the rejoicing of flutes and clarions,

358

and see banners upon the wind and armies marching, and the loveliness of great queens of beauty, and gather dreams and inspiration there, and come again and bow down before the eternal Phantom in the heart of all of us.

For wisdom reneweth herself in beauty.

It will not suffice that you care for these beautiful old tales as one cares for a flower that one plucks by the wayside, that one gathers at whim and idly discards. It will not suffice to like them as we like something which amuses us for a moment, a fantasy at a theatre, a light air lightly played or a song lifting itself from twilights of silence, this painted idyll of what was never was, this facile romance of the obvious or the impossible. These are things of pleasantry, and are good, or may be good, each in its kind: but they are not the things of the heart's desire, nor images of what the soul longs for and thirsts for.

But will you find anything of that which the soul longs for and thirsts for, will you find any unshaken or wavering image of your heart's desire, in the telling of an old tale? Many will ask that; some incredulously, some scornfully, some indifferently.

Perhaps. Perhaps not. It is of least moment what is in the tale: it is of moment what atmosphere of ideal beauty has remained with it out of the mind of the dreamer who shaped it, out of the love of generations·for whom it has been full of a perpetual sweet newness as of summer-dawn, for whom it has been as fresh as moon-dew glistering on banks of thyme along old grassy ways. And it is of supreme moment what we ourselves bring: what every reader who would know the enchantment must bring, what you, dear, if you would know the enchantment, must bring.

Let me for a moment tell you something that bears upon what I say. Long ago, one of the old forgotten gods, the god of enchantment and illusion, made a glory of loveliness, a glory of sound, and a glory of delight. Then he watched seven mortals approach in turn. Three saw in it no loveliness, heard in it no ecstasy, caught from it no rapture. Of three others, one knew an inexplicable delight, and took away the wonder and the memory to be his while he lived: and one heard an ecstasy of sound, and went away rapt, and forgetting all things because of that dream and passion not seen but heard: and the third looked on that loveliness, and ever after his fellows spoke of him as one made insane by impossible dreams, though he had that in his life which rose in a white flame, and quenched his thirst at wells of the spirit, and rejoiced continually. But of the seven one only saw the glory as the god of enchantment and illusion had made it, seeing in it the spirit that is Beauty, and hearing in it the soul of Music, and uplifted by it to the rapture that is the passion of delight. And lest that evil Destiny which puts dust upon dreams, and silence upon sweet airs, and still songs, and makes the hand idle, and the mind an eddying leaf, and the spirit as foam upon the sea, should take from this dreamer what he had won, the god of enchantment and illusion gave the man a broken heart, and a mind filled with the sighing of weariness, and sorrow to be his secret friend and the silence upon his pillow by night.

I have told you this to help you to understand that it is what we bring to the enchantment that matters more than what the enchantment may disclose. And, when you have been kissed by sorrow—may the darker veiled Dread pass you, dear—you will understand why the seventh dreamer who looked upon the secret wonder was of the few whom the gods touch with the hands, of the chosen keepers and guardians of the immortal fire.

No, it will not suffice that you care for them as a flower plucked by the wayside, as a pleasure gathered in idleness, to be for-

gotten when gathered. You must come to
these old tales to seek and to find the surviv-
ing beauty of gathered dreams and a silent
world, the immortality of ideals treasured
once, forgotten now. I do not say, I would
not have you believe, for I do not so think,
that all the old ideals of beauty have stolen
away from the world, as twilight retreats
from the grass in the pale greenness of dawns.
But some have gone, or are changed, and we
do not know them: and some have dimmed.
And, at least I think so, some are so rare
now as to be seen only in a few hearts, like
the star in a woodland pool seen among slim
spears of reed. One does not look into many
enchanted hearts in that uncertain wandering
of ours between the lighting and the ashes of
the brief fire which we come to unknowingly,
and carelessly tend, and regret with unavail-
ing tears, and leave, cold. And I . . . I shall
have bent above the fading warmth, and have
risen at last, cold, and gone away, when that
little wondering heart of yours shall have become a woman's heart: and so I do not know
whether, if I were to look in it, I should see
beyond the shaken reeds of the mind the
depth-held star of the old passion of beauty,
the old longing, the old enchantment. But I
hope so.

And so, if, carrying a heart such as I hope for you and believe is yours, little one, you will bring with you the enchanted secret, the enchantment in your mind, and look into that dim, beautiful enchantment of the past—of a world that ended, that changed long ago, and whose light endures as the travelling light of a star may immeasurably survive the star— I know you will find a compelling beauty in these old tales of the Gael, a beauty of thought against which to lay your thought, a beauty of dream against which to lay your dream, a beauty of desire against which to lay your desire. For they are more than tales of beauty, than tales of wonder. They are the dreams of the enchanted spirit of man, achieved in beauty. Shall the day come when the tale of Deirdrê shall be no more told, when in the firelight moist eyes shall not deepen at the sorrows of Fionnula and her swan-brothers, when men's hearts and women's hearts shall not be quickened by the tale of Ailinn and Bailê Honeymouth, when the madness of Cuchulain shall not trouble, when the love of Emer shall not be the very fragrance of great love, when the song of Niamh shall not enchant?

If so, it is not merely beautiful children of legend we shall lose, not the lovely raiment,

363

but the very beauty and love themselves, the love of beauty, the love of love, the old wondering ecstasy, the lost upliftedness, which once were an ancestral possession in an old, simple, primitive way, and now, or in that way, are no more ours, but are changed for us, as rainbows are changed upon the brows of cloud.

So, little one, come in time to love these things of beauty. Lay your child's heart that is made of morning joy and evening longing to that mother-heart: and when you gather years, as now you gather the little white clan of the grass, it shall be well with you. And you, too, when your time is come, and you in turn pass on the mystery of life to another who will look up from your breast with eyes of still wonder and slowly shaping thought, forget not to tell that other to lay its child's heart of morning joy and evening longing against a more ancient and dream-filled heart than that of any woman, that mother-heart of which I speak to you, the Heart of Beauty.

THE WINGED DESTINY

The Winged Destiny

I

In tragic drama it is authenticity of emotion and not authenticity of episode that matters. It is of lesser moment whether the theme be imaginary, or historically of this country or of that, or of this age or of another age. What does matter is the veritable action of the elemental emotions, and primarily the emotion of the inevitableness of destiny and the emotion of tragical loveliness. One does not need to know the Scandinavian story of Gunhild, or the Arthurian story of Tristran and Yseult, or the Gaelic story of Deirdrê and the Sons of Usna, in order to know the mystery and the silent arrivals of destiny, or to know the emotion of sorrow at the passage of beauty. These emotions are not the properties of drama, which is but a fowler snaring them in a net. These deep elementals are the obscure chorus which plays upon the silent flutes, upon the nerves wherein the soul sits enmeshed. They have their own savage or divine energy, and the man of the woods and the dark girl of the canebrakes know them with the same bowed suspense or uplifted lamentation or joy as do the men and women who have great names and to whom the lords of the imagination have given immortality.

Many kings have desired, and the gods forbidden. Concobar has but lain down where Cæsars have fallen and Pharaohs closed imperial eyes, and many satraps and many tyrants have bent before the wind. All old men who in strength and passion rise up against the bitterness of destiny are the kindred of Lear: those who have kept love as the crown of years, and seen it go from them like a wreath of sand, are of the kin of Concobar. There is not one Lear only, or one Concobar, in the vast stage of life: but a multitude of men who ask, in the dark hour of the Winged Destiny, *Am I in truth a king?* or who, incredulous, whisper, *Love is dead, Love the immortal is dead!*

The tradition of accursed families is not the fantasy of one dramatist or of one country or of one time. The *Oresteia* of Aischylos is no more than a tragic fugue wherein one hears the cries of uncountable threnodies. The doom of the clan of Usna is not less veiled in terror and perpetuated in fatality than the

doom of the Atredai: and even " The Fall of
the House of Ussher " is but a single note of
the same ancient mystery over which Sophocles brooded in the lamentations which eddy
like mournful winds around the House of
Labdacus.

Whether the poet turn to the tragedy
of the Theban dynasty, wherein Laios and
Iokaste and Oidipus move like children of
fire in a wood doomed to flame; or to the
tragedy of the Achaian dynasty wherein Pe-
lops and Atreus, Agamemnon and Menelaos,
Helen and Iphigeneia, Klytaimnestra prophesying and the prophet Kalchas, are like
shadowy figures, crowned with terror and
beauty, on the verge of a dark sea where the
menace of an obscure wind is continually
heard beyond the enchanted shore; or to the
tragedy of Lear weeping, where all kingship
seems as a crown left in the desert to become
the spoil of the adder or a pillow for wandering dust; or to the Celtic tragedy of the
House of Fionn, where Dermid and Grania,
where Oisin and Malveen, are like the winds
and the waters, the rains and the lamentations
of the hills: or to that other and less familiar
Gaelic tragedy, where an old king knows
madness because of garnered love spilt and
wasted, and where a lamp of deathless beauty

shines like a beacon, and where heroes die as leaves fall, and where a wind of prophesying is like the sound of dark birds flying over dark trees in the darkness of forgotten woods —whether one turn to these, or to the doom of the House of Malatesta, or to the doom of the House of Macbeth, or to the doom of the House of Ravenswood, one turns in vain if he be blind and deaf to the same elemental forces as they move through the blood that has to-day's warmth in it, that are the same powers, though they be known of the obscure and the silent, and are committed like wandering flame to the torch of a ballad as well as to the starry march of the compelling words of genius; are of the same dominion, though that be in the shaken hearts of islesfolk and mountaineers, and not with kings in Mykê-nai, or by the thrones of Tamburlaine and Aurungzebe, or with great lords and broken nobles and thanes.

The poet, the dramatist, is not able—is not yet able—to express in beauty and convey in symbol the visible energy of these emotions without resort to the artifice of men and women set in array, with harmonious and arbitrary speech given to them, and a background of illusion made unreal by being made emphatic.

If one were to express the passion of re-
morse under the signal of a Voice lamenting,
or the passion of tears under the signal of a
Cry, and be content to give no name to these
protagonists and to deny them the background of history or legend: and were to
unite them in the sequence of significant and
essential things which is drama in action, but
in a sequence of suggestion and symbol rather
than of statement and pageant: he would be
told that he had mistaken the method of lyrical music passing into musical drama for
the method of verbal emotion passing into
poetic drama. But that is too subtle a dream
for realisation to seem possible yet, save for
those who, hungering after the wild honey
of the mind and thirsting for the remoter
springs, foresee a time when the imagination
shall lay aside words and pigments and clay,
as raiment needless during the festivals of the
spirit, and express itself in the thoughts which
inhabit words—as light inhabits water or as
greenness inhabits grass.

But so long as the imagination dwells in
the accepted convention that imposes upon
us the use of events which chime to the bells
of the past, and the use of names which are at
once congruous and traditional . . . in this
convention of episode and phrase in the con-

cert of action and suspense . . . it will be
well ever and again to turn to those ancestral
themes of destiny past which so many generations have slipt like sea-going winds over
pastures, and upon which the thoughts of
many minds have fallen in secret dews. I do
not say, for I do not so think, that there might
not be drama as moving whether it deal with
the event of to-day and the accent of the hour
as with a remote accent recovered and with
remote event. But, to many minds, there
must always be a supreme attraction in great
themes of the drama of destiny as familiar to
us as the tales of faerie and wonder to the
mind of childhood. The mind, however, need
not be bondager to formal tradition. I know
one who can evoke modern dramatic scenes
by the mere iterance of the great musical
names of the imagination. . . . Menelaos,
Helen, Klytaimnestra, Andromache, Kassandra, Orestes, Blind Oidipus, Elektra, Kreusa,
and the like. This is not because these names
are in themselves esoteric symbols, or are
built of letters of revelation as the fabled
tower of Ys was built of evocatory letters
made of wind and water, of brownness of
earth, of greenness of grass, and of dew, all
of which the druids held in the hollows of the
five vowels. And here, he says, is his delight.

" For I do not live only in the past, but in the present, in these dramas of the mind. The names stand for the elemental passions, and I can come to them through my own gates of to-day as well as through the ancient portals of Aischylos or Sophocles or Euripides: and for background I prefer the flame-light and the sound of the wind to any of the crude illusions of stagecraft."

It is no doubt in this attitude that Racine, so French in the accent of his classical genius, looked at the old drama which was his inspiration; that Mr. Swinburne and Mr. Bridges, so English in the accent of their genius, have looked at it; that Etchegaray, in Spain, looked at it before he produced his troubled modern *Elektra* which is so remote in shapen thought and coloured semblance from the colour and idea of its prototype; that Gabriele D'Annunzio looked at it before he became obsessed with the old terrible idea of the tangled feet of Destiny, so that a tuft of grass might withhold or a breath from stirred dust empoison, and wrote that most perturbing of all modern dramas, *La Città Morta*.

That sense of the fatality which may have become native to certain localities where Destiny has been fulfilled, which is the funda-

373

mental idea of *La Città Morta,* has been felt by others also of our day. Readers of Walter Pater's " Apollo in Picardy," for example, will remember how when the Prior Saint-Jean was about to be transferred to " the wild lands " where lay the " Obedience " of Notre-Dame-de-Pratis, he was warned by the old Abbot to take heed of his ways when he was come to that place—for " the mere contact of one's feet with soil might change one." Elsewhere the same writer reminds us how the Greeks had a special word for the Fate which accompanied one who will come to a violent end, how the common Destinies of men, **Moîpa,** *Moerae,* accompany all men indifferently; but **Kῆρ,** the extraordinary Destiny, one's Doom, has a scent for distant blood-shedding—" and, to be in at a sanguinary death, one of their number came forth to the very cradle, followed persistently all the way, over the waves, through powder and shot, through the rose-gardens;—where not? Looking back, one might trace the red footsteps all along, side by side."

This sense of a doom which is not only an implacable personal fatality but can be a terrible and incomprehensible Fate which will involve innocent and guilty, a whole house, a whole clan, a race even, which will even em-

bitter the wind, add a more cruel and relentless terror to the sea, which, most appalling
of all, will tangle its trailing threads in the
roots of grass and in the green life of flower
and weed, because, there, that was once accomplished which was the sowing of seed or
the reaping of whirlwind—this sense finds
expression in a deep and terrifying sigh
throughout literature, from the fierce singers
of Israel to the last Gaelic rhapsode, from the
first of the dramatists of destiny even to the
latest.

II

There is no inherent reason why a poet of
to-day should not overtake the same themes
as Aischylos overtook from Phrynicus, and
Sophocles from Aischylos, and Euripides
from all three. The difficulty is not in the
remoteness of the theme, still less in the essential substance. It is in the mistaken idea
that the ancient formal method is inevitable,
and in the mistaken idea that a theme sustained on essential and elemental things and
therefore independent of unique circumstance
can be exhausted by the flashing upon it of
one great light. Kassandra and Helen and
Iphigeneia . . . they live: they are not dead

375

It is not the themes that have receded but the imaginations that have quailed.

Merely to parody the Greek tragedians, by taking a great theme and putting one's presumption and weakness beside it—that is another thing altogether. One hesitates, after Shelley and Robert Browning, after Mr. Swinburne and Mr. Robert Bridges, to say that no modern English poet has achieved a play with a Greek heart . . . no play written as a nineteenth century Sophocles or Euripides or Agathon would have written it. Even on *Prometheus Unbound* and *Atalanta in Calydon*, even on *Erechtheus*, the Gothic genius of the North has laid a touch as delicate as frost yet as durable as fire on the brows of immemorial rock. Perhaps the plays of Mr. Bridges are more truly classical than any modern drama since Racine. But their flame is flame seen in a mirror: we see the glow, we are intellectually warmed by it, but we do not feel it . . . our minds only, not our hearts that should burn, our nerves that should thrill, respond.

The reason, I do not doubt, is mainly a psychical rather than an intellectual difficulty. It is the indwelling spirit and not the magnetic mind that is wayward and eager to evade the compelling wand of the imagina-

tion. For the spirit is not under the spell
of tradition. It wishes to go its own way.
Tradition says, if you would write of the
slaying of Klytaimnestra you must present a
recognisable Elektra and a recognisable
Orestes and Dioskoroi against a recognisable
background: but to the spirit Elektra and
Orestes are simply abstract terms of the
theatre of the imagination, the Dioskoroi are
august powers, winnowers of fate, and the
old Greek background is but a remembered
semblance of a living stage that is not to-
day what it was yesterday or shall be to-
morrow, and yet is ever in essentials the
same.

III

We are, I believe, turning towards a new
theatre. The theatre of Ibsen, and all it
stands for, is become outworn as a compelling influence. Its inherent tendency to demonstrate intellectually from a series of incon-
trovertible material facts is not adequate for
those who would see in the drama the means
to demonstrate symbolically from a sequence
of intuitive perception. A subtle French
critic, writing of the theatre of Ibsen, appre-
ciates it as a theatre more negative than posi-

377

tive, more revolutionary than foundational, more intellectual than religious. "A ce théâtre amer et sec," he adds, "l'âme moderne ne peut étancher toutes ses soifs d'infini et d'absolu."

I think that, there, the right thing is said, as well as the significant indication given. "More intellectual than religious": that is, more congruous with the method of the mirror that gathers and reveals certain facets of the spirit, than with the spirit who as in a glass darkly looks into the mirror. "More intellectual than religious": that is, more persuaded by the sight that reveals the visible than by the vision that perceives what materially is not visible. "At this bitter and parched theatre of the intellect, the modern soul cannot quench its thirst for the infinite and absolute": and that is the reason, alone adequate, why to-day the minds of men are turning to a new drama, wherein thoughts and ideas and intuitions shall play a more significant part than the acted similitudes of the lesser emotions that are not so much the incalculable life of the soul as the conditioned energies of the body. The Psychic drama shall not be less nervous: but the emotional energy shall be along the nerves of the spirit, which sees beneath and above and beyond,

378

rather than merely along the nerves of the material life, which sees only that which is in the line of sight.

And as I have written elsewhere, it may well be that, in a day of outworn conventions, many of us are ready to turn gladly from the scenic illusions of the stage-carpenter and the palpable illusions of the playwright, to the ever-new illusions of the dreaming mind, woven in a new intense dramatic reality against imagined tapestries

> . . . dream-coloured dramas of the mind
> Best seen against imagined tapestries . . .

against revealing shadows and tragic glooms and radiances as real, and as near, as the crude symbols of painted boards and stereotyped phrase in which we still have a receding pleasure.

I think the profoundest utterance I know, witnessing to the fundamentally psychical nature of the drama, is a phrase of Chateaubriand which I came upon recently in Book v. of his *Mémoires* . . . " to recover the desert I took refuge in the theatre." The whole effort of a civilisation become anæmic and disillusioned must be to " recover the desert." That is a central truth, perceived now of many who are still the few. This great writer knew that in the *théâtre de l'âme* lay the subtlest and most searching means for the imagination to compel reality to dreams, to compel actuality to vision, to compel to the symbolic congregation of words the bewildered throng of wandering and illusive thoughts and ideas. By "the desert" he meant that wilderness, that actual or symbolic solitude, to which the creative imagination goes as the curlew to the wastes or as the mew to foam and wind.

Other writers speak of " nature " and " solitude " as though regarding them as sanctuaries where the passions may, like the wild falcons, cover their faces with their wings, and be still. Chateaubriand was of those few who look upon the solitudes of nature as enchanted lands, where terror walks with beauty, and where one sees on the dew the marks of invisible and hurrying feet. He was of those who looked upon solitude as, of old, anchorites looked upon waste places where the vulture had her eyrie and the hyena wailed and in desolate twilights the lioness filled the dark with the hunger of her young. " Be upon your guard against solitude : the great passions are solitary, and to transport them to the desert is to restore them to their triumph."

IV

It is in " the desert," whether in the wilderness of the unpeopled waste or in that of the mind where the imagination wanders like a lonely hunter on the trail of the obscure and the unknown, that the whisper of Destiny is supremely audible. It is on the eddying air. It is in the sigh of the grass. The green branch whispers it. It is in the brown leaf, on the grey wind.

When we are companioned or are in crowds, when we are in the fellowship of our illusions, when we can banish " the desert," shut out the wilderness, we turn from this perturbing thought, this Idea, so vast and menacing. We talk lightly, then, of the fatality of things. Our egotisms, even, feed on the ground-flame: we speak of " the fatality that made me do this "; " my usual fate that has brought this about "; " there is a fatality in this date, in that number, in the inevitable event, in what has occurred." If we speak of Fate, it is as an omnipresent force, indifferent at best, jealous it may be, perhaps hostile, even malign. But oftenest we disguise Destiny in Luck, and feel as safe in the use of the subterfuge as we feel uneasy in that of the sinister thing for which it stands.

The Winged Destiny

It is only when we turn to imaginative literature, to the drama in particular, that we can hear Destiny as a theme, as a present reality. To many minds it is a solace, a wall, rather, behind their weakness, that "a force greater than ourselves" is responsible for vicissitude, misfortune, miscarriage, circumstance, temperament even, even mien of mind and body. It is not we, they say, but Destiny who willed it so. For many others, who would refuse this confusion of the invited, the what but compelled fatalities, with the obscure Destiny which works afar off, at long range, behind many years it may be, perhaps even a generation or more, many generations even, and whose slow, inevitable workings are as relentless as they are inscrutable, there is a "fatalism" hardly less disastrous. They will not admit the feeble plea of the weak, but in their hearts they say "our best shall be set at nought, our strength shall avail nothing, in the end." It is only when we turn aside from the shifting images which make up the phantasmagoria of life, and look, though it be as in a glass darkly, into our own hearts, that we may have an imagination of the Winged Destiny: that spiritual force which is at once as remote from us, as far above us, as the dancing fires of the Pleiades, and yet in which

382

we have our being and by which we are controlled and toward which we inevitably move, even as our little world with all our universe about it and beyond it moves orderly to the incalculable rein of one of these little dancing fires.

In life, as in that pictorial show of life in flashing or dimmed mirrors which we call drama, or poetry, or this or that art, there is no arbitrary destiny so omnipotent that the soul cannot proudly meet it, none, it may be, that the soul cannot overcome. But, alas, it is not the soul that is called upon to meet Fate, as we call the terrible logic of rhythmic order, but our distempered selves, and our frail wills, and our vain, impossible dreams.

V

It is easy, then, by the illusions of the imagination, to avoid the dread shadow. Man has shaped and coloured many beautiful dreams, as much, perhaps, to elude this shadow as to create enchantment. Is it not for this, in so great a part, that he has taken the sigh of the sea and the cadence of the wind and the murmur of the leaf, and lamentations and delight and whispers, and made Music;

383

that he has taken from the silent flower and wave-haunted shell, and wrought so the colour and sound of verse; that he has surprised the secret of light and shade, and the secret of the columnar suspense of the cypress in moonlight or the single image of life silhouetted against dawn or sunglow, and the secret of the sombre avenues of pine-forest at sunset or moonrise, and the secret of the swaying branch and the blue smoke of woods and the wave of the sea, and created painting and sculpture and architecture and the dance?

But below all art there is an austere whisper: How would it be with you, O Soul, in the wilderness; how would it be with you alone there, naked amid the great silence and before the eternal shadow, and with no least of your illusions to hide the one or inhabit the other? It is here, in this spiritual wilderness, whether of an actual or symbolical desert, that the soul may know the mystery of the Winged Destiny. No poor fatalities wander here: here Fate herself does not reach, but leans brooding on the silent horizon.

Long ago, to Delphi, where that recovered memory sleeps beneath the "Shining Rocks" and dreams from the slopes of Parnassos to the meeting of the seas, a sculptor came who had fashioned a beautiful image which troubled all who looked upon it. His master, Agathôn, had made a statue, and some called it Eros and some Destiny. But now the younger man's work was held to be more beautiful, to be strange and beautiful to disquietude, to trouble the soul. Some thought it to be Anteros. In that day, in sculpture, only the Son of Ouranos and Aphroditê knew the symbolic beauty of wings. This winged one, was he that most ancient and dread god, imaged in changeless youth, Eros? Or was he that mysterious otherself, or a sombre brother, son of one older than Ouranos, Anteros?

Men wondered, for no one could say. The sculptor had suddenly laid aside life when he laid aside the chisel. He was a man of deep meanings, they knew. When, a year before, in the city of Athena, Agathôn had made for a Thracian prince his statue of Destiny, that image had been a woman, but with the brows and mien of Athena herself. Only, the down-looking eyes were all but closed. This other Destiny was a youth, they saw, but with uplifted face, and eyes looking out through time and change and circumstance: young, yet with weight of deep thought on the brows: serene, yet somehow appalling, as though a most an-

385

cient presence out of eternity looked from the newly carven marble. He was winged too, with great wings, as though he had come from afar, and was but a moment earth-lit. They would have acclaimed Anteros, but that the sculptor's handman said the statue was of The Winged Destiny. Long afterward, the wandering priest of an obscure faith, preaching before what had been the great Pythian fane, told his hearers that Agathón had meant Nemesis, the Following Fate: but that this other pagan dreamer, whose glory was now safe at Delphi, meant a deeper mystery, the Following Love. The stern Mistress of the veiled eyes was Retribution: the Divine Youth was Redemption. The one was born of Man and the Spirit of Time: the other was born of God and the Spirit of Eternity.

VI

I, too, in common doubtless with many of my readers, have thus pondered often, and perplexedly, this problem of destiny in the uses of the imagination, above all in tragic drama, and the deeper and more complicated problem of destiny in life. The more I have thought, the more it is borne in upon me that, in its final expression, the secret of Destiny must be sought within, in the interior life: in a word, that Destiny, as we commonly understand it, is but the vague term of a quality of spiritual energy, and not the designation of an immutable and inevitable force. I turned with eagerness, as doubtless many another turned, to M. Maeterlinck's *La Sagesse et la Destinée,* when that remarkable book was published; to find there a solution of, or at least a signal clue to the heart of the mystery. But, amid much that is beautiful and no little that is significant in interpretation and direction, I found nothing uttered with the authenticity of one who has put away visions because he has attained the source of visions, nothing revealed in the signature of the absolute. That fine book, indeed, in itself knows a continual hesitancy in nomenclature even, for the author speaks now of " le Destin " and now of " la Destinée," apparently by the one meaning that immaterial and secret and divine manifestation which we call Fate, the incommensurable vision and irresistible will of the Unknown; and, by the other, that material and obvious and mortal sequence of circumstance which we indicate in Fatality.

It is clear that he found; it is clear, I think, that each of us, pondering individually this

problem, must find; it is possible that of old
the Greek tragedians, those masters of illusion in the eternal drama of our mortal
" yea " and the immortal " nay," found, and
more intimately than we have found . . . the
same distinction which, soon or late, con-
fronts every thinker: the distinction between
the Destiny, or the Fate, which compels
through the invisible and the untraceable, and
the lesser destiny or fatality, which from
without allures, or from within impels the
overmastering throng of recognised or recognisable forces and influences, the things of our
inheritance, of our creation, the things of our
passions, the things of our desire.

But, surely, there is a further reach than
this for the questing mind. In Destiny itself
—in that great, abstract, overwhelming mystery of Fate, sitting as one enthroned above
the turmoil of the lesser destinies of time
and circumstance and the unceasing maelstrom of the myriad inextricable fatalities—
are there not two mighty forces at work? Is
there not the sombre and inscrutable Genius
of this world, which weaves with time and
races and empires, with life and death and
change, and in the weft of whose web our
swift-passing age, our race, our history, are
no more than vivid gleams for a moment

388

turned to the light? And is there not also a Winged Destiny, a Creature of the Eternal, inhabiting infinitude, so vast and incommensurable that no eye can perceive, no imagination limn, no thought overtake, and yet that can descend upon your soul or mine as dew upon blades of grass, as wind among the multitudinous leaves, as the voice of sea and forest that can rise to the silence of mountain-brows or sink in whispers through the silence of a child's sleep?—a Destiny that has no concern with crowns and empires and the proud dreams of men, but only with the soul, that flitting shadow, more intangible than dew, yet whose breath shall see the wasting of hills and the drought of oceans.

It is because I believe there is, in Fate, first the destiny which we make and invite, and name fatality: and above it the Destiny which calls to us as a tide calling in the night, and to which we respond from within, as creatures that must inevitably go with that tide, whether we know it or believe in it or ignore it, but yet who on that tide may compel our own way, and avoid the whirlpool, and attain the fortunate shores: and, beyond this, the Winged Destiny, which leans from Eternity into Time, and whispers to the soul through symbol and intuition the inconceivable mystery of the divine silence—it is because of this belief that I have placed these few words at the end of this book.

For, throughout, there breathes in it, I hope, not only the faith in the things which the spirit may compel and dreams achieve; not only the belief that the secret of redemption, alike for the individual, the generation, and the race, lies in the well in each heart and not in the clouds that float on the dim horizons of the mind of man; but also the belief, the faith, that for each of us, for all, there is the Winged Destiny, the Shepherd with whom, in the dark hour, we must go at last, to whose call we must answer when the familiar passions and desires and longings are as dust on the wind, and only that remains which so little we consider, only that little shaken flame of the spirit, which is yet of the things that do not pass, which is of the things immortal.

BIBLIOGRAPHICAL NOTE TO FIRST EDITION

As explained in the text, the short paper called "Celtic" has already appeared in book-form (*The Divine Adventure: Iona*, etc.), and is now, with the courteous consent of Messrs. Chapman and Hall, reprinted in its completed state, as the second of the three papers collectively entitled "For the Beauty of an Idea." The present first part of this dissertation on the Celtic destiny appeared (without certain revisions and added matter) as a foreword to an American reprint of the "Celtic" essay (Mr. Mosher, Portland, Maine). Of "The Sunset of Old Tales" series, one or two are printed for the first time; others, under the same general title, appeared in *The Fortnightly Review*, where, also, respectively at a later and at an earlier date, have appeared "The Woman at the Crossways" and (Section III.) "The Four Winds of Eirinn." "The Wayfarer" is reprinted from *Cosmopolis*. Of "The Children of Water" series, "Mäya" is printed for the first time; five appeared in *The Contemporary Review*, and "The Lynn of Dreams" in Mr. Mosher's reprint of *By Sundown Shores* (from *The Divine Adventure* volume); while "Sorrow on the Wind" (as also from Section III., "A Triad" and "Aileen") first appeared in *Country Life*.

In the third section ("Anima Celtica"), "The Shadowy Waters" (under the title "The Later

Work of Mr. Yeats"), and part of "The Gaelic
Heart," have appeared in *The North American Review*. "Seumas" is reprinted from the American
volume, *By Sundown Shores*, already alluded to.
"The Gael and His Heritage" appeared in *The Nineteenth Century* for November, 1900. "The Ancient
Beauty" formed the introduction to the American
(Mr. Mosher's) edition of my retold version of the
old tale of Deirdrê and the Sons of Usna; and a
portion of the earlier part of *The Winged Destiny*
(since revised and adapted), appeared as an introductory note on "Fatality in Tragic Drama," to
Mr. Mosher's American edition of my drama, *The
House of Usna*.   F. M.

NOTE

BY MRS. WILLIAM SHARP

The first edition of *The Winged Destiny* was published in 1904 (the second in 1905), by Messrs. Chapman and Hall. Into the present edition two "studies" have been added: 1. "The Awakening of Angus Òg," from the volume of Spiritual Tales (P. Geddes and Colleagues, 1897, and David Nutt, 1904), contributed originally to the winter number of *The Evergreen* (P. Geddes & Col., 1896), a quarterly edited for one year by William Sharp. 2. "The Two Old Songs of May," which appeared in the *Academy* in 1905. "The Wayfarer" was written for *Cosmopolis*, June, 1898; in 1904 a revised version, prepared for *The Winged Destiny*, was published separately by Mr. Mosher in 1906, and it was prefaced with a sonnet written by Mr. Alfred Noyes. This "In Memoriam" sonnet, through the courtesy of Mr. Noyes, will be found at the end of Vol. VII. of this authorized edition of the writings of William Sharp, under the pseudonym of "Fiona Macleod."

www.ingramcontent.com/pod-product-compliance
Lightning Source LLC
Chambersburg PA
CBHW081321090426
42737CB00017B/2996